THE POLITICAL AND SOCIAL IDEAS
OF JULES VERNE

THE POLITICAL AND SOCIAL IDEAS OF

JULES VERNE

Jean Chesneaux

Translated by THOMAS WIKELEY

with 41 illustrations
from the original editions of novels
by Jules Verne

GIFT OF
GEORGE I. ALDEN
TRUST

THAMES AND HUDSON · LONDON

Several of the chapters in this book are revisions of articles published previously in various journals:

Chapter II: 'Science, machines et progrès chez Jules Verne', in *La Pensée*, July 1966.
Chapter III: 'Ioul Vern i 1848 Traditsia' ('Jules Verne et la tradition de 1848'), in *Frantsuski Ezhegodnik 1967, French Yearbook for 1967*, Moscow 1968, Académia Naouk, pp. 108–22.
Chapter IV: 'Jules Verne et la tradition du socialisme utopique', in *L'Homme et la société*, July 1966.
Chapter V (and parts of Chapters VII and IX): 'Critique sociale et thèmes anarchistes chez Jules Verne', in *Le Mouvement social*, July 1966.
Chapter VI: 'Jules Verne et les peuples coloniaux', in *Démocratie nouvelle*, January 1967.
Chapter IX: 'Jules Verne's Image of the United States', in *Yale Review of French Studies*, No. 49, 1969.
Chapter X: 'L'or et l'argent chez Jules Verne, archétypes ou critique sociale', in *Les Lettres nouvelles*, 1970, No. 2.

The Jules Verne archives are not accessible. Some of Verne's letters have been published by his niece, Mme Allotte de La Fuÿe, in her biography, *Jules Verne, sa vie, son œuvre*. Others have been discovered by Mme S. Vierne, who has been kind enough to inform me of their contents. I am exceedingly grateful to her. Except where otherwise indicated, the letters quoted in this book originate with Mme Vierne.

J.C.

Translated from the French, *Une lecture politique de Jules Verne*
© Librairie François Maspero, Paris, 1971
English translation © Thames and Hudson Limited, 1972

All rights reserved. No part of this publication may be reproduced or transmitted in any form or by any means, electronic or mechanical, including photocopy, recording or any information storage and retrieval system, without permission in writing from the publisher.

ISBN 0 500 01084 6

Text filmset by Keyspools Ltd, Golborne, Lancs
Printed by BAS Printers, Stockbridge, Hampshire

Contents

	Political Chronology	8
I	The bourgeois façade and what it concealed	11
II	Science and its machines	23
III	The 1848 tradition	45
IV	The echo of utopian socialism	69
V	Libertarian individualism	87
VI	Colonial people: 'good savages' and 'bad savages'	112
VII	Chance and providence	127
VIII	Nationalism and Internationalism	140
IX	The American mirage and the American peril	150
X	Gold and silver	165
XI	Progress or pessimism: the future of mankind	181
XII	A political interpretation of Jules Verne	196
	Notes to the text	209
	Bibliography	216
	List of illustrations	219
	Index	221

Engraved frontispiece by Bertrand; this appeared in several editions of Verne's novels.

'But now that he was come into that city and that land, and was the king thereof, he found the freedom and the vividness all too soon worn out, and monotonous for want of linkage with anything firm in his feelings and memories. He was a king in Ooth-Nargai, but found no meaning therein, and drooped always for the old familiar things of England that had shaped his youth. All his kingdom would he give for the sound of Cornish church bells over the downs, and all the thousand minarets of Celephais for the steep homely roofs of the village near his home.'

The Dream Quest of Unknown Kadath by H. P. Lovecraft
(Ballantine Books, 101 Fifth Avenue, New York, N.Y. 1970)

Political Chronology

People's struggles and political crises of the nineteenth century and their relevance to the *Voyages extraordinaires*. Titles of novels in which the episode cited plays an essential role are indicated in small capitals; those in which an episode is mentioned only marginally or occasionally are indicated in italics.

AFRICA

1835–55	Trek of the Boers driven from Natal by the British and forced to withdraw into the Orange Free State and the Transvaal	THE SOUTHERN STAR MYSTERY (1884)
1863	Discovery of the diamond mines of Griqualand	Ibid.
1850–60	Resistance of el-Hadj-Omar to the French attempts at the conquest of Senegal; defeat of el-Hadj-Omar	*Five Weeks in a Balloon* (1863)
1850–60	Humanitarian campaigns against the African slave trade; end of the great trade	THE BOY CAPTAIN (1878)
1880–90	Development of the activity of the Muslim millenarian sect of Senussi in Libya and Tripolitania	*Mathias Sandorf* (1885)
1880–90	French penetration into the south of Tunisia	THE INVASION OF THE SEA (1905)
1885–95	French colonization of western Africa as a whole	*The Astonishing Adventures of the Barsac Mission* (1920)

AMERICA

1837	Armed revolt of French Canadians against the British authorities	FAMILY WITHOUT A NAME (1889)
1850–60	End of Araucan nationalism, establishment of Chilean authority in the Andes	*The Children of Captain Grant* (1867–68)
1859	John Brown's raid on Harper's Ferry	*20,000 Leagues under the Sea* (1870) *An Eccentric's Will* (1899)

1860–65	Civil War in the United States; victory of the Union anti-slavery forces	*From the Earth to the Moon* (1865) THE MYSTERIOUS ISLAND (1874) THE BLOCKADE RUNNERS (1875) NORTH AGAINST SOUTH (1887)
1867	Sale of Alaska and other Russian territories in America to the United States	*Caesar Cascabel* (1890)
1879	Cession of Swedish Antilles to France	*Travelling Scholarships* (1903)
1881	Partition of the Magellan territories and Tierra del Fuego between the Argentine Republic and Chile	*The Survivors of the 'Jonathan'* (1909)
1889	Emperor Pedro II of Brazil is overthrown by a republican rebellion and abdicates	*Propeller Island* (1895)
1897	Klondike gold rush across Chilkoot Pass	THE VOLCANO OF GOLD (1906)
1890–1900	The United States 'big stick' policy against Central America and in the Caribbean	*Propeller Island* (1895) (1895) *Travelling Scholarships* (1903)

ASIA

1799	Napoleon's expedition against Acre	*Master Antifer* (1894)
1833–39	Syrian Wars; Mehmet Ali repels the Turkish armies and imposes Egyptian autonomy	Ibid.
1851–64	The Taiping rebellion	*The Tribulations of a Chinese Gentleman* (1879)
1857–59	The Indian Mutiny	*20,000 Leagues under the Sea* (1870) THE MYSTERIOUS ISLAND (1874) THE STEAM HOUSE (1880)
1860–70	Conflicts between Russia and the Central Asian emirates (Bokhara, Khiva)	MICHAEL STROGOFF (1876)
1860–70	Modernization movement in China (*Yangwu*)	*The Tribulations of a Chinese Gentleman* (1879)
1870–75	Muslim insurrection in Chinese Turkestan	*Claudius Bombarnac* (1892)
1870–80	Conflict between the Old Turks (conservative) and Young Turks (modernists)	KERABAN THE INFLEXIBLE (1883)
1880–81	English expedition against Herat, Afghanistan	*The Clipper of the Clouds* (1886)

EUROPE

1820–25	Greek War of Independence	ISLANDS ON FIRE (1884)
1848	Peasant revolt led by Sandor Rosza in Transylvania	*The Carpathian Castle* (1892)
1854–56	Crimean War (France and Britain against Russia)	*Measuring a Meridian* (1872)
1850–60	Hungarian national independence movement	MATHIAS SANDORF (1885)
19th century	Scottish nationalist movement	*The Children of Captain Grant* (1867–68)
		The Green Ray (1882)
1868	Cretan insurrection against Turkish domination	*20,000 Leagues under the Sea* (1870)
1870–71	The Franco-Prussian War	*The Begum's Fortune* (1879)
		The Superb Orinoco (1898)
1850–80	Irish nationalist movement; agrarian agitation; Fenian uprising	FOUNDLING MICK (1893)
		The Brothers Kip (1902)
1870–90	Anti-Tsarist conspiracies and Nihilist movement in Russia	*Michael Strogoff* (1876)
		Caesar Cascabel (1890)
		A Drama in Livonia (1904)
1880–90	Slav revival movement in the Baltic provinces (formerly Germanized) of Russia	A DRAMA IN LIVONIA (1904)
1880–90	Progress of socialist propaganda in France	*The Survivors of the 'Jonathan'* (1909)
1890–95	Rise of the Anarchist movement; waves of assassination attempts against the King of Italy, the Tsar of Russia, the Presidents of France and the United States, etc.	THE SURVIVORS OF THE 'JONATHAN' (1909)
1880–1900	Bulgarian nationalist movement (leading in 1908 to Bulgarian independence)	A DANUBE PILOT (1908)
1870–1900	Norwegian nationalist movement (leading in 1905 to Norwegian independence)	*A Lottery Ticket* (1886)

OCEANIA

1850–60	Maori uprisings against British domination in New Zealand	*The Children of Captain Grant* (1867–68)
1851	Australian gold rush	*The Children of Captain Grant* (1867–68)
19th century	Liquidation of autochthonous Australian and Tasmanian populations	Ibid.
		Mistress Branican (1891)
		Propeller Island (1895) ✓
1885	Partition of the Papuan Islands between Germany and Britain	*Propeller Island* (1895) ✓
1885	New Zealand gold rush	*The Brothers Kip* (1902)

CHAPTER I

The bourgeois façade and what it concealed

'A nice, quiet middle-class gentleman, fond of white pudding and Nantes bacon . . .',[1] that is how Jules Verne appeared to the eighteen-year-old Aristide Briand*, then studying at Nantes with Verne's son Michel and acting as the latter's 'correspondent' with the school authorities. And that, indeed, is just what Verne's family circumstances, his literary career, his friendships and his way of life make him appear to us now: a good nineteenth-century bourgeois.[2]

His father was a Nantes lawyer born at Provins. His mother came from the Nantes bourgeoisie; her family, the Allottes, had made a fortune out of trade with the colonies in the eighteenth century, and had only recently added to their name the pseudo-noble title of 'de la Fuÿe' from a dovecote on one of their estates. His uncles, relatives and friends bore such names as De la Celle de Châteaubourg, Du Crest de Villeneuve, Fleury (a Parisian stockbroker who had married his sister, Marie), and Guillon. His wife's family was just as middle-class as his own: in 1857 he had married a wealthy widow from Amiens, Honorine Morel, *née* Du Fraysne de Viane.

His professional life was also bourgeois, despite some temporary aberrations which, however, hardly exceeded the limits then permitted to the son of a good family. He studied law in Paris between 1848 and 1850, a large part of his time being spent 'in the bars of the Latin Quarter'. At the age of 23 he took a job as secretary to the Théâtre-Lyrique, after refusing to join his father's firm and giving up his legal studies. Earning his living mainly by his pen, during the period 1850–55 he wrote numerous songs, theatrical sketches, operettas, curtain-raisers and short stories, most of them as conventional and as colourless as the rest of such fashionable productions during the Second Empire. After his marriage he settled down in the most conventional way and took a job with a Paris stockbroker whose partner he later became. Until 1862 he handled a lot of real estate business. In that year he met the publisher Hetzel, who

* Aristide Briand, 1862–1932, French Socialist statesman best known for his international activities after the First World War.

agreed to present his first great novel *Five Weeks in a Balloon*. Despite the fact that the meeting was a turning point in his intellectual life and that his plan to write the *Voyages extraordinaires* was a project of great originality and daring, this second literary career, which was to last for forty years, continued to follow a very bourgeois and conventional pattern. A 'treaty' was signed; the publisher undertook to pay, and to pay well, while the author was to put his nose to the grindstone and produce three, later two, books a year, year in and year out, whether inspiration came to him or not. For Jules Verne from the start it was a question of 'earning money'; to his friends at the stock exchange he said:

> I am going to leave you. I have had an idea which Girardin* says should come to every man every day, and which I have only had once in my whole life. I have written a novel of a new kind, all my own. If it is a success, it will be the vein of gold leading me to a gold-mine. Then I will go on writing, writing without a break, while you will go on buying shares just before they start to go down and selling them just before they begin to go up. I leave the stock exchange.³

Thus it was a question of literary production in the economic sense of the word, and not just one of those feverish imaginings which he, a child of the nineteenth century, might have during sleepless nights.

The people Jules Verne knew and his way of life seem at first sight to be just as bourgeois as all the rest. He kept company with fashionable musicians, newspaper men, financiers, prominent politicians: Léo Delibes, Victor Massé, Hignard, Guéroult, Raoul-Duval the Paris Deputy, Wallut the Director of the *Musée des Familles*, Pelouze the Director of the Mint, Joessel the Director of the Forges d'Indret.* One of his family biographers, with patent satisfaction, calls him 'the favourite of Princes': the Count of Paris and his sons, the Duke of Montpensier and the other members of the Orléans family.* He bought several pleasure boats. The first was nothing more than a refurbished fishing boat, but *Saint-Michel III* was a sumptuous yacht, bought by Verne from the Marquis Des Préaux in 1877 at the time when the 'golden rain' was falling upon him (the phrase is that of his niece). He enjoyed pleasure cruising, and received titled personages on his yacht such as the Archduke Louis-Salvador of Habsburg, brother of the last Grand Duke of Tuscany.

---

*Emile de Girardin, 1806–1881, French publicist and politician.

*Léo Delibes, 1836–1891, and Félix Marie (called Victor) Massé, 1822–1884, French composers.

*Charles-Edmond-Raoul Duval, called Raoul-Duval, 1807–1893, French politician.

*Théophile-Jules Pelouze, 1807–1867, French chemist.

*The family of Louis Philippe, 1773–1850, king of France 1830–1848.

He sold the yacht to the Prince of Montenegro in 1886. Stopping at Rome during a Mediterranean tour, he presented himself respectfully for an audience with Pope Leo XIII. At Amiens, whither he retired in 1872, he lived in the most conventional bourgeois comfort:

> It is my wife's wish that I should live at Amiens, a nice, well-regulated, good-tempered town with a friendly and educated society. One is close enough to Paris to feel its influence without having to put up with its unbearable noise and sterile agitation.⁴

He was elected a member of the local Academy, and he assiduously cultivated the society of the good bourgeois of Picardy. He gave big fancy-dress balls, he became a fashionable personage honoured by the French Academy, his works translated into twenty languages. His novels were adapted for stage presentation at the Châtelet Theatre and brought him easy 'Parisian' successes.

Such professions of political faith as he took the trouble to formulate seem to have been drawn straight from the same respectable bourgeois society. The partisans of the *Commune* filled him with horror:

> The Mobile Guard will deal with those hotheads. A republic is the only system of government that has the right to show no mercy to such wild beasts, since it is the government chosen by the majority of the flock.⁵

> As for their policy, that will come to an end. It was necessary for this socialist movement to take place. Well, now it is over, it will be defeated; and if the government of the Republic, as is its duty and its right, employs terrible measures of repression, republican France will have fifty years of internal peace.⁶

In 1887 he declared: 'I, a conservative, will vote for Ferry.'* During the crisis brought about by the Dreyfus affair,* he was on the side of the Conservatives and became a member of the right-wing, anti-Dreyfus French Patriotic League. In 1895 he wrote: 'I am anti-Dreyfus to the bottom of my soul.'⁷

In answer to questions from his young Italian friend and correspondent, Mario Turiello, he wrote in 1898:

> I prefer to reply to this question rather than to the other one, the one about the Dreyfus affair. It is better not to mention that one, alas!

---

*Jules François Camille Ferry, 1832–1893, French lawyer and politician.

*Alfred Dreyfus, 1859–1935, Jewish officer in the French army, who was accused in 1894 of treason on forged evidence and sent to Devil's Island after being sentenced to detention for life. Right-wing society considered him guilty even when the falsity of the charges was proven. The Dreyfus affair split the whole French bourgeoisie of the period.

> I have long held that whatever may happen in future, the affair has been well and truly dealt with.⁸

He was therefore completely satisfied with the verdict against Dreyfus, and he disapproved of the pro-Dreyfus attitude of his friend and lawyer, Raymond Poincaré*:

> What kind of New Year's Day will it be with our poor country fallen into such a state of anarchy? I simply don't know. But it is quite simply abominable, and I cannot tell you how surprised and upset I am by Poincaré's action.⁹

In the same way he disapproved of President Loubet's* visit to Italy, a gesture of solidarity with the Italian monarchy and of circumspect hostility to the Holy See.¹⁰

Even in the sphere of literature he was on the side of the conservatives, and he supported the banalities of Nisard* in his criticism of Jean-Jacques Rousseau; he wrote to Mario Turiello:

> You have studied the works of Jean-Jacques Rousseau. Very well! And you have very personal opinions about him. So be it! I do not share them. If Rousseau was a great writer, he was a miserable creature as a private person, and most of the ideas he propagated are detestable. I am on the side of M. Nisard rather than on yours.¹¹

It might be asked whether the election of Jules Verne to the Town Council of Amiens in 1888, on a programme with socialist and radical tendencies, alters in any way the impression derived from so many professions of conservative faith. Does it not reveal to us that Jules Verne was at heart a progressive (as Marcel Moré¹² thinks, for instance), does it not show us a Jules Verne at last giving expression to his innate sympathy with left-wing ideas? This is far from certain. No erudite son of Picardy has yet told us what items, exactly, were included in that famous programme, and it was perhaps only Verne's conservative-minded family who thought it 'ultra-red'. The candidate himself did all he could to reassure his friends, and he made it clear, for instance, that he had not renounced his Orleanist sympathies:

> My only purpose is to make myself useful and to bring certain urban reforms to a satisfactory conclusion. Why must politics and Christianity always intrude into administrative matters? You know me well enough to realize that I have not changed on the essential points. In social matters my taste is order; in politics this is my

---

*Raymond Poincaré, 1860–1932, one of the leading twentieth-century French statesmen.

*Emile Loubet, 1838–1929, French politician, moderate republican, President of the Republic 1899–1906.

*Désiré Nisard, 1806–1888, French literary critic.

hope: to create within the present government a reasonable party, balancing respect for justice and religious belief with consideration for people, the arts and life itself. Believe me, I do not hide my opinion about the laws of exile, and I am also resolved to defend in the same way, and on every occasion, each person's freedom of conscience. My 'prestige', as you kindly call it, will therefore be used only in the service of respectable causes.[13]

Even though Verne entered local politics in Picardy by joining what was doubtless an incongruous coalition, almost certainly including real extremists, he proved during the following years to be consistently on the side of the moderates. His election in 1888 was therefore neither the outcome of a rash impulse, nor of a temporary escapade into the ranks of the 'reds'. In 1895, for instance, when he took part in the elections caused by the Mayor's death, he did not support the extremist parties:

The town takes up much of my time. . . . Shall I still be a municipal councillor in two months' time? I am not sure, and the fight against the combined forces of socialism and radicalism will not be easy.[14]

He was equally active, and still on the side of the moderates, in 1897, and he gave no sign that his election in 1888 had implied any line of political thinking inconsistent with his position at that time:

We have unseated the Mayor in a campaign into which I put a lot of work. We will see what comes of it. In any case, it can't be worse than before, and at least the moderates have won.[15]

In our present state of knowledge, therefore, there is nothing to show that the 1888 election had the effect of separating Verne from those bourgeois circles in Picardy among whom he had come to make his home. He showed similar respect for the conventions in the exercise of his academic functions. Thus, on 8 January 1875, in his capacity as Director of the Academy, he replied officially, and very pompously, to the inaugural address of a lawyer, Gustave Dubois, who had just been admitted as a member of that illustrious company.

I cannot but congratulate myself that it falls to me to reply to such a distinguished lawyer as yourself. . . . Therefore, in your own words, I salute you as the mouthpiece of rights ignored, of misfortune undeserved and of misery begging for human forgiveness. That, Sir, is what you are, in company with your honourable colleagues of the legal profession in Amiens. . . .

A little later, he congratulated a new member of the Academy on his opposition to the Paris *Commune*:

In your protest against the horrors of the *Commune*, you say that 'the members of that sect have been murdering the ministers of

Religion, as if the death of martyrs had ever done anything else than increase the influence of Religion', and you are absolutely right, Sir.

In passing, Verne declared himself in favour of copyright – so harshly, indeed, that his heirs can only have congratulated themselves on the protection they enjoyed under rules which, according to his wishes, had been progressively tightened up:

> Many good men have shared Lamartine's opinion that the copyright of a book creates for its author the same rights as the ownership of a house vests in the owner. This is not the place to discuss the matter, but allow me to believe that the last word has not been said on the subject. M. Berville [the deceased member of the Academy whose place the new member was taking] extended for twenty years after the death of the author the rights of his heirs. Today the period is thirty years, and everything leads us to suppose that it will be increased. . . .

This lovely piece of Picardy eloquence concludes:

> Yes, Sir, you were right to use the epithet 'conservative' in speaking of the Republic of Letters, for indeed it conserves its supporters in the best sense of the word. If equality cannot exist within that Republic, there is at least a place for all who value language, and talent therein is ageless.[16]

Just as conventional are the many anti-feminist clichés in a speech made by Verne in 1893 for the prize-giving at a girls' school in Amiens:

> To fill their hearts with love for the French fatherland and – as the Minister of Education recently said at the inauguration of the Le Puy Girls' School – to teach them to be valiant and disinterested women, ready to contribute their spirit, their knowledge and their virtue to the cause of their country's greatness . . .
>
> What you are learning from your mistresses is preparing you gradually to fulfil your destined role. Thanks to them, when the responsibility of bringing up a family falls into your hands, you will fulfil it in the only true way in which a woman should make her influence felt in society. . . .
>
> Little girls and big ones, be careful not to lose your way by running after the sciences, . . . do not plunge too deeply into science, that 'sublime emptiness' in the words of the great poet, wherein a man may sometimes lose himself. . . .
>
> What is one to think of those women who throw themselves into social struggles, at a time when decent citizens becoming involved in the rat-race are spattered with insults? . . . It is better for you to

turn your abilities to the creation of a pleasant family home and hearth.[17]

Jules Verne's ideas about the treatment of servants are also typical of a certain bourgeois system of organizing social relationships. The master-servant relationship, which is everywhere appearent in the *Voyages extraordinaires*,[18] can only arise in the context of a prosperous middle class. By the nature of things, the lower classes cannot have experience of this kind of salaried service; the nobility, on the other hand, and the other ruling classes have far too many servants to allow individual master-servant relationships to develop. In affluent households, the only possible attitude the master and mistress of the house can adopt towards their 'people' is that of collective, and therefore distant, condescension. The individual servant, however, drawing pay while nevertheless remaining a person in his own right, exactly reflects a certain economic status, that of the middle bourgeoisie with which Verne felt himself so much in sympathy. In his novels – and here we foreshadow the method used in the rest of this book, namely that of trying to show that an author's work as a whole reflects a certain view of the world – Verne paints many pictures of masters and servants, antagonistic to each other but nevertheless inseparable, such as Dr Fergusson and his faithful Joe who does not hesitate to jump into an African lake to lighten his master's balloon and thus save his life (*Five Weeks in a Balloon*); similarly, Conseil (well portrayed in the film by Peter Lorre) is so devoted to the service of Professor Arronax that he leaps into the sea when his master falls overboard from the deck of his ship as the result of the collision with *Nautilus* (*20,000 Leagues under the Sea*); or Madge, nurse and adopted mother of the intrepid Mrs Barnett, who follows her mistress to the edge of the frozen Arctic Ocean (*The Fur Country*); and Xaris, devoted to young Hadjine Elizondo like a faithful dog (*Islands on Fire*); Ben Zouf from Montmartre, the batman and *alter ego* of Captain Servadac; Rotzko, an old soldier and the companion of Count Frantz de Telek (*Carpathian Castle*); also Martial, another old soldier with a dog-like fidelity to young Jeanne de Kermor, the daughter of his former colonel (*The Superb Orinoco*). The Catalan businessman, Clovis Dardentor, has Patrick, his 'liveried mentor', always beside him:

> Indeed they could not do without each other, although it would be difficult to conceive of two more dissimilar natures. It was not his pay which tied Patrick to the house at Perpignan, although he was well paid; it was the certainty that his master had absolute confidence in him, a confidence which he well deserved.

The same attachment unites master and servant from both sides of the Atlantic as, for instance, the devoted Turk and the irascible American

Commodore Urrican: 'One of those faithful dogs which make even more noise than their master when the latter shouts at someone in anger'.

Thus Jules Verne, the son of a lawyer, and a former stockbroker, a fashionable author and a conventional member of the Academy, an opponent of the *communards*, the Dreyfusards and the suffragettes, a declared supporter of the social order, presents a solid, bourgeois façade, coherent, reassuring and seemingly in complete harmony with his environment and the times he lived in.

Is he really the same man who conceived the promethean audacities of Hatteras in the polar regions, of Liddenbrock, deep within the terrestrial globe, who hotly denounced 'the worship of gold'? Was it he who put into Nemo's mouth those proud words of defiance:

> I am not what you call a civilized man. I have broken entirely with society for reasons which I alone have the right to judge. I do not obey its rules, and I ask you never to mention them to me.

Had he then a secret, this nice, quiet little bourgeois who amused Aristide Briand? He certainly maintained a surprising secretiveness about himself: 'The story of my life is not very interesting, nor would the tale of my travels be more so. A writer is of interest to his country and to the world only as a writer'.[19] Thus he wrote to his young Italian correspondent, Turiello. When the latter's tactless enthusiasm resulted in further questions, Verne was a little annoyed that the obstinate Italian should make use of the *Voyages extraordinaires* to exercise his talents as a literary critic: 'Why are you so persistently interested in my works?'[20] 'I wonder why you seem to concentrate your literary abilities upon my books.'[21]

In one of his first letters to Turiello he even says 'I feel that I am the least known of men',[22] an admission, perhaps, that in his subconscious mind he glimpsed abysses which he himself hesitated to explore.

However bourgeois Verne's character may appear to us at first sight, however banal his life may have seemed in his own eyes, he nevertheless passed through a number of moral crises which, although we know little about them, serve to explain the sharp rebuffs he gave to Turiello. A closer look at Jules Verne reveals a more complex personality than his young friend Aristide Briand suspected.

These crises have been analyzed fairly thoroughly by his biographers, in particular by Mme Allotte de la Fuÿe and Marcel Moré – although singularly little autobiographical material exists, and the discreet circumspection of those who control Verne's family archives does not make the task of research any easier. It is therefore not necessary to deal with these episodes in detail; the fact, however, that they were serious enough to bring Verne into conflict with his family and social environment is confirmation enough that the bourgeois façade behind which he liked to shelter did, in fact, hide many secrets. And that is the reason for the investigation which is the main purpose of this book, namely to examine Jules Verne's novels as constituent elements of a certain political view of the world. This view will, in fact, prove to be much stronger and more politically unconventional than could have been guessed from the very ordinary appearance presented by the author at first sight.

The earliest of the crises, and perhaps the most indicative of an extreme independence of character, took place in 1839 when the young Jules Verne tried to escape from the stuffy family atmosphere, taking a job as a cabin boy on a ship about to sail. He was found just in time, and received physical punishment at his father's hands, but the eleven-year-old child may well have been marked for life by this episode.

Of equal importance was the failure of his very conventional marriage to that good bourgeoise (*she* had no secrets), Honorine Du Fraysne de Viane. He soon detached himself from his wife, although without making a complete break, and became more and more solitary, living as a stranger in his own home. His solitude was doubtless mitigated for a time by 'the unique siren', of whose mysterious existence we learn from only a few allusions; she was, however, separated from Verne by another crisis of which hardly anything is known (did the affair break up, did she die?). It was about this time also that another family drama took place: in 1886 Verne's nephew, to whom he was deeply attached, fired a revolver at him; he was badly wounded in the leg, of which he never recovered complete use, and the psychological effects proved just as lasting. This series of intimate crises is not widely known since Verne burned many of his personal papers; but towards the end of his life an increasing melancholy is evident:

> I have too many and too weighty reasons for sadness to be able to join in the family pleasures at Nantes [he wrote to his brother in 1894] – I cannot bear anything frivolous; there has been a profound change in me, and I have suffered blows from which I shall never recover.[23]

Even though so little is known about them, these crises were sufficiently obvious to attract the attention of critics and commentators. For some time past, a good deal has been written about Verne's 'secret'. Already Pierre Louÿs,* in his study of Verne's handwriting, pointed out certain traits of character far removed from ordinary bourgeois mentality: a

---

*Pierre Louis Louÿs, 1870–1925, French writer.

lack of proportion, a certain secretiveness, a liking for solitude and great strength of will:

—an underground revolutionary;
—intrepidity and fearless courage;
—resolute, but secret determination – against everything;
—unvarying purpose;
—perseverance in action;
—tenacity in the face of obstacles;
—solitary and unspoken pride;
—turning the key on inmost thoughts at the end of the signature.[24]

Raymond Roussel* says that he was strongly impressed by Verne when he met the latter during his period of military service at Amiens, and he also stresses the hidden depths of meaning in the *Voyages extraordinaires*, deploring the fact that they should traditionally be looked on as 'reading matter for children'.[25]

> It is just as monstrous to give them to children to read as it is to give them the Fables of La Fontaine, which are so profound that few adults are capable of appreciating them.[26]

The surrealists and their successors sought the secret of Verne in initiatory themes and 'hermetic meanings'. Michel Butor* has pointed out the importance of such surrealist themes as the central fire and the central point;[27] he has most aptly compared the best passages of Henri Michaux* with Verne's description of the submarine fauna and flora seen from the portholes of *Nautilus*, or the account of the electric storm which appeared to make it impossible to reach the Pole. M. Carrouges has used psychoanalysis in an attempt to explain the presence in the *Voyages extraordinaires* of such themes as the island, the 'field of treasure', the search for a father, the metallic force.[28] M. Cellier, M. Brion and especially S. Vierne have drawn attention to the initiatory significance of novels such as *Journey to the Centre of the Earth*.[29]

Marcel Moré, for his part, in two books of profound new analysis,[30] has drawn attention to the presence in all the novels of two fundamental psychoanalytic themes: the search for the 'perfect father' (reflecting the relationship which had grown up between Verne and Hetzel), and the despairing friendship which can unite two brothers (Jules Verne was in fact very close to his brother Paul). Lord Glenarvan is the 'perfect father' for young Robert Grant, even if both of them are bent on finding

---

*Raymond Roussel, 1877–1933, French writer, considered a precursor of Surrealism.

*Michel Butor, b. 1926, French novelist.

*Henri Michaux, b. 1899, French poet and painter of Belgian origin, who has written of various imaginary journeys.

the latter's natural father, Captain Grant. Cyrus Smith is the 'perfect father' for the young naturalist Harbert. Equally frequent is the recurrence of the theme of the two brothers: the two Raos (*The Steam House*), the two Texars (*North against South*), the captains named Guy (*An Antarctic Mystery*), etc.

All these studies are not only 'interesting', 'suggestive' and all the other adjectives learned men in universities affect when faced with new and slightly disconcerting ideas (or just plain ideas). They seem to us above all absolutely justified. They definitely remove Jules Verne from the category of 'children's books' in which his writings have been placed for far too long; and particularly they underline the great richness of his work.

Nevertheless, the world of the *Voyages extraordinaires* has been known to us for so long, and so thoroughly, that we have been tempted to try another kind of interpretation, a political one. The alibi of 'science-fiction' is as inadequate as that of children's books when we come to describe *Known and Unknown Worlds* (*Mondes connus et inconnus*). Or rather, as P. Macherey has shown, Verne's very lively interest in the problem of forecasting scientific developments is an integral part of a specific political analysis of the relationship between society and nature.[31] Science and its machines are, indeed, at the base of Verne's plan for his work, but only in so far as they serve to extend it to the level of the body politic as a whole. The description of the latter contained in the *Voyages extraordinaires* certainly goes deeper than is realized by those who carry their enquiries no further than Verne's 'bourgeois façade', for example, Professor P. Sorlin[32] who sees in Verne a French chauvinist naïvely describing in his works the merits of the French and of the tricolour flag ... an untroubled colonialist. Our interpretation of Jules Verne's novels – the good, and the less good – will on the contrary bring us up against the black flag more often than the tricolour, will reveal a constant concern to question the value of national chauvinism and state-controlled colonialism, and will make plain the author's view that heroism and nobility are to be found only in the ranks of anti-colonialism (Nemo, the Rao brothers, Hodjar, etc.). What we hope to show is that in Jules Verne's writings three different methods of analysis, three groups of references and resonances, constantly recur: the '48 tradition, the echo of Utopian socialism, and libertarian individualism. The careful reader will find that these three currents of thought are always present in Verne's novels. Omnipresent, too, are the big social and political problems which pre-occupied the minds of men in the last third of the nineteenth century: the destiny of the coloured races; the destiny, too, of the United States, for so long a mirage and already a danger; the conflict between nationalism and internationalism; and, finally, the role of the power of finance in human undertakings. These are the four political problems we have taken into consideration, and in the novels we find solutions to them which are often varied and original, and always interesting. It is the *Voyages extraordinaires* we mean, and not Jules Verne as a private person. Indeed, the political horizon revealed by that immense work is infinitely richer and more diverse than the one in which the respectable bourgeois of Nantes and Amiens seemed to move.

CHAPTER II

Science and its machines

The well-known Democrat publisher Hetzel was immediately interested when, in the autumn of 1862, a young, almost unknown author submitted to him the manuscript of *Five Weeks in a Balloon*, for this constituted the outline of a plan – to bring science into the field of literature – the vast developments of which the author himself probably did not realize at the time. In his preface to *The Adventures of Captain Hatteras* (1866), Hetzel underlined the great interest and novelty of this idea:

... The novels of M. Jules Verne have come just at the right time. When an eager public can be seen flocking to attend lectures given at a thousand different places in France, and when our newspapers carry reports of the proceedings of the Academy of Sciences alongside articles dealing with the arts and the theatre, it is surely time for us to realize that the idea of art for art's sake no longer meets the needs of the time we live in, and that the day has come when science must take its rightful place in literature. To M. Jules Verne goes the merit of being the first to tread this new ground. ...

M. Verne's subsequent books will be added to this series as they appear, a series which we will be careful to keep always up to date. The books already printed, together with those still to appear, will cover between them the whole ground the author had in mind when he gave to his work the sub-title of *Travels in Known and Unknown Worlds*. His plan in fact is to sum up all the information gathered by modern science in the fields of geography, geology, physics and astronomy, and to rewrite ... the history of the universe.

No doubt Verne's idea was somewhat less of an innovation than his publisher, for obvious reasons of publicity, tried to make out. There had been forerunners and precedents, in particular among the first French writers of scientific prophecy such as La Follie,* Nogaret,*

---

*Louis Guillaume de la Follie, d. 1780, French amateur chemist, member of the Académie de Rouen.
*François-Félix Nogaret, 1740–1831, French writer and poet.

Lemercier, while great writers such as Voltaire and Balzac are well known to have been interested in science.[33] In its own way Balzac's *Comédie Humaine* sets out to be a scientific study of mankind and society, and it contains a good many descriptions of scientists and scientific themes. But science as such is nowhere present, or rather omnipresent, in any great work of French literature to the extent that it is in the *Voyages extraordinaires*.

The literary construction of Verne's novels already reveals this omnipresence of science. It would in fact be a great mistake to think that scientific themes appear only in those novels dealing specifically with scientific forecasts; these are indeed in a minority (twenty out of sixty-four) although they are, of course, essential to the understanding of Verne's 'project'. Science enters as a basic factor into the romantic composition and plots of all Verne's books: scientific theories, scientific enigmas, scientific solutions.

The plots turn upon scientific theories needing to be proved or disproved. This 'experimental' quality is the main point of interest in *Captain Hatteras* (to verify the existence of an ice-free body of water in the Polar regions), in *A Journey to the Centre of the Earth* (to check whether the theory of the central fire is correct), in *The Clipper of the Clouds* (to decide between the partisans and the opponents of heavier-than-air flying machines), in *The Southern Star Mystery* (to prove the possibility of producing diamonds in the laboratory by synthesis from a gaseous flux of carbon). Similarly, the opening chapters of *The Superb Orinoco* turn upon a dispute among geographers about the upper course of the Orinoco River in Venezuelan territory while Dr Johausen's theories about the language of monkeys lead to the discovery of *The Village in the Tree Tops*.

Many of the journeys are based on scientific activities and techniques; not only imaginary activities such as those of Nemo, Robur, Professor Liddenbrock, Dr Fergusson, Barbicane, but also exploits implying a complete mastery of the scientific techniques then known. Such, for instance, is the case with the difficult triangulation work carried to a successful conclusion in South Africa by a group of English and Russian astronomers; chapter XIX of the novel is headed 'Triangulate or die'. A similar case is that of the ingenious Dr Clawbonny who manages to light a fire by delicately cutting a lens out of a bit of ice with which he then focuses the rays of the polar sun.

Verne is adept at making use of natural disturbances and scientific enigmas: for instance, the comet Gallia which passes close to the earth and tears out bits of the terrestrial crust, completely changing the system of days and nights, and leaving the victims of the disaster to wonder

The weighing of the comet Gallia (*Hector Servadac*), illustrating Verne's intense interest and faith in science.

about it without understanding what has happened (*Hector Servadac*). Another instance is the change in the itinerary of the brig *Pilgrim* (*The Boy Captain*) whose compass is put out of order by an evil-doer hiding a piece of iron close to it, with the result that the ship makes landfall in Africa after rounding Cape Horn; the passengers are brought face to face with innumerable botanical and zoological enigmas. It is the same with the settlers of Fort Espérance (*The Fur Country*) who have built their sub-Polar establishment on an ice island attached to the land, but which breaks away from it; for a long time they are unable to understand all the changes in the natural order of things that they experience in this new 'land'.

Science provides both plot and dénouement, and also the solution for desperate situations. It is the error made by the scientist Paganel in the nomenclature of the Pacific islands which gives meaning to the seemingly useless journey of Lord Glenarvan in his search for Captain Grant. It is the astronomer Black's knowledge of physics which enables the survivors on the ice island, when they are within sight of the Kamchatka coast, to delay the melting of the ice by the use of compressed air. It is the efficiency of the human retina, examining a huge enlargement of the photograph taken immediately after the murder, which leads to the discovery of the true identity of the murderers of Captain Gibson (*The Brothers Kip*). It is the nature of fresh water, which does not mix with salt water, that saves the desperate survivors from the shipwreck of the *Chancellor* who think they are on the point of dying of thirst in the middle of the Atlantic although their raft has already reached the waters of the Amazon. Many more instances could be given of such 'marvellous events' which owe nothing to fairy tales or to the supernatural; they are 'scientific marvels', if one may risk such an expression. The hackneyed phrase, 'a miracle of science', is here used in its most literal and rational sense.

Although affairs of the heart have only a small place in Verne's writings, he even uses science as a factor for success or failure in such matters. It is thanks to his scientific accomplishments that the engineer Cyprien Méré wins the love of young Alice in *The Southern Star Mystery*; he courts her while teaching her chemistry. On the contrary, it is his stupid pedantry and elementary knowledge of science which prevent the ridiculous Aristobulus Ursiclos from carrying to a successful conclusion his plan to marry Helena Campbell (*The Green Ray*).

Finally, it is from science that Verne draws his best characters. It has often been said (and most recently by P. Macherey) that Verne is not, generally speaking, much interested in the finer points of psychology; his preference is for vast undertakings, wide horizons, unforeseen adventures, while the characters taking part in them are hardly more than conventional and fairly banal outlines of men and women, having no real human depths. It is not by chance that the only characters in Verne's books who are firmly established from the literary point of view, who really come alive, who stir our imagination and fascinate us, are scientists and engineers: the 'terribly eccentric' Professor Liddenbrock, for instance, whose goodness of heart is for long hidden by his irritability, and whose human qualities are only discovered by his nephew when they are thousands of metres below the surface of the ground. Then there is Dr Clawbonny, 'lively and talkative with his heart in his hand', whose good humour and moral staying-power are so important for the success of Hatteras's expedition:

> This worthy man was the life and soul of their little world, radiating sincerity and probity. His companions had absolute confidence in

Dr Samuel Fergusson and his companions crossing the Niger in their balloon (*Five Weeks in a Balloon*).

him; his words, his actions and his habits exerted such an influence over them that the six men, forsaken six degrees from the Pole, came to look on their conditions of life as being nothing out of the ordinary.

Other characters drawn with the same vigour are those of Dr Fergusson, courageously launching out into the African skies; the geographer Paganel who, in a fit of absent-mindedness, joins the expedition setting out to search for Captain Grant; the engineer Cyrus Smith, to whose prudence, know-how and toughness the survivors of the crash owe their lives; and above all, Captain Nemo, untamed, strange, violent yet cultured. All these are 'characters'. Indeed, they are among the most brilliant creations in the whole of literature. In the world of the *Voyages extraordinaires* they are magnificent embodiments of science who, at one stroke, ensure for science a prominent place in literature.

In Verne's novels, however, science plays a much bigger role than that of a simple literary motive, however masterfully the author may have used it for that purpose. It is science itself which he presents, in the seemingly dry-as-dust form of scientific reports and scientific popularizations. In accordance with Hetzel's phrase quoted above, Verne did not hesitate to 'sum up all the information gathered by modern science' for the benefit of his readers.

Of all the sciences, it is perhaps geography which was closest to Verne's heart, and to it he dedicated several special works not included in the *Voyages extraordinaires*, such as an *Illustrated Geography of France* in two volumes, a *History of Great Journeys and Great Travellers* in three parts. Above all, almost all his novels contain long didactic explanations of a purely geographical character drawn from the extensive records which he had collected and which he kept carefully up to date (e.g. with the aid of the review *Le Tour du monde*). His treatment of geography was, no doubt, purely descriptive and still very far from the interdisciplinary method of exposition used by French geographers starting with Vidal de La Blache.* Nevertheless, it plays a leading role in Verne's writings, and it helped greatly to familiarize his young readers with northern India (*The Steam House*), eastern China (*The Tribulations of a Chinese Gentleman*), Oceania (*Propeller Island, Mistress Branican*), central Africa (*Five Weeks in a Balloon, The Boy Captain*), the Polar regions (*Captain Hatteras*), Russia in Europe and Asia (*Michael Strogoff, Keraban the Inflexible*), and South America (*The Giant Raft, The Superb Orinoco*), etc.

Geography is allied to cartography, and Paganel, in *The Children of Captain Grant*, waxes lyrical about the pleasures of the latter:

> Can there be a truer satisfaction, a more real pleasure than that experienced by a navigator when he points on his ship's charts the discoveries he has made? He sees new lands forming bit by bit under his eyes and, so to speak, emerging from the waves, island by island, cape by cape! At first the outlines are vague, broken, interrupted. Here there is a lonely encampment, an isolated bay, and further on a gulf lost in space. Then the discoveries complete each other, the lines join up, the dots on the chart give place to a solid line; the bays become openings in a known coastline, the capes jut out from fixed shores; finally, the new continent with its lakes, its streams, its rivers,

*Paul Vidal de La Blache, 1845–1918, French geographer.

its mountains, its valleys and its plains, its villages, its cities and its capitals, unfurls on the map of the world in all its magnificence and splendour.

That is to say that cartography is the activity by which, above all others, mankind takes possession of the earth; thus it is not surprising, as we shall see later, that this form of science holds an important place in Verne's writings. The naming of geographical features and the drawing of a map, however summary, is always an important event, almost a solemnity, in the life of the small communities which Verne sends to live in unknown lands as the result of a catastrophe or an adventure: the survivors of the air-crash in *The Mysterious Island*, the colonists of *The Second Fatherland*, Hatteras and his companions. In many cases Verne himself took the trouble to draw, with evident relish, maps of these imaginary lands, maps which were carefully reproduced by his publisher, Hetzel.

Triangulation is a more elaborate and scientific method in this taking possession of the surface of the globe, and it is given great prominence in *Measuring a Meridian*, a novel rightly considered to be one of the least 'romantic' in the whole series. The purpose and methods of triangulation needed for measuring the terrestrial meridian are explained in this novel with some severity for the sole object of educating the reader, and with no fear that he may become bored.

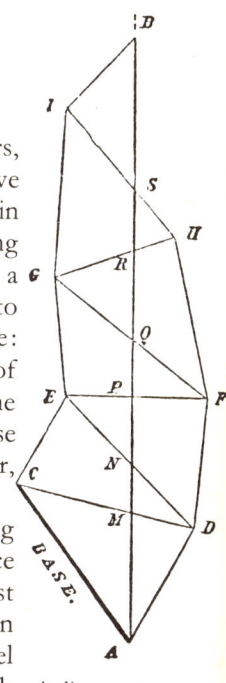

A diagram to explain the measuring of a meridian.

After geography, astronomy is certainly the branch of science in which Verne was most deeply interested. His novels contain many chapters designed to popularize astronomy. *Round the Moon*, an even less romantic novel than the one just referred to, is a novel without 'action', and necessarily so because the protagonists are shut up in their space-craft; it is basically nothing more than a long series of popular lectures on lunar astronomy. Those who have read *Hector Servadac* have nothing more to learn on the subject of comets, just as readers of *The Fur Country* will know all about eclipses. As a British critic has noted, Jules Verne's meditative and speculative turn of mind was incontestably fascinated by 'the eternal silence of infinite space'.[34]

Verne also devotes a great deal of space to the 'natural sciences': zoology, botany, mineralogy. It is with obvious pleasure that numbers of animal and vegetable species are listed and described in *20,000 Leagues under the Sea* (where submarine fauna and flora are concerned), in *The Boy Captain* (referring to Africa), and in many other novels. The *Journey to the Centre of the Earth* is copiously interspersed with geological digressions and descriptions; chapter III of *Black Diamonds* ('the sub-soil of the United Kingdom') is a piece of anthology brilliantly summarizing the theories commonly accepted in Verne's day about the origin of coal.

These long lists of zoological and botanical names, these long descriptions of volcanic, geological or meteorological phenomena provide Verne, paradoxically, with an opportunity for letting his poetic fancy run free, for losing himself in technical terms and strange assonances. We need do no more than refer to those passages in *20,000 Leagues under the Sea* and *Captain Hatteras* which have rightly impressed the literary sensibilities of Michel Butor and Pierre Macherey; they have absolutely nothing at all to do with children's books.

On the other hand, certain branches of science are not nearly so lengthily and systematically treated. Chemistry gets a showing occasionally, for instance in the explanation of the properties of carbon (*The Southern Star Mystery*), the theory of fire-damp (*Black Diamonds*) and certain episodes in *The Mysterious Island*. The departure of Michel Ardan and his companions for the moon provides an opportunity to initiate the reader into the principles of ballistics. The mathematical theory of probabilities is used to extract the meaning of coded documents in *The Giant Raft*. But Verne was clearly less well founded in physics, chemistry, biology and mathematics than in the natural sciences of geography and astronomy, or at least he gave them a less prominent place in his works. What he was interested in, above all, was those branches of knowledge which describe the earth and the universe and enable the enumeration of their riches and potentialities. This brief account of the passages in Verne's works devoted to scientific popularization already leads to the thought that he was principally concerned with the relationship between mankind and the universe and the former's hopes of being able to exploit the latter.

The didactic nature of the passages we have quoted, and consequently the didactic nature of the *Voyages extraordinaires* as a whole, derives also from the care with which Verne sought to retrace in detail the history of man's acquisition of scientific knowledge, instead of just presenting it as it was known at the time. Clawbonny entertains his companions, and Hatteras keeps up their morale, by telling them the story of Polar expeditions. Elsewhere we are given the history of triangulation, or of attempts to fly (*The Clipper of the Clouds*). Verne had a very acute, and very modern, appreciation of the cumulative nature of scientific research, of its collective acquisitiveness. He says with reference to Robur's airship: 'Without the groping experiments of his predecessors, could an engineer ever have conceived so perfect an apparatus?'

The same point is amusingly made in *The Children of Captain Grant* when Paganel is challenged to give the names of a hundred explorers of the Australian continent. The long list he gives – for he wins his bet – reads like a list of martyrs; in the last analysis, it is an acknowledgment of the collective character of these voyages of discovery, which are individual exploits in appearance only.

Verne is thus deeply convinced of the necessity for a scientific and rational exploration of the universe, and he does his best to carry his readers with him by making familiar the material world around them.

The members of the international expedition meet in *Measuring a Meridian*.

He has the very greatest respect for scientific truth, as is shown in the episode where Cyprien Méré discovers – or thinks he has discovered – a way of synthesizing diamonds and refuses, even at the risk of endangering his own life, to keep his discovery secret, whatever the consequences to the diamond industry:

> If I kept the secret of my discovery to myself, I would be no better than a forger! I would be selling underweight, and I would be deceiving the public about the quality of the goods! The discoveries made by a scientist do not belong to him, they belong to everybody.

The firing of the projectile in *From the Earth to the Moon*.

To keep for oneself, for one's personal profit, the least part of them, would be to commit the vilest act of which man is capable....

Thus, although there may be room in the *Voyages extraordinaires* for scientific mistakes as necessary steps towards further progress, and although such mistakes, as has been said, may be skilfully used by the author as a factor in his plots, there is no room at all for scientific imposture. Science does not tolerate forgeries; it insists on the very strictest intellectual integrity.

It is not, however, Verne's sole purpose to widen his readers' scientific knowledge, to develop their feeling and respect for science, and to give the latter its place in literature. He uses science in his writings to raise in the most general way the question of the relationship between man and the natural universe around him. This relationship between man and nature is, according to both Butor and Macherey, and indeed it seems so to us, indisputably the basic theme of the *Voyages extraordinaires*, after setting aside a certain number of alibis and illusions, of which the label 'children's books' is by no means the least.

Verne does not think of nature as having a real existence apart from man and being hostile to him. The natural universe and the human universe are related to each other and in some way consubstantial; they may be analyzed in identical terms as, for example, the following beautiful description of basalt formations in Iceland, quoted by Macherey; the wonders of the Stapi Fjord are evoked in terms intentionally borrowed from human architecture (*Journey to the Centre of the Earth*):

> Everyone knows that basalt is a brown rock of igneous origin. It occurs in formations of surprisingly regular shape, as if nature had followed the laws of geometry and, like a human workman, had made use of set-squares, compasses and plumb-lines. If everywhere else she plays the artist, piling up great, disorderly masses of rock in the strangest of shapes like irregular cones and imperfect pyramids, in this place nature seems to have wished to give an example of regularity. Long before the first architects of earliest times, she here created order of the purest kind, unsurpassed by the splendours of Babylon and the wonders of Greece.
>
> The walls of the Fjord and the whole coastline of the peninsula consisted of a series of vertical columns, beautifully proportioned and rising to a height of thirty feet; they supported an archivolt of horizontal columns overhanging the sea like a half-dome. Under this natural *impluvium* can be seen a series of admirably shaped, ogival openings through which the sea foams. Some sections of basalt columns have been torn from their places by the ocean's fury and litter the ground like the ruins of some ancient temple, ruins forever young and undamaged by the passage of the centuries.

Far from being man's enemy, nature provides inexhaustible resources of wealth and power which human agency may exploit to the fullest extent. Thus mankind's role, to quote the felicitous expression used by Butor, is 'to fulfil the world's age-old desire'.[35] In the last analysis, it is human endeavour, not some abstract concatenation of natural circumstances, which will decide the fate of the world. Dr Clawbonny, discussing the habitability of the Polar regions (*Captain Hatteras*), says:

> ... I do not believe that there are any uninhabitable countries. By his selfless devotion, generation after generation, using all the

resources of scientific agriculture, man will end by making such lands fertile.... Were you now to visit the lands which were famous in the earliest days of the world, the site of Thebes, or of Nineveh or Babylon, in those valleys made fertile by our ancestors, you would think it impossible that men could ever have lived there, and the atmosphere itself has become vitiated since men deserted them. It is a general law of nature that countries where people have never lived are unhealthy and sterile, like those where man no longer lives. Take good note of it, it is men who make their own country, by their presence, by their customs, by their industry, and I will even say by their very breath. Little by little, by the mere act of breathing, man changes and improves the exhalations of the soil and the conditions of the atmosphere. Therefore, I can agree that there may exist lands which have never been inhabited, but never places which are uninhabitable.[36]

One of Verne's best novels, *The Mysterious Island*, is also one of the most significant; it is a sort of parable about man's progressive mastery over nature. The island is a microcosm, a symbolic recapitulation of all the animal, vegetable and mineral resources of the earth ('... one might call it a résumé of a continent in all its aspects'). All this natural wealth is there to be utilized by the survivors of the shipwreck; 'this is nature's gift to us, and this is her share of the common tasks', says Cyrus Smith, pulling out of his pocket specimens of iron-ore, pyrites, clay, lime and carbon, when he returns from an expedition into the mountains. It is, however, the scientific knowledge of the colonists, in particular that of the engineer Cyrus Smith and of the young naturalist Harbert, which is to enable them to exploit such resources and turn to good use the possibilities offered by the island. It is by his knowledge, by his adeptness, that man can master nature:

> They did not even possess the tools necessary to make tools, and they were not even in that state of nature where, given time, a minimum of effort is needed. Time was running out on them since they had to provide for the immediate necessities of existence; and if, thanks to their previous experience, they had no need to invent anything, they had everything to manufacture.

The creative activities of the colonists, therefore, serve to underline the allegorical nature of the novel by recapitulating the successive technological victories of mankind: pottery; metallurgy, by smelting ore and carbon in a fire worked by bellows made from sealskin; chemistry, by producing sulphuric acid and nitroglycerine with the help of pyrites, and by manufacturing candles and soap; carpentry, wicker-work, sugar. Then later there will come glass, weaving, water-wheels and fulling-mills, windmills, shipbuilding and even the electric telegraph.

Professor Cyrus Smith gives a lecture on how a grain found by one of the survivors of the air-crash will proliferate and provide food for the group (*The Mysterious Island*).

Such for Verne is the deepest meaning of progress: the modification of the relationship between men and nature, much more than a change in the relations between man and man or in the structure of human societies. It is this conception of progress as the progressive domination of nature by man which is held by the travellers in the 'Steel Giant' looking forward to the day when the Himalayas will be conquered (*The Steam House*):

> It will be accomplished, just as one day men will travel to the North and South Poles.
> —Of course.
> —As men will reach to the deepest parts of the oceans.
> —Without any doubt.
> —As they will travel to the centre of the earth.
> —Bravo, Hod!
> —As everything will be accomplished, I added.
> —Even journeys to each of the planets of the solar system, replied Captain Hod, whom nothing could stop.
> —No, Captain, I replied. Man is a simple dweller upon the earth and cannot go beyond its limits. Although he is tied to its surface, however, there is nothing to prevent him discovering all its secrets.
> —He can and must, Banks continued. Everything within the limit of possibility must, and shall be accomplished. Then when man has nothing more to learn about the globe he lives on . . .
> —He will disappear, together with the spheroid which will hold no more mysteries for him, replied Captain Hod.
> —No, indeed, said Banks. He will then enjoy it as a master and take better advantage of it.

Dr Fergusson, as he flies over Africa in his balloon and foresees the day when the natural resources not only of Europe, but also of America, will have been exhausted, has a similar vision of human progress:

> Then Africa will supply new races of men with the riches accumulated within her bosom during the centuries. The climates now deadly to foreigners will be purified by the rotation of crops and by drainage; those scattered bits of water will be joined up together so as to form a navigable waterway. And this land over which we are gliding, richer, more vital and more fertile than all others, will become a great realm where there will be discoveries even more astonishing than the discovery of steam power and electricity.

Verne's faith in the progress of science is so strong that he even includes China in its future development, thus contradicting all the commonly held clichés of his day about Chinese conservative habits and resistance to change. His only novel dealing with China (*The Tribulations of a Chinese Gentleman*) has as its hero a young man from Shanghai who is passionately interested in new techniques. 'Kin Fo was a man of progress who welcomed every modern Western invention...' He held shares in a Chinese steam navigation company, he had installed telephones between the different buildings of his *yamen* (residence), together with electric bells; he used a phonograph to communicate with his fiancée in Peking.

Verne thus includes Asia in the field of action of future progress, and thereby demonstrates, it may be said in passing, that he possessed a very lively and modern feeling for world affairs and political problems. The way of progress is open to Asia as it is to Europe, and man is free to follow it, like the Chinaman Kin Fo, or to turn his back on it like his antithesis, the Turk Keraban. *Keraban the Inflexible* is a narrow-minded conservative who refuses to travel in a train or to wear Western clothes: 'He is a faithful member of the Old Turk Party who refuse to admit that there is any good in modern things whether in the field of ideas or of customs, and who protest against all the inventions of modern industry.'

The universe described in the *Voyages extraordinaires*, thus forcibly linked to the idea of progress, is a universe where the line between the conquests already achieved by science, and those which have not yet been achieved, is constantly moving. This is the idea underlying the lofty formula which does duty as a sub-title for the whole collection: *Known and Unknown Worlds* (*Les mondes connus et inconnus*). Verne was acutely aware of the dialectic between present and future knowledge. For him, according to Macherey, 'the future bathes in the present'. This is what the reader is told in the very first page of *Carpathian Castle*:

> This story is not fantastic, it is only romantic. It would be a mistake to conclude from its improbability that it cannot be a true story. We are living in days when anything can happen – one may almost say that everything has happened. If our tale seems improbable today, it need not be so tomorrow, thanks to the resources science will make available in the future, and nobody will then think of calling it fanciful.

This faith in the future of science was yet again stated by Verne when he made his hero Robur disappear in his aircraft under the eyes of a crowd of Americans who had overwhelmed him with sarcasm and whom the engineer thought were too little advanced to be worthy of sharing his secret (*The Clipper of the Clouds*). 'Robur', he says, 'is the future of science, the science perhaps of tomorrow. It is the certain store of knowledge awaiting us in the future.'

If progress means a continually increasing degree of mastery over the natural world, the scientist and the engineer are preeminently the agents of progress, the real heroes of modern times. The knowledge and skill of Verne's scientists enables them to take advantage of all the natural resources of the planet. Morally and intellectually they are characters of the highest standing. They are like 'well-tempered steel', such as Barbicane and Nicholl (*Round the Moon*); 'men of uncommon stamp', like Professor Liddenbrock. Such scientists are not narrowly specialized, but men of vast scientific culture, 'polytechnicians'. Liddenbrock was 'a real scientist, combining a genius for geology with the eye of a mineralogist.' Dr Clawbonny, when asked to join a Polar expedition, takes advantage of the occasion to reveal the encyclopaedic extent of his learning: 'I am offered the chance of completing, or rather of refreshing, my knowledge of medicine, surgery, history, geography, botany, mineralogy, mechanics and hydrography. Very well, I accept.' Dr Fergusson also, the first-born of the long line of demiurges who dominate the *Voyages extraordinaires*, is 'a man of character . . . Never at a loss . . . A member of the Church militant, . . . spending his time in research rather than in discussion, discovery rather than discourse'; he considered that 'obstacles are there to be overcome, and as for danger, who can hope to avoid it? Life itself is dangerous.'

It is the figure of Cyrus Smith which best sums up all these intellectual and moral qualities of Verne's scientists: to encyclopaedic learning he adds a taste for theorizing about vast subjects, and the ability to work with his hands; he is a man of good humour and moral rectitude (*The Mysterious Island*):

> He had one of those handsome, 'numismatic' faces which seem made to be reproduced on medals, with keen eyes, a serious mouth, and the looks of a scientist of the militant school. He was one of those engineers who had chosen to start his career by handling hammer and pick-axe, like those generals who choose to start their careers as private soldiers. In addition to possessing quick wits, he was supremely competent in the use of his hands. Truly a man of action as well as a thinker, he coped effortlessly with all difficulties in the plenitude of his vitality, and he had that lively doggedness which defies all ill-luck. Very well educated, very practical, very *débrouillard* [resourceful], to use French military jargon, he was a superb character because, while able to control himself under all circumstances, in him were fulfilled to the highest degree the three conditions which, between them, determine human action: an active body and mind, impetuous courage and great strength of will.

It is through machines that man exercises control over nature. The *Voyages extraordinaires* are populated by machines as much as by scientists, travellers and engineers. Verne was writing at a time when the machine gave promise of extending human possibilities, without yet seeming to threaten human life and ecology. There was no question then of polluting living waters, nor of degrading the countryside nor the seashore with masses of industrial refuse. That is why, far from comparing noisy machinery unfavourably with the quiet harmony of the countryside and life under conditions of simple nature, Verne never allows an opportunity to pass for proving that machines can be integrated into the world of nature, thereby extending it, even if going beyond it.

There is one image of which he is particularly fond, and which is highly symbolic of this integration of machinery with nature: it is the smoke from a train rolling around trees and adding itself to the natural shapes of the vegetation. In *Black Diamonds*, the description of the abandoned coal-mine with which the novel opens, suggests the same organic unity of machinery with nature; the galleries and mine shafts are as ruggedly romantic as the natural caves of the Scottish mountains rising over the mine. The coal-bearing seams are described as if they were a living organism ('the carcass of a fantastically enormous mastodon whence all the organs it had in life have been removed, leaving only the skeleton'). The last bit of coal is like 'the last drop of blood'. In *Carpathian Castle*, the electric machinery designed by the owner of the old township with a view to frightening away the local peasantry is intimately integrated with the romantic landscape of rocks and cliffs, and with the medieval ruins above them.

But machinery is integrated with nature only so as to extend it and surpass it. Such is the case with the 'Steel Giant', a kind of train whose locomotive is shaped like a gigantic elephant, and whose carriages are models of Hindu temples (*The Steam House*). This symbolism is intentional, even if Verne attributes the choice of the shapes to a Rajah's fancy. The steel elephant is copied from nature but surpasses it:

> 'One horse-power mechanical,' the engineer Banks declared with pride, 'is equivalent to the force exerted by three or four natural horses, and this power can be increased even more. Mechanical horse-power is not affected by fatigue, nor illness; in all weathers, at all latitudes, in sunshine, rain and snow, it goes on working and never gets worn out.'

It is the same with *Nautilus*, which moves through the deeps of the sea as easily as the creatures who live there, drawing motive power from the products of the sea and also food for its passengers, but which at the same time transcends the natural conditions ruling the lives of the submarine fauna (*20,000 Leagues under the Sea*). When the submarine's presence is reported, it is taken for a gigantic narwhal, and a specialist from the Paris museum is called in only to discover the mistake when he is invited on board. As for the paddle wheels of the giant liner *Great Eastern*, they seem to belong to some fantastic creature rather than to a bit of machinery conceived by human reason (*A Floating City*):

> Their elegant casing, the solidly seated hub serving as the main point of support for the whole system, the intersecting stays designed to

The 'Steel Giant', a train in the form of an elephant and Hindu temples, the whim of the Rajah of Bhutan (*The Steam House*).

maintain the distance between the triple felloes, the halo of red spokes, all this mechanism half-hidden in the shadow of the wide paddle boxes, impressed the mind of the viewer and evoked the idea of some strange and mysterious power.

Such a dialectic of machinery as both fulfilling and overtaking nature is perfectly analyzed by Robur in his attempt to prove that heavier-than-air flying machines are superior to dirigible balloons; he reminds his opponents that the concept of a balloon was never used by nature when producing creatures with the power of flight, and that such creatures

The transatlantic liner *Great Eastern*, which Verne describes in *A Floating City*.

are always heavier than air. If 'the laws of nature' are to be the pattern for the construction of flying machines, they should not, however, be 'slavishly copied'.

If machines thus fulfil nature, they become at the same time part of human life and extend human potentialities. Machines are no more antagonistic to mankind than they are to nature; and here again Verne likes to illustrate his idea by the use of stylistic effects which are of great significance, whatever their literary value may be. He often makes use of metaphors conjuring up the image of the man-machine. Such is the case with Dr Clawbonny: 'At whatever cost, he simply had to be able to

41

express his thoughts openly, otherwise the machine might blow up.' Of Colonel Everest (*Measuring a Meridian*), Verne says: 'This astronomer's life was mathematically regulated hour by hour. There was nothing unexpected about him. In everything he moved with the precision and punctuality of a heavenly body passing the meridian.' Of the Russian astronomer, Nicolas Palander: 'Forever absorbed in his calculations, he could have been an admirably organized machine; but he was more than a machine, he was a sort of universal abacus or computer.'

It is with the character of Phileas Fogg that Verne carried to its furthest point the portrait of the man-machine (*Around the World in Eighty Days*). Fogg's whole life is that of a well-regulated, extremely precise machine; he functions 'without friction', i.e. in his social relationships; his clothes are numbered, his daily time-table is minutely regulated, and he has surrounded himself in his daily life with an even more complex machinery of numerous speaking tubes and other technical arrangements.

In his story *Mr D Sharp and Miss E Flat* there is an even more striking description of the 'mechanization' of human personality. A music teacher who dabbles in magic repairs the organ of a little village in the Swiss Alps, adding to it a new register, of children's voices. He obtains this result, however, by shutting up each of the village children in an organ pipe and making them permanently sing the same note. Their voices are heard when he depresses the keys of the organ. 'I am only an instrument in the hands of the organist', one of the voices declares, 'when he strikes the key-board it is as if a valve in my heart opened!'

Thus if there is no insurmountable barrier, no difference in kind, between man and machine – or between nature and machine – the essential function of the latter in Verne's works is to establish and extend man's control over nature. This is not the place to make a list of Verne's scientific forecasts, nor of the innumerable machines and mechanisms thought up by him (that has been done elsewhere),[37] but it is worthwhile investigating the purpose they were designed to fulfil.

These machines of Verne's serve in the first place to increase man's mobility, to help him overcome the contradiction of space-time by means of speed, to move through the air, in the water or in the least hospitable regions of the earth. *Nautilus* dives into the depths of the sea (its motto is *mobilis in mobili*), in the same way as the 'electrics' of Mathias Sandorf. Fergusson's balloon and Robur's aircraft move through the air, and Barbicane's lunar module even escapes out of it. The 'Steel Giant' traverses the forests and mountains of India without altering its line of progress, and the 'Terror', Robur's second vehicle, can travel with equal ease in water, on the land or in the air.

In the second place, Verne's inventions allow men to communicate with each other beyond space and time. Such is the purpose of the apparatus, in *Carpathian Castle*, designed to allow Rodolphe de Gortz to continue to see and hear the singer from whom he has been separated by death; a secret telephone links the castle to the inn, and the only purpose of all the other mysterious machinery in the castle is to guard this photophonograph from prying eyes. Similarly, Mathias Sandorf gives orders to his crew by a kind of radio, while the town council of Franceville (*The Begum's Fortune*) conducts its sessions by means of a kind of 'telex', each councillor remaining in his own house.

Finally, Verne's machines and inventions are conceived with a view to increasing man's creature comforts and improving the conditions of his everyday life. It is significant that the first real bit of machinery constructed by the colonists in *The Mysterious Island* is a lift. *Nautilus* is not only a model of mobility, but also a model of comfort, and it is the same with Robur's 'Albatross'.

Verne's machines are thus designed for travel, communication and comfort with the sole object of giving each man greater control over nature, and of widening the natural and physical conditions governing human life. With the two exceptions of Stahlstadt and Blackland, of which we will speak later, his machines are not designed to serve the purposes of great captains of industry or large-scale manufacturers. In other words, Verne's machines and mechanical arrangements *do not produce surplus value*.[38] It is surprising that an author of the stature of Macherey should not have mentioned this fundamental point, when the rest of his work is such an interesting contribution to the Marxist interpretation of the *Voyages extraordinaires*. For the machines in these stories do not generally require any human labour; they exploit the resources of nature, not the labour of man. This point is underlined by the fact that Verne hardly ever enters into any detail about how the machines were made; this is very typical, and was the norm in the society in which he lived. The construction of *Nautilus* was 'sub-contracted' piecemeal to the best workshops of the Ruhr, Sweden, Liverpool, Glasgow and New York before being secretly assembled by Nemo and his companions. The originality of Verne's ideas about future scientific developments is apparent in his use of electricity as the motive power for his machines. Fifty years before his predictions came to be realized by science, he was vaunting the uses of electrical power and utilizing the idea to great advantage. With the exception of the 'Steel Giant', almost all his machines work by electricity. He did not, however, see electricity only as an avant-garde technique, a victory for science and the human mind, but as a short-cut towards the mastery of nature; it also avoided the necessity of having to provide an answer to awkward questions about the role of labour in a modern mechanized world. *Nautilus*' batteries operate directly from sea-water, while Robur's are recharged by a mysterious process, like those in *Carpathian Castle*, or those others which work the fantastic arc-lamps of the subterranean coal-mine in *Black Diamonds*.

Verne's machines, at least in his earlier works, have no effect upon social relationships, which is the reason why, at this stage, his predictions of scientific developments are not linked with any similar predictions in the politico-social field. Later, it was to be different; his attitudes towards science, machines and progress were to become increasingly pessimistic, and he wrote eventually about 'cities of perdition' such as Stahlstadt, Milliard City and Blackland.

Modern though they may be from a technical point of view, Verne's machines also have something archaic about them. They are the expression of human ingenuity, of man's wish to free himself from the restraints of nature; they increase man's control over space and time, but they do not enslave humanity and they are not bound to the implacable necessities of large-scale capitalist production.

Verne's engineers are closer to the Renaissance engineers of the da Vinci type than they are to the captains of industry, like Eiffel,* of Verne's own time. His inventions are the direct descendants of those of Leonardo and, before him, of Hero of Alexandria,[39] and they are unrelated to the requirements of nineteenth-century industry on the grand scale.

---

*Gustave Eiffel, 1832–1923, French engineer, specialist in metal construction; the tower in Paris named after him was constructed for the Universal Exposition of 1887–89.

CHAPTER III

The 1848 tradition

... They were portraits, portraits of those great men of history who had lived only to devote all their time to a great human ideal: Kozciusko, the hero who died with the words *Finis Poloniae* on his lips; Botzaris, the Leonidas of modern Greece; O'Connell, the Irish patriot; Washington, the founder of the United States; Manin, the Italian patriot; Lincoln, killed by a bullet from a slave-owner's gun; and finally John Brown, that martyr to the liberation of the black races, hanging on his gibbet as so frighteningly depicted by Victor Hugo.[40]

These etchings hanging in Captain Nemo's study are one of the keys to the political system of the *Voyages extraordinaires*: sympathy for the struggle of oppressed peoples, of whom Nemo is the self-declared champion – for the revolt of the 'slave races', whom he proposes to liberate.[41] *20,000 Leagues under the Sea* is in fact one of the books which most clearly reveal these deep-lying tendencies; in using his rebellious hero's preferences to acclaim those 'heroic souls', Verne was expressing a political opinion all the more deliberate because the novel was written in the days of the Second Empire with a government in power which, although its absolute character was then (1868) becoming attenuated, none the less still carried, in the eyes of advanced thinkers, the stigma of the infamous 1851 take-over.

It is not by chance that Verne was sympathetic towards the ideas of 1848, particularly in regard to nationalist movements in Europe. Born in 1828, he was twenty at the time when 'the peoples' springtime' began, and it was with the '48 revolution that his political consciousness awoke, an event accelerated by the fact that he was in Paris at the time for the purpose of sitting for his law exams. In the Spring of 1848 the atmosphere of Paris was in strong contrast to the peaceful bourgeois way of life he had always known in Nantes. He was still influenced by that *milieu*, witness his membership of a students' club in the Rue de Poitiers which was anti-revolutionary in character, and his declaration that he favoured 'the quiet moderation of M. Thiers* and his associates, because they represent law and order.'⁴² Nevertheless, in addition to the fact that we need not interpret too literally a statement intended for the eyes of his parents, on whom he was still financially dependent, it is permissible to conjecture that he could not have failed to think deeply about all that sudden political agitation going on around him. Furthermore, on his next visit to Paris in the autumn of 1848 to continue his studies, he took all possible steps not to miss the great romantic festivities organized by Lamartine* in the Place de la Concorde in honour of the new Republican constitution. Along with one of his friends, he tried to stow away on a special train reserved for the representatives of the provincial national guards; he was very bitter at being made to get off and at not reaching Paris until the evening of the festival 'when the last candles were smoking'.⁴³

Three years later, his hostile reaction to Napoleon III's seizure of power shows that he was still faithful to 'the peoples' springtime':

> Don't believe a word of the newspapers which may reach you, or of the public proclamations. Serious street battles took place on Thursday and houses were destroyed by gunfire! ... It is a scandal, and public anger against the President is widespread, and also against the army which has disgraced itself on this occasion. This is perhaps the first time that right and legality are on the side of the insurgents. Many people have died, most of them persons of good standing. I do not know how it will all end! but I don't really ... [illegible], and in any case one dare not say a word for risk of hanging.
>
> ... Napoleon has already failed with the publication of his second decree; this no longer makes it obligatory for each ballot paper to carry the name and qualifications of the voter, an obligation which used to infringe the liberty of conscience of all civil servants who might otherwise have voted for him for fear of losing their jobs.⁴⁴

The company which Verne frequented in Paris at the beginning of his creative period (starting in 1865) also influenced him in the direction of the '48 tradition. His publisher, Hetzel, who also acted as his literary adviser and mentor, and for whom he had deep admiration, had been in 1848 principal private secretary to Lamartine, then Minister for Foreign Affairs in the provisional government,⁴⁵ a post he relinquished when Louis-Napoleon was elected President of the Republic, though he continued his active opposition to the latter's ambitions. At the time of

---

*Adolphe Thiers, 1797–1877, French statesman active in the government under Louis-Philippe, supported the election of Louis Bonaparte in December 1848, President of the Republic 1871–1873.

*Alphonse de Lamartine, 1790–1869, French poet who served in the provisional government after the rising of 1848.

the *coup d'état* in December 1851, Hetzel had been put under arrest for some hours but managed to reach Belgium, from which he returned only in 1860. In 1864 he started publishing a review for young people called *Magasin d'Education et de Récréation*,[46] of which Jules Verne became a co-director with Jean Macé who, several years later, founded the League of Education. It was in such republican-minded circles with their '48 tradition that Verne's social contacts principally lay towards the end of the Empire, and it was among them that he first met, for example, his great friend Nadar,* another victim of the 1851 proscriptions, who was famous for his skill as a photographer and for his attempts as an aviator. A certain nostalgia for the hopes of 1848 is also implicit in the critical summing-up made by Verne just before the Empire came to an end:

> ... Yes, that is what the Empire has brought us to after eighteen years of power: a thousand million in the bank, trade and industry at an end; eighty stocks on the market paying no interest, not to mention those which are still likely to fail; a military statute which takes us back to the times of the Huns and Visigoths; the prospect of a series of stupid wars.[47]

Verne had republicans and democrats among his friends in places far beyond the frontiers of France. He was, for example, in close relations with the Russian woman democrat Vovtchok (1833–1907) who was almost exactly his contemporary and who translated some fifteen of his novels into Russian during his lifetime. Marko Vovtchok was married to a Ukrainian writer, A. V. Markovitch; she had contacts with the Russian revolutionary-democrats in the 1860s, took an active part in the struggle for the abolition of serfdom in Russia and dedicated several of her books to that problem; she was known as the 'Harriet Beecher Stowe of serfdom'. She collaborated also with Hetzel in the production of his *Magasin d'Education et de Récréation*.[48]

In the opinion of his family, Verne had three consuming passions: 'freedom, music and the sea',[49] a trinity which certainly also bears the imprint of '48 romanticism. The sea, to which he devoted so much space in his books, fascinated him with its limitless horizons, its 'pure, health-giving breath', its 'supreme tranquillity'. In the enthusiastic words of Captain Nemo: 'There alone is freedom; there I recognize no master, there I am free!'

Great as was his love of pleasure cruising, Verne was also passionately fond of music, as are several of his heroes: Captain Nemo himself, for instance, lost in dreams at the keyboard of his organ, or the 'concert quartet' whose performance is so perfect that it leads to their being

---

*Nadar, pseudonym of Félix Tournachon, 1820–1910, French photographer, writer, draughtsman and aeronaut; the first Impressionist exhibition, 1874, took place in his studio.

kidnapped by the multi-millionaires of *Propeller Island*.⁵⁰ But with Verne's third passion, freedom, we move away from personal adventures and aesthetic emotion to the sphere of politics.

Nationalist movements are often described in the world of the *Voyages extraordinaires*, sometimes only anecdotally, but always with perfect clarity. Thus, the peasant revolts in Transylvania are brought into *Carpathian Castle* in order to give depth to the strange figure of Baron Rodolphe de Gortz; the latter had formerly taken part himself in an insurrection in the company of the bandit Rosza Sandor, and 'had not forgotten his Transylvanian homeland during all his long peregrinations'. The hostility felt by the Hungarians for the Austrians and Germans serves as background to *The Secret of Wilhelm Storitz*. Nemo, when his *Nautilus* is cruising in Mediterranean waters, is able to help the Cretan insurgents in 1868 thanks to the gold he had wrested from the wrecks of galleons in Vigo Bay. Scottish nationalism is dealt with in *The Children of Captain Grant*: the latter tried to found a colony of 'independent' Scotsmen since 'his country's interests could never be the same as those of the Anglo-Saxons'; in his own country he was a national hero ('All Scotland will join me in the attempt to save this great-hearted man who has devoted his life to her', says his compatriot Lord Glenarvan as he starts out to look for him). The brave Sinn Fein rebels of Ireland are described in *The Brothers Kip*, two blameless men who, in the English penal settlement of Port Arthur in the Pacific, get to know the Irish rebels who were 'tracked down without mercy' and 'treated with excessive severity'; when Irish revolutionaries from the United States manage to free their comrades, the two brothers seize the opportunity to leave with them. Finally, in *A Lottery Ticket* Verne gives pride of place to the Norwegian separatists 'most solicitous of their prerogatives' at the time when Norway, under the regime instituted by the Act of Vienna, was subject to the Crown of Sweden, from which she was to gain her freedom only in 1905. One of the characters of the novel is Professor Hog who 'had constantly and unshakably opposed the encroachments of Sweden'; Verne noted in this connection that 'so marked was the difference between the two peoples that the Swedish flag was flown on neither Norwegian buildings nor ships.'

All this indicates that Verne was extremely well informed about the struggles for freedom and the national sensibilities of the smaller peoples of Europe – to the point even, as with Scotland, of going beyond the real course of history. In the same way, in *The Hunt for the Meteor*, he imagines that Greenland has broken away from Denmark and has become an independent state.

In all these cases, however, national movements are mentioned only briefly in novels with a central theme of a quite different nature, viz. the forecasting of scientific developments as in *20,000 Leagues under the Sea, Carpathian Castle, Wilhelm Storitz*; while romantic adventure is the main theme of *A Lottery Ticket, The Brothers Kip* and *The Children of Captain Grant*. On the other hand, in six of his novels, including some of the most important, liberation movements among the oppressed peoples of Europe provide the central theme and the main plot: Greek independence in *Islands on Fire*, Hungarian nationalism in *Mathias Sandorf*, Bulgarian struggles against Turkish oppression in *The Danube Pilot*, Irish nationalism in *Foundling Mick*, the national struggles between Baltic barons and Russian peasants in *A Drama in Livonia*, the nationalist movement against British domination in French Canada in 1837 in *Family without a Name*. In all these novels Verne underlines the force of national sentiment:

> It seems that the Greeks draw from the unstable soil of their land an instinct for physical and moral restlessness which can carry them to the greatest excesses in an heroic cause. It is, nevertheless, true that thanks to their natural qualities of indomitable courage, patriotism and love of freedom, they have been able to build an independent state out of those provinces which, for so many centuries, bowed beneath Ottoman domination. (*Islands on Fire*)

Similarly in *Mathias Sandorf* he brings out the strength of Hungarian nationalism, the feeling of being neither Slavs nor Germans, together with fidelity to the Catholic Church and the use of the Hungarian language:

> The Hungarians still speak their ancient language, a mother-tongue which is soft, harmonious and capable of expressing the beauties of poetry; less rich than German, but more concise and vigorous, a language which from the fourteenth to the sixteenth century was used in place of Latin for legal and official documents until it attained the status of a national language.

The opening chapter of *Family without a Name* ('Some Facts, Some Dates') is a forceful summary of the struggle for independence of the French Canadians, 'outraged by Great Britain' since the annexation of 1763. Verne criticized the narrow-minded view of the English authorities who 'can see nothing more important that the activities of a subversive faction when what they are dealing with is a national upsurge'. He likewise salutes the courage and selflessness of patriots such as Mathias Sandorf, a great aristocrat who had sacrificed all his property in the cause of Hungarian freedom and who, vilely betrayed by a paid informer, addresses his companions as he faces death: 'My friends, I may be the cause of your deaths, but it is not for me to ask your pardon for this. The independence of Hungary is at stake. Our cause is just and it is our duty to uphold it. It will be an honour to die for it.'

Serge Ladko (*The Danube Pilot*) is a similar character: a young Bulgarian who is the leader of the nationalist party in his native town of

Jean-without-a-Name, the hero of Verne's novel about the French Canadian uprising of 1837, *Family without a Name*.

Rutschuk in the Danube delta ('he had also the moral qualities of a leader: speed in decision, prudence in action, a passionate love for his country'). Such also is the mysterious 'Jean-without-a-name', a guerilla leader described in such a way as to make him appear a very modern militant revolutionary, who is the soul of French Canadian resistance to English power ('a veritable legend had grown up around this character and this gave him an extraordinary influence over the masses'). In point of fact, he is the son of a traitor to the French Canadian cause, and is seeking to expiate his father's crime.

Redolent as they are of revolutionary romanticism and entirely in accord with the 1848 tradition, these novels give, by antithesis, an equally important place to the policy of brutal repression by the foreign Power whose control of the country is threatened by the nationalist movement: the proud English aristocrats in Canada, the Austrian police and their dealings with shady characters from whom they learn about Sandorf's plottings, and above all the Turks whose Chios massacres are denounced in the same way as their Bulgarian massacres fifty years later.

In all these novels, nationalist struggles are more than a mere framework designed to make the plot livelier by adding some picturesque historical material. They provide the mainspring of the action. Nationalist movements are the factor which determines the quality and lives of the characters, the psychology of the scenes, even the rhythm of the book. *A Drama in Livonia* is a detective novel turning upon an error of justice; but the accused is a Slav, his presumed victim is an employee of the biggest German bank in Riga, and the whole affair has intense political undertones. *Islands on Fire* is dominated by the patriotic struggle of the old Greek peasant woman, Andronica Starkos, against her son Nicolas, alias the pirate Sacratif, who is both a traitor to Greece and a slave dealer. Mathias Sandorf is another Monte-Cristo, but he seeks to avenge a whole people and not simply a personal injustice. All the strange events of Ladko's journey on the Danube, when he assumes the disguise of the fisherman Ilya Brush, can be explained by the fact that he is one of the leaders of the Bulgarian nationalist party. The despair and hopes of 'foundling Mick' are inseparable from the destiny of the whole Irish people. The dramatic power of *Family without a Name* springs from the fact that these three French Canadian patriots, a mother and her two sons, intend to give their lives for the French Canadian homeland, and they are all the more ready to do so because the head of the family had earlier betrayed the nationalist cause for money.

Only an author as well versed as Verne in the history of the nationalist struggles of his day could have used that knowledge to such advantage in the composition of his books.

Jules Verne does not, however, consider nationalist struggles as being simply manifestations in support of abstract ideas; on the contrary, he attaches great importance to their social significance and the social context in which they take place. In *Islands on Fire*, the Turks are not only foreigners and detested as such by the Greeks under their rule, they are also slave-owners and accomplices of the pirates in the archipelago who are making fortunes, thanks to the complicity of the Ottoman authorities, by selling in Africa thousands of innocent captives. French Canadian separatism is presented as a democratic and popular movement with an essentially peasant social basis; its slogans are: 'Run, tyrants, the people are awakening! A bloody struggle rather than oppression by corrupt power!'

In *A Drama in Livonia* Verne shows even more clearly his acute sense of social realities; chapter VI of the novel is called 'Slavs and Germans', and could just as well be 'Classes and Nations'. We are given a very skilful and clear analysis of the social forces facing each other in Riga and in Livonia generally: on the one side, the 'privileged classes' of the nobility and the bourgeoisie, who are of German origin and 'have imposed themselves in the Baltic provinces'; on the other side we have the working people of the suburbs of Riga, who are of Slav origin, and above all the Livonian peasantry 'forming the real native population', both of whom are exploited by the great German feudal barons. The Germans, says Verne (who had a taste for figures), 'own in Livonia alone the greater part of the countryside extending to at least 400,000 hectares,' whereas in the three Baltic provinces at the end of the nineteenth century only some 150,000 out of two million inhabitants were of German origin, including the nobility, the merchants and the bourgeoisie.

The Livonian peasants, on the other hand, lead miserable lives:

> Those poor moujiks! In their miserable hovels they have to put up with summer's heat and winter's cold, with the rain and the snow at all times. And what can be said about their food? Black and flabby bread made of husks with, ever so seldom, a few mouthfuls of bacon or salt beef. What an existence!

The antagonism between the German and Slav communities, arising from national differences, is thus accentuated by the social antagonism between the people of property and the workers:

> In the Baltic provinces the nobility, the honorary citizens, the bourgeoisie and the merchants are almost exclusively of Teutonic origin. Although these Germans managed to convert the people to Catholicism first, and then to Protestantism, they have never been able to turn them into Germans. The Estonians, those brothers of the Finns, and the Letts, nearly all of them sedentary husbandmen, take no pains to hide their racial antipathy for those who rule over them.

This antagonism is the dominating feature in the municipal politics of the city of Riga when two of the most important characters in the novel are in competition for the post of mayor: the wealthy German banker, Johausen, and Nicolef, the professor from Moscow, who is poor but highly thought of by his compatriots. In the university of Dorpat a similar antagonism exists between the different student 'nations', those of Germanic origin and the Slavs (there are barely fifty of the latter as against 900 of the former): 'The struggle between German and Slavic tendencies showed signs of becoming more marked in university circles.' Even in the ranks of the police this national rivalry could be felt, most of the policemen being of German extraction, and more than one of them 'very prone in the exercise of his duty to favour the citizens of his own race as against the Russians in Livonia.'

In *Foundling Mick*, the social factor in the Irish nationalist problem and its economic basis are just as clearly described. The hero is an orphan boy adopted by an Irish farming family. Their landlord, however, is an Englishman, Lord Rockingham, and Verne makes it obvious that the exploitation of the Irish peasantry by absentee landlords is the key to the Irish nationalist problem at that time: 'the result of this absenteeism is that the money produced by Irish labour goes out of the country and is of no profit to Ireland'). A bad winter like that of 1880/81 brings distress and famine, and 'the nationalist movement tends to become stronger in the counties; that is what happens each time the shadow of famine rises over the Irish countryside.'

The MacCarthy family, who adopted foundling Mick, are unable to pay their taxes or the rent for their farm; the bailiff refuses to give them time to pay, with the result that the family are evicted by the English police. This is the 'abominable eviction' of which Verne gives a detailed and moving description. 'After so many evictions like this, so frequent and carried out in a manner amounting to ferocity, why should any one be surprised that so much hate has gathered in the hearts of the Irish peasants?' All that the MacCarthy family can do is to emigrate to Australia where their subsequent life is a succession of miseries.

Foundling Mick, by means of the subterfuge of the nationalist struggle, also contains the only mention in the whole of Verne's universe of the class struggle of the proletariat as such. We have already noted, indeed, the virtual absence of the working classes in the *Voyages extraordinaires*. This is the result of the da Vinci character of Verne's machines, most of which are concerned with making life more comfortable for individual people rather than with industrial production, reflecting at the same time the Saint-Simonian tendencies of Verne's ideas. The miners of New Aberfoyle, for example, live in idyllic social conditions of progress through work. The workers in the Blackland 'factory' (*The Barsac Mission*) are the victims of a despotic tyrant rather than of economic exploitation by big industrialists; when they finally resort to action under the leadership of Camaret and his faithful overseer, Rigaut, the revolt assumes an essentially political character. As for the miners and metal workers of Stahlstadt (*The Begum's Fortune*), they are positively crushed under the iron heel of a great capitalist industrial magnate, Herr Schultze; the episode of the young miner asphyxiated by carbonic gas leaves us in no doubt about this. But they are well paid and seem to have no revolutionary ideas. If, on the other hand, Verne's picture of the workers' revolt in Belfast includes a description of working-class insurrections, and not just of the hardships under which they live, as is the case in *The Begum's Fortune*, it is because he wishes to underline the idea that nationalist movements 'reinforce' social discontent:[51]

> The street was barred by a closely packed crowd. He had to find a way through the noisy mass of people. It was pay day, and a number of working men and women had gathered. They had just listened to an announcement that their pay was to be cut from the following week, and this had exasperated them to the highest degree.
>
> The reader should know that this industry of growing and spinning flax had been brought to Ireland, and principally to Belfast, long ago by Protestant refugees from France after the revocation of the Edict of Nantes. These families still have a considerable stake in several such factories. This particular factory was the property of an Anglican company. Now, as the majority of the workmen were Catholics, it is easy to understand why the latter were pressing their protests with a frightening degree of violence.
>
> Soon the shouts turned to threats and stones were thrown at the doors and windows of the factory. At this moment several squads of police entered the street to break up the meeting and arrest the ringleaders.
>
> Afraid of missing his train, Foundling Mick tried to get away but could not do so. He had to huddle in a doorway to avoid being trampled, thrown down and crushed beneath the police charge. Five or six workmen fell beside the wall after being brutally struck.

The social basis of nationalist struggles is searchingly analyzed in *Foundling Mick*; it is in fact in this novel that hostility towards the nobility, a factor evident throughout the *Voyages extraordinaires*, is most strongly expressed. This very bourgeois dislike of the nobility is the reason why Verne makes such caricatures of Lord Glandover (*The Begum's Fortune*), Sir Edward Turner (*Caesar Cascabel*), Sir Francis Trevelyan (*Claudius Bombarnac*) and Lt. Franz von Grawert (*Flight to France*), a point which has been picked up with a very acute sense of class by M. Ghislain de Diesbach, an author who is socially related to these illustrious victims of Verne's irony.[52] Diesbach also points out that, even when they are not ridiculous, most of Verne's aristocrats die without heirs, as if their caste had been stricken with a kind of historical sterility: Frantz de Telek and Rodolphe de Gortz, the Marquis of Vaudreuil and Lord Glenarvan. This severe treatment meted out to members of the nobility is in fact a basically bourgeois trait, provided that the bourgeoisie is defined (which M. de Diesbach failed to do) in its historical sense, the result of historical experience, that is, as a social category born

The English aristocracy in Verne's novel about Irish nationalism, *Foundling Mick*: Lord and Lady Piborne and their son.

out of the struggle against the nobility. The '48 tradition is here in direct line of descent from the tradition of 1789–93. In *Foundling Mick* Lord Piborne is both hateful and ridiculous:

> His Lordship of Piborne is fifty years old – fifty years to be added to the several centuries which his noble family can muster in direct line of descent without once having lost their noble status. An important member of the House of Lords, it is in good faith that he deplores the loss of ancient feudal privileges, the era of fiefs, dues, freeholds and domains, when his ancestors were the dispensers of justice, enjoying the homage of each and all of their liege vassals.

> Tall, thin, smooth-faced, eyes lustreless from long exercise in the expression of disdain, of few words and curt, Lord Piborne is a typical representative of those haughty gentlemen moulded in the semblance of their old parchments. . . . [His son] has regular and quite insignificant features and, even though grown up, gives no sign of vivacity nor intelligence. He is indeed the natural issue to be born to a Marquis and a Marchioness two centuries behind everyone else, obstinate opponents of all modern progress, true Tories from pre-Cromwellian times, incapable of change . . . He has none of the good qualities of youth, no spontaneous generosity, no liveliness of heart, none of the enthusiasms of youth. . . .
>
> Such persons are certainly becoming rarer, these high-born gentlemen whose destiny it is to become very distinguished nonentities, but they are still to be found, and Count Ashton Piborne is one of them.

Verne did not select these qualities of arrogance and stupidity by chance; he chose them for their deep social connotations which he explains with perfect clarity, namely the double national and social oppression of the Irish peasantry by the great Anglo-Saxon landlords settled in the island since the seventeenth century.

Foundling Mick is at the same time a vindication of mercantile capitalism carried to the intentionally paradoxical point where an eleven-year-old boy makes a fortune in the City of Belfast, having started as a simple barrow-boy. The 'august imbecility' of Lord Piborne and the 'beautiful profits' made by the little gentleman are linked together by very logical, solid and historical ties, almost as conclusive as the demonstration of a problem by a teacher in the classroom: the national and social liberation of the Irish people runs *pari passu* with the expression of anti-feudal sentiments and the fight against the feudal system, as well as with admiration for the profits of capitalism.

The antithesis of Ireland, with its feudal society, is to be found in Norway, and the praise lavished on that country by Verne underlines his basic political outlook (*A Lottery Ticket*):

> Norway has no aristocracy; but if democracy is dominant there, that does not prevent it from being aristocratic in the highest degree. All are equal at the top, instead of being equal at the bottom. A genealogical tree is still shown, even in the humblest shanty, as proof that the family has not degenerated, although its roots are once again deep in common earth; on it can be seen the quarterings of the noble families of feudal days from whom these simple peasants trace their descent.

Verne's opposition to slavery is one more reason to think of him as a spiritual heir to the ideas of the 1848 revolution. It is well known that the abolition of slavery, proposed by Schœlcher,* was one of the first Acts passed by the provisional government in Paris.

Much space is given to the question of slavery in Verne's writings. It forms the central theme of two important novels: *North against South* and *The Boy Captain*; it is often mentioned elsewhere and it always provides an opportunity for denouncing 'the odious traffic', 'the hateful exportation of slaves'. In *The Boy Captain* America as the land of freedom is symbolically contrasted with Africa, 'the Africa of the slave-dealers and slaves'.

The Weldon family and the young sailor Dick Sand, together with six free Negroes from the United States, thought they were travelling to America by way of the Pacific, but their ship is thrown out of course as the result of treachery and they land in Africa on the shore of a Portuguese colony, where slavery still prevailed at the time the action is supposed to have taken place (around 1880). Verne here relates in some detail the history of the traffic in African slaves; he also describes the Portuguese slave-traders, the convoys of captives, of whom many die on the road, the brutality of the overseers (*havildars*) and the slave markets.

As we have already seen, the slave trade is also denounced in *Islands on Fire*. The traffic in slaves, tolerated if not encouraged by the Ottoman authorities, was at its height around 1825 in all the Eastern Mediterranean. One of the main episodes of the novel (Chapter XII) takes place in the slave market at Scarpanto when the crew and passengers of a ship captured by pirates are offered for sale, including Hadjine the young daughter of a rich Corfu banker; during the auction two men bid against each other, the 'phil-hellenic' Henry d'Albaret who is a French officer engaged to Hadjine, and the slave-trader, Nicolas Starchos, who is after the girl's fortune. Verne was 30 years old when the Civil War broke out in the United States, and it made a strong impression on him. The abolitionist movement in America appears many times in his work. As we have seen, John Brown, hero of the ill-fated raid in 1859 against the Southern arsenal of Harpers Ferry, who was hanged after his defeat, is one of the men whose portraits are to be seen in Captain Nemo's study, along with that of Abraham Lincoln. John Brown is also honoured by Verne in another novel, *An Eccentric's Will*. Six persons compete in a vast game of which the squares on the board are the States of the Union. The chance of the game sends Max Réal, the most appealing of the competitors, to Richmond, Virginia. On the way he makes a 'pilgrimage' to

---

*Victor Schœlcher, 1804–1893, French politician, proscribed in 1851 for having opposed re-establishment of the Empire.

Martinsburg City 'wishing to pay his respects to a hero,' whose memory he salutes thus:

> John Brown was the first to raise the anti-slavery banner at the start of the Civil War. The Virginia planters tracked him down like a wild beast. He only had some twenty men with him. . . . After fighting with astonishing courage, badly wounded and unable to struggle on, he was captured and dragged to a town near Charleston where, on 2 December 1859, he suffered death by hanging – a death which the gibbet itself could not dishonour, and the glorious fame of which will be remembered from age to age. It is to the memory of this man who died a martyr in the cause of liberty and human freedom that I wished to pay my respects as a patriot.

Verne's vigorous support for patriots is also evident at the start of *The Mysterious Island*: the abolitionist survivors of the air-crash are prisoners in the Confederate capital, Richmond; they manage to escape by means of a balloon from which they fall into the middle of the Pacific as the result of a storm. These five men are typical of Verne's heroes with their skill, their ingenuity, their physical and moral stamina; at the same time, on the political plane, they are opponents of slavery.

The Civil War also furnishes the theme for a story written by Verne in his younger days, *The Blockade Runners*, in which he states that in his opinion the question of slavery is 'the principal issue' in the Civil War, and is more basic than the economic rivalry between North and South and the question of customs duties; he thus adopts a position typical of the ideals of '48, but which cannot be reconciled with the findings of historical research. One of the characters tries to enter the port of Charleston to arrange the escape of a prisoner held by the Southern forces. The fact that he travels on an English ship which forces the blockade in order to buy cotton in the port, does not prevent him from expressing lively disapproval of those who profit from such traffic: 'You are just as much to blame when you sell opium to the Chinese, thereby degrading them, as you are now when you are selling to the South the means to continue fighting in a criminal cause.'

In *North against South*, the whole novel is taken up with the struggle between the slave owners and the anti-slavery forces. James Burbank, a Florida plantation owner, is the target for the hatred of a Southern slave-owner named Texar. Challenged by the latter, Burbank sets all his labourers free, an act all the more courageous since he is in Southern territory, where the local whites become increasingly opposed to the idea of abolition as the Union army approaches Florida. When he tells the slaves that they are free, his words are a real echo of the generous and humanitarian traditions of 1848:

> As you know, my friends, a civil war between the peoples of the United States has already lasted a long time and a great deal of blood

A battle scene from *Islands on Fire*, showing Lt Henry d'Albaret, the phil-hellenic French officer.

has been shed. The real issue at stake in this war has been the question of slavery. The South, thinking only of what it believes to be its interests, wishes slavery to continue. The North, in the name of humanity, wishes to see it abolished in America. God has favoured the defenders of a just cause, and victory has already more than once crowned the efforts of those who are fighting for the liberation of a whole section of the human race. Everyone knows that I have, in loyalty to my family origins, long shared the Northern view without having been in a position to give effect to it. Now, circumstances enable me to hasten the moment when I can act in conformity with my opinions. Listen, therefore, to what I have to tell you in the name of all my family:

As from this 28th day of February 1862, the slaves on this plantation are freed from all servitudes. They are free men. There are no men who are not free at Camdless Bay.

Verne was thus absolutely and unreservedly opposed to slavery, but only from strictly humanitarian motives. He takes up a position of principle. He is not interested in questions of the productivity of labour, and he never suggests that the slave-owners had, or could have had, an interest in freeing their slaves as a means of increasing their efficiency as labourers.

This idealist and humanitarian outlook finds expression not only in the context of slavery, but is manifest in all Jules Verne's romantic works. He is a firm believer in the interdependence of all human beings, thereby showing himself a true heir to those who in 1848 added the word 'fraternity' to 'equality' and 'freedom' in the motto of the new French Republic.

This theme of interdependence and brotherhood comes into play, for instance, when people involved in some catastrophe are struggling to escape death. Such is the case with the survivors of the air-crash in *The Mysterious Island* when five Americans (an engineer, a sailor, a journalist, an economist and the latter's black servant) all live together in the most perfect harmony. It is due to this, as much as to the discreet help of Captain Nemo, that they are able to organize their life on the island in relative material comfort; even better, the old misanthrope Nemo is touched by the way they stand together, and it is this which makes him decide to help them.

The same thing happens in the case of Hatteras and his companions who start off on foot for the North Pole after the loss of their ship. Only their brotherly understanding gives them the strength to come through the trials and tribulations of a long, harsh winter on the ice. Even the early rivalry between Hatteras and the American captain, Altamont, whose derelict ship provided the party with invaluable supplies, finally dies away and is replaced by a 'brotherly' friendliness. Brotherly co-operation of this kind is an even more imperious necessity, the condition *sine qua non*, of survival for the unfortunate garrison of Fort Espérance, who thought they had founded a factory on the shores of the Arctic Ocean on behalf of the Hudson's Bay Company, and then found that they had, in fact, installed themselves on an ice-island; the latter becomes detached from the land and drifts away in the most dangerous circumstances. The party's safety depends upon their friendly co-operation with each other (*The Fur Country*).

In *Two Years' Holiday*, it is a party of children who learn at an early age the irreplaceable value of the great law of human interdependence. Pupils of a boarding school in New Zealand, they are thrust into the Pacific after the brig, in which they were sleeping during the absence ashore of all the crew, becomes detached from its moorings. The storm carries them to a desert island where they organize their lives like a society of adults, dividing the necessary chores among the members of the party, electing a leader, etc. At one time they divide into rival factions, but become fraternally reconciled on the arrival of pirates, from whom they manage to escape only with great difficulty.

Even stranger is the predicament in which the characters of *Hector Servadac* find themselves. Carried away by a comet passing very close to the earth, their safety depends, here again, upon the establishment of good relations among the survivors. This is not too difficult to achieve between a French officer of the army in Algiers and his batman, a group of Spaniards from Ceuta, a Russian Count and the crew of his yacht which has been cruising in the region. It is thanks to their solidarity that they are in the end able to reach the earth again when the comet has completed its orbit. On the other hand, the English garrison of Gibraltar, also carried away by the comet after the cataclysm, are lost as the result of their arrogance and refusal to co-operate with the other temporary inhabitants of the comet *Gallia*, or even to believe in the reality of the adventure. Those Englishmen are destined 'to revolve in space for ever', a conclusion which could hardly fail to please Verne's anti-British sentiments.

Similarly, the relations among the members of new social communities, several of which were dreamed up by Verne and included in his books, are governed by brotherhood and good understanding: the miners of New Aberfoyle in their gigantic coal-bearing caverns, who organize themselves into a harmonious society (*Black Diamonds*); the colonizers of *The Second Fatherland* somewhere in the Indian Ocean; the Indians of the Santa Juana mission in the high reaches of the Orinoco, who are civilized and organized by a former soldier of the French army turned missionary as the result of family troubles (*The Superb Orinoco*).

Finally, it is the conception of the brotherhood of men which dictates a man's behaviour towards those suffering from poverty, oppression and obscurantism. In *Caesar Cascabel*, a simple strolling player returning to Europe from California by way of the Bering Straits, befriends without hesitation, and well knowing the risk of doing so, a Russian prince sought by the Tsarist police for his subversive political activities. In *The Southern Star Mystery*, the engineer Cyprien Méré extends the same generous treatment to some Kaffir labourers who are being ill-treated and exploited by the diamond-mining firms of Griqualand. Even the obstinate and inflexible Phileas Fogg in *Around the World in Eighty Days* shows the same sense of human solidarity when it is a question of saving the young widow of a Rajah, whose duty it is to follow her husband into death in accordance with the Hindu rite of *suttee*. On another occasion, he does not hesitate to risk losing his bet in order to save his faithful servant, Passepartout, from the marauding bands of Sioux who have just captured him during the crossing of the Far West of America.

Title-page of the first edition of *Hector Servadac*.

(*Left*) Phileas Fogg at the Reform Club, where the wager of *Around the World in Eighty Days* is made.

The romanticism which imbues all Verne's work, and from which, surprisingly, attention has been diverted by his purely scientific contributions to literature,[53] is another proof of his attachment to the politico-literary tradition of 1848. The formula chosen by Jean Cassou as the title for the first chapter of his study of the spiritual values of 1848, 'Secret and Accursed Things',[54] could equally well be applied to the world of the *Voyages extraordinaires* or at least to many of its aspects.

Verne's landscapes are eminently romantic.[55] Windswept plains stretch to the horizon in monotonous immensity: the Russian steppe in *Michael Strogoff*, the Kalahari desert in *Measuring a Meridian*, the plains of Australia in *The Children of Captain Grant* and *Mistress Branican*. There are the rugged mountain landscapes of Scotland (*The Green Ray, Black Diamonds*), or of Transylvania (*Carpathian Castle*) and Norway (*A Lottery Ticket*); there are the frozen spaces of the Arctic zone (*Captain Hatteras, Caesar Cascabel*). Verne is fond of storms: the storm which drives the whaling ship *Saint-Enoch* to follow the hypothetical traces of the great sea-serpent (*The Tales of Jean-Marie Cabidoulin*), the storm which allows a fugitive from the Siberian penal settlements to cross the Russian frontier into Livonia (*A Drama in Livonia*), the one which blows onto the north-eastern shore of Siberia the ice-floe carrying Caesar Cascabel, the one which hurls Cyrus Smith and his companions into the middle of the Pacific (*The Mysterious Island*), the one which is challenged by the engineer Robur in his aircraft and in which he finally meets his death (*Master of the World*), the one which tests the strength of the gigantic liner Great Eastern (*A Floating City*), and many others. Caves also, those mysterious, freak formations beneath the earth's surface, provide Verne with one of his favourite settings for many of the episodes in his novels: the colonizers of *The Second Fatherland* find shelter in just such a romantic setting, as do Hector Servadac and his company on their comet, the Kaffirs who hide their treasure in a cave (*The Southern Star Mystery*), and the survivors of the shipwreck in *The Mysterious Island*. In *Black Diamonds* a series of caves provides room for a whole township, and in *Journey to the Centre of the Earth* caves are the landmarks in a fantastic expedition.

Verne's taste for decaying castles and ruins is also in the romantic tradition: the castle keep at Pisino where Mathias Sandorf and his companions are imprisoned pending their execution; the abandoned Spanish fortress hidden away in the flooded forests of Florida which serve as the haunt of Texar the Highwayman (*North against South*); the ruins of Dundonald Castle in Scotland with its 'fiery women' who frighten the superstitious local peasantry (*Black Diamonds*); the fortress of Ripore in central India (*The Steam House*); and above all the extraordinary *Carpathian Castle*, that old, haunted stronghold which is the scene of a whole series of fantastic events.

The world of the *Voyages extraordinaires* is also filled with romantic episodes and romantic characters. We have, for example, the deaths of

Frantz de Telek staring across at the mysterious castle of Rodolphe de Gortz (*The Carpathian Castle*).

Jean and his sweetheart Clary plunging over Niagara Falls to their deaths in the burning boat (*Family without a Name*).

Clary de Vaudreuil and Jean-without-a-name whose boat hurtles over Niagara Falls (*The Family without a Name*); the promethean death of Robur, felled by lightning aboard his flying machine during a tempest (*Master of the World*); Captain Grant's shouts piercing the night when the rescue ship fails to depart from his island; the nearly inaudible cries of the Eskimo girl trying to warn her friends that they are being carried away from the coast without knowing it (*The Fur Country*). Verne also has a liking for outcasts and people who are lonely and misunderstood: the watchmater Zacharius, damned by his pact with Satan; the alchemist Wilhelm Storitz; the engineers Thomas Roch (*For the Flag*) and Robur;

political exiles like Vladimir Yanof (*A Drama in Livonia*), Serge Narkine (*Caesar Cascabel*) and Ladko (*A Danube Pilot*).

Even more romantic in conception, and more surprising coming from the pen of a novelist normally so attracted to scientific progress and positive knowledge, are the ethereal feminine characters appearing so often in his books – imaginary beings, or taken from real life, we just do not know: young Nell of *Black Diamonds*, who has been brought up in the total darkness of a cave, and is at first mistaken for a *brownie*, a spirit of the mine, by those who meet her; the apparition of the mysterious 'lady in black' who arouses the interest of the passengers on the *Great Eastern*, and turns out to be a poor madwoman shut up by her husband; the 'wandering flame' is another romantic picture of a madwoman venerated by the Indians, who is eventually discovered to have survived the Cawnpore massacre at the time of the Indian Mutiny (*The Steam House*); the even more shadowy figure of Myra, forced against her will to drink a philtre which makes her invisible, at least until the birth of her child returns her to her normal appearance (*Wilhelm Storitz' Secret*); finally, the purely artificial figure of the Italian singer, La Stilla, whose voice and physical appearance could still be admired after her death by Rodolphe de Gortz, thanks to a number of machines (*Carpathian Castle*).

In the same way, it seems to us that Kenneth Allott was quite right in his study of Jules Verne to consider as a purely romantic poem the description in *A Journey to the Centre of the Earth* of young Axel, relaxing on the raft that carries him over the underground sea he discovered with his companion, the geologist Liddenbrock; he sees in reverse order the changes which have taken place during the geological cycles of the earth:

> The centuries flash past like days! I am going back along the series of the earth's transformations. The plants disappear; the granite rocks become soft, changing from solid to liquid under the influence of greater heat; the waters rush to the surface of the globe and begin to boil and turn to steam; the vapours cover the earth which is soon nothing more than a mass of gases, white-hot and as immense and as brilliant as the sun!
>
> In the middle of this nebulous mass, fourteen hundred thousand times bigger than the globe which it will one day become, I am swept out into interplanetary space. My body becomes refined, sublimated, in its turn and, like some weightless atom, becomes part of those vaporous immensities forever revolving in flaming orbits through infinite space.

Verne was a man of 1848 whose literary career continued well into the period of imperialism. He lived in a world infinitely wider, more complex and more disrupted by social and international contradictions than that of the '48 generation; the world of George Sand and Michelet,* of Flora Tristan and Victor Hugo.* It was a world which witnessed the explosive expansion of Europe over the whole planet. Thus Verne's humanitarian sentiments, deriving from the ideals of '48, were not confined to the nationalist movements in Europe, but included similar popular movements in the other continents. The pages of his novels deal with the Indian Mutiny as well as with the Irish Sinn Fein, the revolt of the people of Kashgaria in 1875 under the leadership of Yakub Beg against the Manchu dynasty, the nationalist aspirations of the Livonians, the nationalist revolt against English encroachments by both the French Canadians and the Boers. Today we are perhaps more sensitive to the world-wide significance of this list, living in a time when conflicts everywhere impinge on our horizon: Vietnam and Bolivia, Turin and Prague, Portuguese Africa and Northern Ireland. But this same planetary outlook and awareness can already be seen in Verne's writings, although he did not follow through this train of thought. He realized the strength of popular movements in the 'Third World', to use that anachronism. He may have been in secret sympathy with the struggles of colonial peoples. But in the end it was Progress which claimed him, and that implied Western domination. It is this conclusion which emerges from a study of his attitude to colonial populations.

---

*George Sand (Aurore Dupin, Baronne du Dudevant), 1804–1876, French novelist and revolutionary in the early days of 1848.

*Jules Michelet, 1798–1874, French historian.

*Victor Marie Hugo, 1802–1885, French poet and novelist, republican and representative of the Romantic movement.

CHAPTER IV

The echo of utopian socialism

'Steam and electricity for all tasks; in place of the exploitation of man by man, the exploitation of the globe by mankind': can there be a better summary of the *Voyages extraordinaires* than this famous phrase of Saint-Simon?[56] For Jules Verne, the systematic development of the resources of the world was the essential mission of mankind. Nature, far from being hostile, exists to supply man with inexhaustible reserves of wealth and power, enabling him to develop his activities to the utmost. It is towards such control over nature and the fulfilment of all its potentialities that the exploits of Captain Nemo and the engineer Robur are directed, together with the exploration of inaccessible places, such as the centre of the earth or the Polar regions, by the geologist Liddenbrock or Captain Hatteras, and also the activities of the colonizers in *The Mysterious Island*. For all these Vernean characters it is clearly a question of *careful, regulated, fraternal co-operation in the exploitation of the globe in the light of scientific knowledge*, a formula which was used in 1828 in *The Producer*, the first newspaper published by the followers of Saint-Simon.[57]

If men are thus capable of making effective use of the resources of the planet, this result can only be achieved by their labour and their knowledge. Both these Saint-Simonian themes of work and science have an essential place in the *Voyages extraordinaires*.

One of the mottoes of the followers of Saint-Simon was 'Down with idlers', and the founder of their school of thought used to refer to the fable of the bees winning their war against the hornets.[58] *The Mysterious Island* is in fact a Saint-Simonian parable, a hymn to the glory of labour. The underlying purpose of the novel is to show how, by their dogged endurance and labour, the five survivors of the air-crash, starting without any resources at all, are able to re-live a sort of summary of all the stages of human technological development: the case of tools supplied secretly by Captain Nemo for Cyrus Smith and his companions only appears on the scene after they have proved their readiness and zeal for work. 'You love this island', Nemo tells them when he is dying, 'You have changed it by your efforts and it is truly yours.'

Verne's veneration for work, evident throughout this novel, is further underlined by the contrast between it and the theme of a much later work, *Propeller Island* (1895). The latter is a kind of antithesis of the first island, a city of perdition, a floating island inhabited only by idle American multi-millionaires supplied with unheard-of luxury, whose wealth enables them to buy anything they want, including the services of intellectuals and artists. The island is destined to perish as the result of its inherent contradictions; it breaks into pieces when the two rival clans of millionaires competing for the government are unable to agree upon the course the island should take.

In *The Mysterious Island*, on the other hand, society develops in peace as the result of the labours of the inhabitants, although their work would have been in vain without the many-sided technological accomplishments of the engineer, Cyrus Smith. For Verne, scientists are the real, promethean heroes of modern times and, here again, he is linked directly to the Saint-Simonian vision of a world 'administered by scientists'.[59] Nemo, Liddenbrock, Fergusson, Robur, Cyrus Smith, Clawbonny are the élite of mankind, even if sometimes rejected.

The little community of shipwrecked survivors in *The Mysterious Island* has no more than symbolic importance: it comes into being through exceptional circumstances, and will disappear in the same way. In several of his books, however, Verne invented whole imaginary societies of people whose existence depends upon technology and labour, and who are actively following the road to progress: Franceville, the pattern of what a city should be (*The Begum's Fortune*); Coal City in its subterranean mine (*Black Diamonds*); the secret base of Antekirtta (*Mathias Sandorf*). All these are authentic scientific colonies such as the Saint-Simonians, and other currents of utopian socialism, dreamed of founding in Africa or America. It is a further pointer to Verne's interest in such ideas that in all three novels the cities in question escape disaster by a hairbreadth. Franceville just escapes destruction by a bomb filled with liquid carbonic gas made by the ruler of the rival city of Stahlstadt, a German thirsting for world domination. Coal City is endangered by the hatred of an old miner who dislikes progress, and tries several times to destroy the subterranean city; Antekirtta is attacked by Senussi raiders from Tripolitania under the leadership of the man who once delivered Sandorf into the hands of the Austrian police, and the city is saved only after a fierce struggle. The three cities, having surmounted all these dangers, are in Verne's eyes symbols of future progress, and it is worth our while to examine them briefly in closer detail.

Of the three, it is Franceville which is most fully described and whose utopian character is most systematically emphasized. A worthy French academic, Dr Sarrasin, learns while he is attending an international scientific congress that he has inherited a fabulous fortune; he announces, 'I look upon myself as a trustee of science . . . It is not to me that this

The ideal and idyllic city of Franceville in *The Begum's Fortune* (see p. 177).

money rightly belongs, it belongs to mankind, to progress', and he consequently decides to devote the unexpected fortune 'to designing a modern city on strictly scientific lines'.

This model city is founded by him in Oregon on land granted by the United States. The site selected provides yet another indication of Verne's attachment to the tradition of *Le Voyage en Icarie* by Cabet* and other attempts to found new societies on American soil. Franceville

---

*Etienne Cabet, 1788–1856, French socialist who sought to establish a Utopian community first in Texas, then in Illinois; died in St Louis, Mo.

follows to the letter the most modern rules for urban construction and hygiene. The walls of the buildings are of patent hollow brick, no house is more than two storeys high, each house stands in its own grounds planted with trees, and is reserved for a single family. The town plan is 'simple and regular'.

> Anyone wishing to be allowed to become a resident of Franceville needs only – but this is essential – to produce good references, be trained in a useful or liberal profession, in industry, science or art, and must undertake to observe the laws of the city. Idlers are not tolerated.
>
> The most important public buildings are the cathedral, some chapels, the museums, the libraries, the schools and the gymnasia, all luxuriously fitted out in a decent and hygienic manner worthy of a great city. . . .
>
> The main preoccupation of the founders of Franceville is to keep the place clean, individually and collectively. To clean and clean unceasingly, to remove and destroy as soon as formed the noxious emanations constantly arising in built-up areas, this is the main job of the central government. . . .
>
> Each citizen is given on arrival a little booklet in which, in simple and clear language, are explained the most important principles of life according to the findings of science. This shows that a perfect balance of all activities is one of the requirements of healthful living; that periods of work and of relaxation are equally necessary to the organs of the body; that the brain must work, as well as the muscles, until both are tired; that nine-tenths of illnesses are due to contagion transmitted by the air or by food.

Verne is dealing here with a very cautious form of utopian society, and he tells us nothing about the economic basis of the new city; he is content to say that 'all kinds of industry and commerce may be freely practised'. The government is organized on a rather vague democratic basis with a City Council, from which all important matters are referred to a plenary assembly of all the citizens. Hence it is a primary democracy in the manner of the old Swiss cantons. We are given details of only one government organization with repressive powers, namely the health police, who have very extensive powers and are recruited from the ranks of 'experienced men, real scientists, trained for the job in teachers' training colleges.' Franceville is nevertheless differentiated from the banal predictions of the hygienists by the importance attached to both work and knowledge and the 'down with idlers' attitude, thus tying it in with the Saint-Simonian tradition. The city is 'a gathering of happy, free, independent people', fully approved of by the *New York Herald*, which was in those days a daily newspaper of advanced views.

The miners' dwellings in Coal City, built inside a Scottish coal-mine (*Black Diamonds*).

On the other hand, in the case of the mining town of Coal City in its huge underground cave, the accent is on economic-social relationships, but only so that they may be seen in an atmosphere of class collaboration. The site is an old, abandoned coal-mine, its supply of coal exhausted. When the decision is taken to close the mine, it is the chief engineer, James Starr, who speaks to the miners (the shareholders and directors of the company being kept in the background, in accordance with the formula of Bertolt Brecht):

You have lived in this mine which has been emptied of coal by your labour. Your work has been hard, but not without advantage to you.

Our big family is now to be dispersed.... But do not forget that we have lived together for a long time and that the miners of New Aberfoyle have a duty to help each other.

The idea of *a big family* has a significant connotation in Verne's social thinking. In this novel, written in 1877, he conceives of the workers' interests as being complementary, not antagonistic, to those of the owners of capital. Later in the novel, new seams of coal are discovered and a vast mining city is built underground in a most exalted Saint-Simonian atmosphere of science and labour. The gigantic cave is lighted by two powerful electro-magnetic arc-lamps. The miners return to the abandoned mine, attracted by the assurance that there will be plenty of jobs and by the high wages to be paid as the result of the successful exploitation of the mine.

The people of this city, under the almost patriarchal guidance of the chief engineer, living together in amity and the joy of work, 'constitute one big family with the same interests, the same tastes, and more or less the same financial status.' It is the same term, 'one big family', that flows from Jules Verne's pen, and underlines the timidity of his social concepts.

Mathias Sandorf, transformed into the mysterious Dr Antekirtt, founds the island of Antekirtta after escaping from an Austrian fortress where he was imprisoned for his activities as a Hungarian patriot. This island also is a colony of scientists with utopian overtones, situated at the head of the Gulf of Tripoli; it has been turned into a modern, strongly fortified base and possesses a fleet of ultra-fast torpedo boats powered by electricity. It is electricity, also, which is used to ensure the proper working of all the public services such as transport, lighting, telegraph, etc. The island is run by a council of leading citizens who assist Sandorf ('not their master, but the first among them'). Some of the population live in the countryside, but the majority reside in the capital, Artenak. 'Instead of being built in the American chessboard style, with streets and avenues all running at right-angles to each other, the buildings were placed through the town in no particular order, following the natural contours of the land ... the general effect being cool, pleasant, attractive, and even enticing – a city in the true meaning of the word.' Later in the book we read 'Scientists and inventors came there at Sandorf's request and turned to advantage the discoveries which, without his advice and his wealth, might have remained undeveloped.'

Finally, Verne's power of imagination and his taste for forecasting social developments find expression in an essay entitled *The Ideal Township* which he read at a public meeting of the Amiens Academy on 12 December 1875, during his term as president of that learned society for that year.[60] He was, of course, indulging in no more than a whim when he suggested, for example, that in the year 2000 doctors would be paid only by those of their patients who were in good health, or that the

'Dr Antekirtt' inspecting the fortifications built to protect Antekirtta against the Senussi (*Mathias Sandorf*).

increasingly heavy taxation of bachelors would result in the town's population rising to 450,000. His preoccupation with health matters and urban planning is also evident at a time when he was doubtless already thinking about Franceville of *The Begum's Fortune* which was to be published in 1879, four years later: all the streets are paved and all public thoroughfares are well lighted; the main streets of the town have been widened and lengthened. Verne's attachment to modern scientific developments finds more serious expression, however, in the fact that Latin and Greek have disappeared from the schools' curricula and that 'they teach only purely scientific, commercial and industrial subjects';

it is also expressed in his description of an imaginary exhibition of 'machinery from America carried to the ultimate limit of progress'.

Verne's idea of the methods by which mankind may exercise progressive control over nature include, as Macherey has acutely noted, voyages of discovery, scientific inventions and colonization.[61] His conception of 'colonism', which was the word used in the nineteenth century, once again brings him into line with the Saint-Simonian tradition. For him a 'colonizer' was a man of progress – in the sense employed by Prosper Enfantin, the most active of Saint-Simon's disciples, when he gave his encouragement to the French colonization of Algeria, and made great efforts to revive it. For Paganel, one of the admittedly Saint-Simonian characters of the *Voyages extraordinaires* (was it not he who thought that railway shares were of greater worth than gold nuggets?), to colonize a place meant to develop its potentialities, and it is in the following words that he describes his future life on a desert island (and therefore necessarily exempt from all risk of trouble with 'the natives'):

> I will make a new life for myself. I will hunt, I will fish; in winter I will live in a cave and in summer in a tree. I will have store-rooms for my harvests; in a word, I will colonize the island.

The five inhabitants of Lincoln Island are in the same happy position, since their island has no native inhabitants (*The Mysterious Island*):

> When they reached the island they were nothing but survivors from a shipwreck with no idea of how they were going to force nature to provide the necessities to enable them to eke out a miserable existence. But now, thanks to the scientific knowledge of their leader and their own intelligence, they had become real colonizers furnished with arms and tools, having turned to their own use the animals, plants and minerals of the island, that is to say, the three kingdoms of nature.

The objective was to raise the island to the American standard of life, a development foreshadowed in the place-names they chose (Lincoln Island, etc.):

> We will make this island into a little America [says one of the survivors of the shipwreck]. We will build towns and railways and telegraph lines and, one day, when it has been properly regulated and civilized, we will offer it to the government of the United States.

Paddy O'Moore, an Irish farmer who has settled in Australia with his family, has the same conception of what a colonizer should be. He has fertile land and a home supplied with simple comforts (*The Children of Captain Grant*):

> Living with his hard-working family in buildings which are still new, in an almost virgin countryside, this man is a typical representative of an Irish colonist; weary of the poverty of his homeland,

he has come to seek wealth and happiness on the other side of the oceans; he shares his meals with his servants whom he regards as his equals.

O'Moore is a hard-working farmer who became the owner of some plots of land set aside for immigrants by the Australian government and 'he enjoys complete independence in the freest country in the world.'

In several novels it is soldiers who become the leaders of these colonizing movements, who direct the work of developing the new territories and who organize the social life of the pioneer communities. Does this not bring to mind Enfantin's well-known opinions relating to the 'peaceful army of labourers', to the use of the armed forces for carrying out public works, and to the army, taken as a whole, as the model of what the society of the future should be, with its hierarchy of authority and its discipline? Opinions of this kind were published in 1830–32, particularly in *The Globe*, Enfantin's own newspaper.[62]

In *The Fur Country*, for instance, it is Lt Jasper Hobson who, on behalf of the Hudson's Bay Company, has the responsibility for founding a trading post on the shore of the Arctic Ocean. His authority extends not only over his own company of soldiers, but also over the latter's families and certain other working people. The little colony survives the most terrible catastrophes thanks to its military discipline and its solidarity with its leader. In the same way, in *The Superb Orinoco*, the French Colonel de Kermor, having become Father Espérante, founds a 'mission' – more social than religious – among the Indians living in the virgin forests of Colombia. He organizes a militia and at the same time brings education and medical progress to his parishioners. In *Hector Servadac* it is more a question of survival than of colonization: a handful of Frenchmen, Spaniards and Russians are brought together by chance on a piece of the earth's crust carried away into space by the comet Gallia. It is Servadac, an officer of the French army in Africa, who organizes the social life on the comet in keeping with the Saint-Simonian tradition,* fixing the prices, allotting the living accommodation (in caves), deciding upon migrations (according to the temperature variations), and even taking charge of international relations (since there is also present on the comet the English garrison from Gibraltar).

It is, incidentally, in this novel that Verne mentions the 'Saharan Sea' for the first time, a body of water formed by joining the Shotts of southern Tunisia with the Gulf of Gabès, an idea later used as the theme of *The Invasion of the Sea*. This was a project worked out by an officer of the French army in Africa, Captain Roudaire,* with whose activities

---

*Christophe Louis Léon Juchault de Lamoricière, 1806–1865, French general and politician, was the type of person on whom Servadac could have been based.

*François-Élie Roudaire, 1836–1883, initiator of project for an interior lake in Africa.

and writings Verne was familiar. On the same page, Verne mentions an 'Australian Sea' the purpose of which, likewise, is to bring fertility to a desert basin. These two references to artificial seas, even though hidden away in a footnote, are not fortuitous; they give a certain discreet Saint-Simonian flavour to *Hector Servadac*.

In *The Children of Captain Grant*, the equation of military training with the ability to develop the resources of a colony is given humorous emphasis in the person of the former French sergeant of Basque origin, who is in command of a fort in the pampas on the edge of the zone of colonization; he brings up his twelve children with military discipline, making them drill each day.

Another reason for placing Verne in a certain Saint-Simonian tradition is the importance he gives in his writings to great public works. Already in 1825 *The Producer* was clamouring in its editorials for railways, and it was with railways that the policy of 'practical Saint-Simonism' had its first successes, after its many failures, in the days of the Second Empire when Enfantin sat on the Board of Directors of the Paris-Lyon-Méditerranée line, together with the Péreire brothers and Talabot.*

Railways are one of Verne's favourite topics and they have a privileged place in that long '*meditation on the straight line*', as Macherey describes the *Voyages extraordinaires*. Better than any other means of locomotion, they symbolize man's ability to travel all over the world without being deflected from his purpose, to girdle the globe and write his signature upon it. The British and American railways are described by Phileas Fogg in lyrical terms in *Around the World in Eighty Days* while he is travelling through India and the United States. It is only because railways exist that there is any point in his bet, and he almost loses it when a section of the line is found to be unfinished in central India. Verne's taste for scientific forecasts naturally draws his thoughts to the problems of transcontinental railway connections. In *The Clipper of the Clouds*, looking down from the aircraft *Albatross*, one can see the Trans-Saharan railway under active construction, 'that long ribbon of iron which is to join Algiers to Timbuctoo by way of Laghouat and Gardaïa, and which will later be continued to the Gulf of Guinea.' In *Claudius Bombarnac*, the 'great Trans-Asian railway' has just been inaugurated, and its 6,000 kilometres make it possible to reach Tiflis in thirteen days from Peking – including the Caspian crossing by steamer from Baku to Uzun-Ada. This line passes through Russian Turkestan and western China, thereafter splitting into a branch going to Peking and another to Nanking. It is indeed, to use the words of an American passenger in the train – an

---

*Jacob Emile Péreire, 1800–1875, and Isaac Péreire, 1806–1880, French businessmen, who founded the Crédit Mobilier and built the first railways in France.

*Paulin Talabot, 1799–1885, French engineer, involved in the building of early railways in France.

enthusiastic advocate of railway extension – a question of those 'iron bands which in the end will encircle the globe as if it were a cask of cider or a bale of cotton.'

Other books of the *Voyages extraordinaires* deal with imaginary large-scale public works stemming even more directly from Verne's predictions, such as the gigantic cannon of the Columbiad (*From the Earth to the Moon*) which is 900 feet long and weighs 68,040 tons; it is cast in one piece on the site in Florida by a veritable 'army' of several thousand workmen: 'Colossal though it may be, it was not beyond human capacities.' Verne goes on to describe the various steps in its manufacture with passionate attention to detail. Chapter XV is headed 'Festive

Lt Jasper Hobson, in the traditional Verne posture of the man standing motionless alone, looking out for a relief ship to come to the rescue of his party stranded in the Polar regions (*The Fur Country*).

Casting Day', when 1,200 furnaces stretching for two miles are to pour 136 million pounds of molten metal into the previously prepared cement mould:

> It was a moving and magnificent sight. . . . The earth trembled when that flood of molten metal, smoking to high heaven, turned the moisture in the mould to steam, projecting it in impenetrable clouds of vapour through the vents in the masonry. . . . Any primitive tribesmen wandering beyond the horizon might have thought that a new volcanic crater had formed in the middle of Florida. . . . But it was not that! Man alone was the author of those reddish vapours, those gigantic bursts of flame worthy of a volcano, those noisy tremors reminiscent of an earthquake, and that noise as if hurricanes and tempests were struggling together. It was due to the agency of man that a whole Niagara of molten metal tumbled into an abyss created by him.

Barbicane, Maston and Nicholl, promoters of this enormous undertaking and the journey to the moon, are met with again in a less well-known novel which is nevertheless significant in this particular context: *Upside Down*. With the object of causing the Polar ice to melt, they plan to straighten the earth's axis by harnessing the force of recoil derived from the firing of an enormous cannon; this would not only permit the coal deposits of the Arctic regions to be utilized, but the suppression of the declination of the earth's axis would ensure a more even length of the day and night from season to season, and would create more favourable conditions for human activities. The giant gun on the side of Mount Kilimanjaro is placed with its axis at an angle to the earth's surface – not perpendicular to it as in an earlier novel – or, rather, the gun consists of a tunnel in the rock into which both the charge and the shot will be placed, thereby avoiding the complications of making a real gun. The tunnel is lined with a perfectly bored casing of cast iron, and not far away a cannon ball of 180,000 tons is being cast.

Of course, this is no more than a fancy. Maston makes a mistake in his calculations and the explosion, when it takes place, has no effect at all upon the earth's position. But in two of his last novels, *The Lighthouse at the End of the World* and *The Invasion of the Sea* (the last to be published while he was still alive, in 1905), Verne again deals with the possibility of enormous imaginary undertakings with undoubted social utility: on the one hand, a giant lighthouse at Cape Horn placed on a tower 223 feet above sea level, and visible from a distance of 20 kilometres; on the other, as already mentioned, a canal, linking the Gulf of Gabès to the Shotts of southern Tunisia and those south of Constantine, navigable by sea-going ships. The creation of this 'Saharan Sea' would improve the climate, with beneficial results for agriculture, and at the same time facilitate commercial relations. An engineer named De Schaller, who

A view of the extraordinary cannon proposed by J. T. Maston in *From the Earth to the Moon*.

had studied at the influential *Ecole centrale des Arts et Manufactures*, is in charge of the work and at the same time the moving spirit in the concessionary company responsible for the project. The combination of technician and financier in one character is quite in the tradition of 'practical Saint-Simonism'. The project is successful; at the end of the novel the waterway is finished, and the Tuareg tribesmen, who had attempted to stop the work, drown in it.

The accent thus placed on themes such as the exploitation of the globe by mankind, 'colonism', the necessity for hard work and scientific knowledge, the importance of huge constructions, all bring Verne into line with the authentic Saint-Simonian tradition. Nevertheless, and this is quite clear, the latter exerted only a partial, and very late, influence over him. The working classes, upon whom the founders of the utopian socialist movement expended so much emotion, hardly figure at all in the *Voyages extraordinaires*; they are only mentioned in a few paragraphs of *The Begum's Fortune*. In the other novel dealing with large-scale industrial production, *Black Diamonds*, the workers are described as living in idyllic conditions of class collaboration; at the most, there are a few passing words which could be taken to imply that the author was not quite insensible to the real problems of the world of labour.[64] The question of women's rights and their place in society, to which Fourier* and Enfantin attached so much importance, is likewise very rarely touched upon in Verne's novels. As Marcel Moré has noted, Verne's female characters are conventional and lack both depth and verisimilitude;[65] Verne was in fact something of a misogynist. Finally, Verne pays little attention to all the religious aspects of Saint-Simonism. Despite fairly frequent references to Providence, to the Supreme Being, he is fundamentally a rationalist, an initiate of scientific thought. In many basic respects, therefore, Verne diverges radically from the utopian socialist tradition.

Nevertheless, it is possible to find in the *Voyages extraordinaires* a real echo of Saint-Simonism and Fourierism, although a tardy one (Jules Verne's writings covered the period 1860–1905). The many clues to this which we have extracted from Verne's works are corroborated by what is known of his relations with the last generation of the Saint-Simonians and the interest they aroused in him.

When Verne started on his literary career during the Second Empire, only 'practical Saint-Simonism' had survived;[66] Talabot, the Péreires, Michel Chevalier* and even Enfantin had renounced their utopian dreams in exchange for the solid reality of directorships on the boards of railway companies. De Lesseps,* a captain of industry who seized upon one of the great ideas of Saint-Simonism to make his fortune with the Suez Canal, is typical of the influence of Saint-Simonism with the industrial society of the Second Empire. It is not by chance that Verne was so great an admirer of Lesseps and pays tribute to his name on several occasions,[67] for it was Lesseps, then already a member of the French Academy, who was instrumental in obtaining the Legion of Honour

---

*Charles Fourier, 1772–1837, French philosopher and economist, founder of idealistic co-operative societies.

*Michel Chevalier, 1806–1879, Saint-Simonian economist and politician, supporter of the Empire.

*Ferdinand Marie, Vicomte de Lesseps, 1805–1894, French diplomat and administrator, responsible for the successful Suez Canal, also founded a company to build the Panama Canal, but this failed.

for Verne just before war was declared in 1870.⁶⁸ Nadar, Lesseps' secretary, was a great personal friend of Verne who gives him a place, under the transparent anagram of Michel Ardan, in *From the Earth to the Moon*.

Lesseps and Nadar were not, however, the only friends Verne had in Saint-Simonian and post-Saint-Simonian circles. He was also closely linked with Guéroult, one of Enfantin's earliest disciples who became an influential journalist during the Second Empire and died in 1872 'in the Saint-Simonian faith'.⁶⁹ Another follower of Saint-Simon, Édouard Charton,⁷⁰ was editor of *Le Tour du monde*,* a review which, by its presentation of geographical and ethnographical material in popular form, perpetuated the Saint-Simonian faith in mankind's mission to exploit the world's natural resources; Verne was an assiduous reader of the review, referring to it on several occasions and drawing from it a good deal of his geographical information.

Another scion of the Saint-Simonian family, Henri Duveyrier,* is mentioned several times by Verne, for example in *Mathias Sandorf* in connection with the Senussi fraternity's threat to destroy the scientific colony of Antekirtta.⁷¹ It was Duveyrier who was responsible for Verne's hostility towards the African Mahdist movement.⁷² As representative of the Geographical Society of Paris, Duveyrier accompanied Captain Roudaire in 1874 on a visit to the Shotts south of the Constantine region, and it is certainly not by chance that the information they gathered was used in *The Invasion of the Sea*.⁷³

Verne, a great music lover, seems to have been particularly fond of Félicien David,* whom he mentions several times, particularly in books dealing with North Africa.⁷⁴

Lesseps, Nadar, Guéroult, Duveyrier, David, all these names certainly give us reason to inquire about Verne's relationships with the last generation of Saint-Simonians, although they do not provide a satisfactory answer, at least not until Verne's personal papers are made available for research. Indeed, it is only from his personal correspondence that any accurate idea could be obtained of his relationships with the last of the Saint-Simonians during the period 1860–70. On one other point also, and one not without importance, we can only pose the question, namely, what was the influence on Verne of 'the good Dr Guépin', his fellow-citizen of Nantes who played an important part in that city's political life in 1848 and 1870, and who was well-known as an initiate of Saint-Simonian and Fourierist ideas.⁷⁵

---

*Édouard-Thomas Charton, 1807–1890, French socialist, one-time Saint-Simonian.

*Henri Duveyrier, 1840–1892, French explorer in Africa.

*Félicien David, 1810–1876, French composer, specialist in exotic music.

A very curious book of 992 pages by Dr Guépin was published in 1854 under the title *Philosophy of the Nineteenth Century, an encyclopaedic Study of the World and Mankind*. Readers of this work are entitled to ask themselves whether Verne may not have been greatly influenced by it, whether it did not assist in bringing to maturity his plans for the *Voyages extraordinaires*, and if it did not serve as a sort of staging-post between those novels and the classics of utopian socialism. Dr Guépin declares that 'the whole world belongs to mankind; our globe is an inexhaustible source of heat and magnetism and there is nothing to prevent us exploiting it.' These words link him with Enfantin, who used to say 'the world is our fiancée, our mother'.[76]

Dr Guépin had a burning faith in the future of electricity, which he presents in popular form in a whole long chapter. A forerunner of Verne whose scientific forecasts, as we have seen, take full advantage of this newly discovered natural force, Dr Guépin tries his hand at drawing diagrams for electrical machines, for example, 'electro-extractors' and heat-absorbers'. For him, as later for Verne, machinery is an essential factor in man's exploitation of nature, and he considers the machine invented by Papin* to be 'a mechanical being created by man, a slave invented by him so that one kind of power may be replaced by another, organs of flesh and blood by organs of steel'.

In Dr Guépin's book there is a long summary of the ideas of Saint-Simon, Fourier and their followers. Much of the book is devoted to scientific matters, more than half being taken up with a résumé of the principal information then available on physics, chemistry, zoology, botany, etc. Guépin, who said that 'science provides the means for reconciling all conflicts', ends his book with an appeal for the creation of 'a literature for the age of science'. Referring to the growth of art and letters during the nineteenth century, he concludes with the words: 'Industry, that literature, that writing on the face of the world which broke so suddenly upon the minds of men, may we not imagine now that it will allow us to draw the outline of all works whatever needing to be done on the surface of the planet?' The whole spirit and form of the book, particularly its reference to a literature of science 'which will one day write man's achievements on the face of the earth', distinctly foreshadows Verne's own literary plans. Does it not, indeed, give us in advance a clue to the deeper meaning of Verne's work?

Verne's relations with the utopian socialists, indirect, tardy and partial though they may have been, were not confined to those businessmen who professed 'practical Saint-Simonism'. If it can be shown that Jules Verne had known Dr Guépin, or had at least been influenced by him, we would be justified in supposing that there was a real intellectual link in

---

*Denis Papin, 1647–1714, French inventor.

that direction. Furthermore, the fact that certain pages in Fourier's writings can be compared with material appearing in the *Voyages extraordinaires*, gives us good grounds for inquiring whether the utopian socialists did not exercise a deeper influence on Verne. Fourier, who had a much richer conception of the world than Saint-Simon, and whose political posterity was destined to last much longer, was literally obsessed by man's relationship to the Cosmos, and that was long before Verne gave the same problem a central place in his writings. Fourier was also very interested in the problem of the Northwest Passage of which Verne writes so often, particularly in *Captain Hatteras*. The pages in which Fourier discusses the idea that climatic changes are linked with the extension of agriculture, a process which he describes as 'the refining of the atmosphere resulting from the integral cultivation of the globe', must be read together with Dr Clawbonny's pronouncement that man 'makes the air healthier by the mere fact of breathing it'. Fourier indeed, and long before Verne, was fascinated by the problem of the Polar regions, by the contradiction between their central position and their inaccessibility. There is also Fourier's well-known myth of the 'Northern Crown' – the idea that agriculture moves towards the Pole:

> By the time mankind has succeeded in exploiting the globe beyond the latitude of 60°N, the temperature of the planet will have become much milder and less changeable; animals will be more active in the rutting season; the Aurora Borealis will be much more frequently seen and will be stabilized over the Pole in the shape of a ring or crown.

Dr Clawbonny's words in *Captain Hatteras* about the future of the Polar regions, so laden with poetic utopian ideas, are based upon memories of Fourier. It is surprising that so perspicacious a critic as Butor, who devoted so much attention to *Captain Hatteras*, should have failed to see that novel as being in the Fourier tradition. The connection in that case may indeed be purely fortuitous, but it is difficult to attribute to chance the fact that Fourier, nearly a century before the publication of Verne's *Upside Down* in 1889, had already thought of the possibility of shifting the earth's axis so as to create more favourable conditions for the agricultural activities of mankind:

> Another reason for forecasting the formation of such a crown can be found in the declination of the earth's axis. If such a crown is ever to come into existence, the axis has to be tilted by a twenty-fourth part, or seven and a half degrees, which will confer advantages on both continents. . . . The Gulf of Archangel and the White Sea will become easily accessible. . . . communication by sea will become much easier as far as the mouths of the Obi and the Yenesei, the region having become six degrees warmer as a result of the shift in the earth's axis, to which another six degrees will be added by the

cultivation of eastern Siberia which will then have been made possible. One will then be able to travel by water from end to end of the biggest continent; Chinese exports will move to Lake Baikal from the bend of the Hoang-Ho, and thence be transported to Europe at low cost, travelling down the Angara and the Yenesei.

In *Upside Down*, the main points of which we have already summarized, Barbicane and his comrades plan to displace the earth's axis in just the same direction since the new axis would pass between Greenland and Baffin Bay. The imaginary article in the *New York Sun* commenting favourably on this grandiose project is worth comparing with Fourier's forecast, even to the style of writing employed by Verne:

> All praise to President Barbicane and his colleagues.... They will have made the earth a healthier place to live in, and also more productive; it will then be possible for seed-time to follow immediately after harvest; seeds will germinate without delay, and no more time will be lost because of winter! Not only will the discovery of new coal deposits have enriched the world's resources to ensure, perhaps for many years to come, adequate supplies of that indispensable raw material, but the climatic conditions of our globe will have been transformed to our advantage.

Fourier once drew 'a plan for a town of the sixth period' which foreshadows Verne's ideas about the way in which Franceville should develop. Indeed, Fourier lays down careful rules for the shape of the houses, how far apart they should be, the necessity for building only detached houses and the necessity for the creation of a sanitary police corps. These similarities are too numerous to result from pure chance.

Verne is therefore a true, if distant, heir to the utopian socialists of the first half of the nineteenth century.[77] In many places his writings reveal the influence, and contain many reminders of the ideas and visions of Saint-Simon and Enfantin, Fourier and Guépin. A particular example of this will be dealt with later, namely, the importance attached to the United States by the Saint-Simonians, whose favourite country it was, and by Verne who preferred it to all other lands as the setting for his stories.

It should be noted, however, that the influence of utopian socialism, which is so clearly seen in the earlier *Voyages extraordinaires*, tends to decrease as the century passes. Even if traces of it may still be found in later works such as *Upside Down*, *The Invasion of the Sea*, *The Lighthouse at the End of the World*, the general tone is no longer one of optimism. Between about 1880 and 1890, i.e., the beginning of the age of imperialism, Verne's dreams of the exploitation of nature through science and hard work begin to disintegrate when faced with the power of money and systems of government based on violence.

CHAPTER V

Libertarian individualism

Two seemingly harmless but basic words in Jules Verne's writings are *the sea* and *travel*. To explain the former, it is not necessary to go beyond Verne's memories of childhood when his family were just in time to catch him as he tried to sail as a cabin boy, or beyond the great pleasure he found in cruising.[78] Verne was passionately fond of the sea and said so quite plainly through the mouth of the young Olivier Sinclair in *The Green Ray*:

> The sea is a living creature whose heart beats along the line of the Equator. . . . Of all travel stories, my favourites are those dealing with voyages of discovery in distant seas. . . . Can anything be more wonderful in the whole history of mankind than such discoveries? How marvellous to have been among the first to cross the Atlantic with Columbus, the Pacific with Magellan, the Arctic with Perry, Franklin, d'Urville and so many others! At the sight of a ship putting to sea, whether warship, merchantman or simple launch, my whole being goes on board with it. I think I must have been meant to be a sailor and each day I regret that I did not go to sea when I was a boy.

As for travel, there could be no easier expedient for an author wishing to teach geography than to take his readers over the oceans and continents, skilfully mixing together romantic plots, descriptions of landscapes and copious, sometimes even boring, lists of geographical locations. A closer look, however, makes it clear that for Verne the sea and travel were themes with much deeper connotations. In *Captain Hatteras*, when the Brig *Forward* begins its journey to the Pole, there is this comment:

> To a thinker, a dreamer or a philosopher there can be no more moving sight than a ship setting out. In imagination one can follow it in its tussles with the sea, its struggles with the winds, on a course which does not always end in port.

Thinker, philosopher: the reason for the use of these words seemingly out of context is to be found later, when Nemo's imprecations explain the allusions to be found in *The Adventures of Captain Hatteras*:

> —You like the sea, Captain?
> —Yes, I love it! The sea is everything! It covers seven-tenths of the terrestrial globe. Its breath is healthy and pure. It is an immense desert where man is never alone for he can feel life moving alongside him.... There is perfect peace. Despots have no rights of property over the sea. On its surface they may still try to exercise their iniquitous power, to fight each other, to devour each other, to transport all the horrors of the land; but thirty feet below the surface their dominion ends, their influence fades away. Oh, Sir, you should live in the sea! There alone is freedom! There I recognize no master. There I am free!

The sea is thus a philosophic concept for Verne, not only a tourist one; it is the negation and antithesis of the land with its police-ridden societies and its constraints. To borrow a word from the anarchist circles of the end of the nineteenth century, the sea is a 'free medium' in the highest degree.

As for travel, is a traveller no more than someone seeking his own pleasure and edification? Is he not rather, at a deeper level, a person wishing to escape from the society in which he lives, someone who, even if only temporarily, breaks away from his national, social and family circles? It is not by chance that Verne gives so much space in his novels to characters belonging to wandering and itinerant professions – minor forms of anti-sociability. On the Town Council of Amiens, of which he became a member in 1888, he was able to undertake responsibility for theatre affairs and travelling entertainers. Clowns, mountebanks, itinerant artistes and other 'people of the road' appear many times in the *Voyages extraordinaires*: the two Caterna singers (*Claudius Bombarnac*), the two jugglers, Pointe Pescade and Cap Matifou (*Mathias Sandorf*), Passepartout and his troupe of Long-Noses (*Around the World in Eighty Days*), Caesar Cascabel and his family circus, the 'concert quartet' kidnapped by the millionaires of Standard Island in order to ensure their exclusive services (*Propeller Island*). It is the same with journalists: Blount and Jolivet (*Michael Strogoff*), Gideon Spilett (*The Mysterious Island*), Claudius Bombarnac, Amédée Florence (*The Barsac Mission*). Characters like these, living on the fringes of conventional society, are always described in genial and sympathetic terms:

> How many people have not sometimes dreamt of travelling in a house on wheels like circus performers! How wonderful not to have to bother about hotels, or inns, or doubtful beds, or even more doubtful food, when travelling through a region only sparsely supplied with hamlets or villages! Why is it that the joy of 'land

The acrobats Pointe Pescade and Cap Matifou, who join 'Dr Antekirtt' in *Mathias Sandorf*.

navigation' is experienced only by itinerant show people? (*Caesar Cascabel*)

They do not worry about saving money, these Princes of the Fiddle, these Kings of the Four Strings! They enjoy their adventurous existence, they are sure of a welcome and a profit everywhere and always, rushing from New York to San Francisco, from Quebec to New Orleans, from Nova Scotia to Texas; they are more or less Bohemians, in fact – from that youthful Bohemia of the spirit which is the oldest, the most charming, the most to be envied and the best loved province of our old France! (*Propeller Island*)

On the other hand, government agents and organizations responsible for enforcing social conformity are the objects of Verne's discreet, but quite clear, censure: judges, for example, policemen, mental hospitals and prisons. The judges are most often depicted as pretentious quibblers like Judge Jarriguez in *The Giant Raft*; for them, every accused person is guilty, witness Judge Rona in *The Danube Pilot*, who looks at the prisoner, Ladko, 'as a cat must look at a mouse'. Judge Ordok in *An Eccentric's Will* is petty and obstinate; when the Titbury couple try to explain why they were taking part in an immense game across the territory of the United States, he simply doubles their fine.

Policemen are made to appear cynical and unsympathetic, like Rip in *Family without a Name* who bribes one of the leading plotters to reveal their plan to liberate French Canada. His basic motive is greed:

> His private headquarters were registered under the name of Rip & Co. For him, a police matter was nothing more nor less than a matter of money, which he entered in his accounts like a merchant recording the amount of a bill of exchange – so much for a search, so much for an arrest, and so much for spying on someone.

The same unflattering language is used to describe Brigadier Eck in *A Drama in Livonia* when he is on the track of a political prisoner escaped from Siberia:

> Very keen on his work, well regarded by his superiors, he was implacable in the investigation of those cases entrusted to him; success filled him with pride, and he could not accept defeat. When entrusted with such an important matter as the recapture of an escapee from Siberia, he threw himself into the task with even greater energy.

The policeman Fix, following his prey with the stubborn tenacity of a bloodhound, adds to the merriment of *Around the World in Eighty Days*. At each stop he waits in vain for the warrant which will allow him to arrest Phileas Fogg, who is falsely suspected of a serious robbery. An inexact description of the criminal, which Fix does not take the trouble to check, nearly makes Fogg lose his bet. John Stock, Chief Inspector of Police in Washington, is ridiculous and pompous when he takes up the pursuit of Robur, who has voluntarily outlawed himself. He summons Robur 'in the name of the law' while he is Robur's prisoner on board the *Épouvante*; he is able to claim the glory for Robur's defeat, although he is no more than the plaything of circumstances and manages to take advantage of the storm which throws the flying machine out of kilter (*Master of the World*).

For the Flag contains the only reference by Verne to a mental hospital as a means of social restraint. The American government has had Thomas Roch shut up in an asylum named 'Healthful House', after he has invented a formidable war-weapon and tried in vain to sell it to various governments; he is closely watched in an attempt to discover the secret of his invention. Prisons, however, figure more frequently. Although the convicts in Norfolk Island, an English prison settlement until 1842, live under inhuman conditions, the island becomes a 'granary of abundance' as the result of the labours of these miserable wretches (*The Brothers Kip*). Verne analyzes in some detail the status of the different kinds of prisoners at Port Arthur, the Tasmanian penal settlement to which the brothers Kip are sent. He distinguishes between those sentenced to forced labour, those guilty of misdemeanours ('English magistrates often have heavy hands') who are 'granted the favour of entering the service of some colonist without being paid for their work', and those who achieve better conditions through good conduct. Verne is particularly severe in his strictures on the Port Arthur penitentiary for young offenders, noting that many of the inmates 'are forced into the ways of crime'. Russian prisons figure in *Michael Strogoff* and, above all, in *A Drama in Livonia*, the hero of the latter being an escaped convict. The French prison at Toulouse provides the setting for a story written in his youth, *The Destiny of Jean Morénas*. The dominant note is always that of terror, brutality and inhumanity, and also the profits accruing from convict labour.

This is the reason, Verne notes sympathetically, why the idea of escape, the return to freedom, is so irrepressible, and why escape may sometimes be undertaken in relatively favourable circumstances (*The Blockade Runners*): 'A prisoner is much more possessed by the thought of escape than his gaolers are of preventing him. Consequently a prisoner should always manage to bring off his escape. All the chances are on his side.' It is thanks to this principle of stronger motivation that Vladimir Yanof manages to escape in *A Drama in Livonia*, as do others like Mathias Sandorf, Marcel Bruckmann (*The Begum's Fortune*), Henry Markel's band of murderers (*Travelling Scholarships*) and the two Sinn Feiners of *The Brothers Kip*.

In the *Voyages extraordinaires* Verne gives prominence to judicial error, a frequent theme in the anarchist writings of the period as symbolizing both the conflict between society and the individual, and the fallible character of established justice; no fewer than three of Verne's novels turn on this theme. The Kip brothers, accused of the murder of Captain Hawkins, who had rescued them after their shipwreck, are sentenced on the strength of false evidence arranged by the real murderers. In *The Giant Raft*, the rich planter, Joam Garral, is accused of having attacked, twenty-five years previously and in collusion with some bandits, a diamond convoy whose route was known to him in his official capacity; from Peru he enters Brazilian territory intending to surrender himself to the Brazilian authorities who had earlier sentenced him. Unfortunately, the proof of his innocence is contained in a ciphered document,

The bearded pirate, Ker Karraje, who abducts the 'mad' scientist, Thomas Roch, in *For the Flag*.

the key to the meaning of which has been lost, and which he manages to decipher only at the very last moment. In *A Drama in Livonia* matters move to a tragic finish when the judge, Kersthof, a man of integrity and perspicacity, 'a personification of the law', nevertheless mistakenly sentences the lawyer Dimitri Nicolef for the murder of a banker who spent a night in the same inn as he. The judge is led astray by false evidence manufactured by the real murderer, the innkeeper Kroff.

Verne's attitude to crime and criminals is equivocal. Outlaw bands and pirates frequently figure in his novels and are described in terms which seem to be conventional and unfavourable: 'the dregs of society', 'miserable creatures', 'hardened criminals'. Thus he writes of Bob Harvey's band of ruffians who attack the colonists in *The Mysterious Island*; Ker Karraje's band in *For the Flag* ('criminals of various countries, deserters from colonial military contingents, fugitives from penal settlements, sailors who had deserted their ships'); the 'Kongre band' who attack the keepers of *The Lighthouse at the End of the World*; Harry Markel's gang from Queenstown prison in Ireland, who seize the *Alert*, a ship due to take the children of the London Antilia School on a cruise. Many of these bandits and pirates are sailors. Verne, who felt so strongly about everything to do with navigation, seems to have been obsessed by the problem of authority on ships, and naval mutinies are given considerable space in his writings. In the conditions of complete isolation which are found on a ship, the conflict between authority and insubordination reaches a climax, as on the *Chancellor*, on the *Forward* (*Captain Hatteras*), on *Propeller Island*, on the *Alert*, on the *Halbrane* (*An Antarctic Mystery*), on the *James Cook* (*The Brothers Kip*). In a novel he wrote in his youth, nearly a century before Robert Merle,* Verne gives us a romanticized version of the *Bounty* mutiny which is indisputably sympathetic towards Fletcher Christian and his companions of Pitcairn Island.

If we look a little closer, however, do we not find that the author in fact shows a secret esteem for the vigorous humanity of these outlaws and mutineers?:[79] for the 'savage looks' and the 'violent but spirited' character of Kongre; for the 'wild features' of Harry Markel 'who could have made an honourable career for himself, had he not been thrown into the ways of crime by his terrible passions, by an ungovernable lust for money and by the desire to be his own master'. This hypothesis finds support in the final scene of *The Children of Captain Grant* between the corrupted quartermaster Ayrton, and Lord Glenarvan, leader of the expedition sent to look for the shipwrecked Captain Grant, The 'agreement' reached between them gives Ayrton the assurance that he will not be brought before the courts, in exchange for such information as he is able to give about Captain Grant:

Glenarvan: 'Ayrton, if I agree to your request, will you tell me everything I need to know?'
Ayrton: 'Yes, my Lord, or rather all that I know about Captain Grant and the *Britannia*.'
—The whole truth?
—The whole truth.
—But . . . who will guarantee . . . ?
—I understand your difficulty, my Lord. You will just have to rely

*Robert Merle, b. 1908, French writer.

upon me, upon the word of a criminal! That is true, but what can you do? That is the position. You must take it or leave it.

Thus it is Ayrton who, both morally and humanly, dominates Lord Glenarvan in this conversation; here the leader of a band of convicts imposes his will upon an honourable member of society: 'Ayrton had an answer to every question, forestalling every difficulty, and providing unanswerable arguments against him. As we have seen, he gave every appearance of acting in good faith in this "affair".' And the inner strength he exhibits forces those who were so nearly his victims, and who continue to be his enemies, to treat him with respect: 'That rascal could have been a decent man,' says the Major. 'Yes,' replies Glenarvan: 'he has strength of character and intelligence, faculties which have somehow turned towards evil.'

Verne may never have created a character in the style of Jean Valjean – a 'criminal with a heart of gold' – but he writes of criminals and the world of crime in a rather subtle way. Ayrton is not far from being the central character of *The Children of Captain Grant*, as Marcel Moré has noted but, it seems, without realizing the political implications of such a situation.

In his youthful story, *The Destiny of Jean Morénas*, Verne already reverses conventional value to the benefit of criminals and prison inmates. Jean Morénas has been unjustly sentenced for the murder of his uncle (the theme of judicial error is already apparent), who was in fact killed by Jean's brother Pierre. Filled with remorse, Pierre arranges for Jean to escape without letting him guess who is behind this. Jean returns to his village, only to be present unintentionally when his brother commits another murder. He is accused and arrested for a second time, this time willingly, to prevent his sister-in-law, Marguerite, from breaking her heart. He is sent back to prison.

Verne is aware of, or at least senses with singular clarity, the indeterminate nature of the frontier between 'common law' crimes and political insubordination, between infractions of the civil law and those of the established social order. This ambivalence is brought out in the character of Nemo, but Nemo's case is not as exceptional in the *Voyages extraordinaires* as it often appears. Verne mentions, for example, if only in passing (*Carpathian Castle*), the Transylvanian bandit, Rosza Sandor, a brigand on the lines of Robin Hood and Mandrin,* a former highwayman 'dramatically turned into a hero as a result of the war of independence' (he took part in the people's struggle in Rumania in 1848). The evocation of such a character, and in such terms, is proof of political maturity surprising in a provincial bourgeois of that time. The same can

---

*Louis Mandrin, 1724–1755, French merchant who became a bandit when his business failed.

be said about the Taiping rebellion, described by Verne in a manner reflecting a similar ambiguity between political insurrection and banditry (*Tribulations of a Chinese Gentleman*):

> A formidable revolt was already threatening the reigning dynasty. The Chang-mao, or Taiping, 'the long-haired rebels', gained possession of Nanking in 1853 and of Shanghai in 1855.... Declared enemies of the Tatars, these Taiping were well organized for the rebellion and it was their purpose to replace the Ch'ing dynasty by that of the Wang. They were divided into four separate bands: the first, under a black flag, were the killers; the second, with a red flag, had been given the job of arson; the third, with a yellow flag, were the looters; the fourth, under a white flag, had the responsibility for provisioning the three others.[80]

A careful examination of the *Voyages extraordinaires* from this angle reveals many allusions and episodes which, by implication, call into question the established conventions of society and its institutions. The whole plot of *Keraban the Inflexible* turns on his refusal to accept government dictation which, in this case, involves payment of a tax for crossing the Bosphorus to Constantinople by ferry; the obstinate Keraban prefers to go all the way round the Black Sea by land.

Verne also, in the matter of the ownership of certain diamond-bearing properties, shows the inadequacy of the basis on which such plots of land are distributed and the errors arising from it. Starting with a seemingly marginal case, we are led to realize the conventional, and consequently frail, fortuitous and revocable nature of the private ownership of land. By a judgment of the Kimberley Court, the boundary between the property of the Dutchman Vandergaart and the Englishman Watkins is to follow the 25th Longitude East; it is the Englishman who gets the diamond mine, but a geodesic error subsequently comes to light, and Watkins is ruined when it is corrected (*The Southern Star Mystery*).

Verne's concern with the ownership of private property is made clear in a passage in a witty paper, 'Ten Hours' Shooting', read by him to the Amiens Academy. Verne and his companions had been annoyed at being stopped by a notice reading 'Private Shoot':

> Private shoot, I said to myself. Why private? Is that not after all carrying the right of ownership too far? Private because a passing partridge might have eaten your corn, owner that you are.... Once the harvest has been taken in, should the land not belong to everyone? But seriously, from the point of view of the common law, it seems to me that game, like the water in the rivers and the air surrounding us, belongs to everyone to be enjoyed by everyone. But I would not have dared to express such thoughts in the hearing of my companions. They would have shot me![81]

This passage disappeared from the text in the new edition published in 1882 at the end of the volume including *The Green Ray*. Hetzel was much more acutely aware than Verne himself of the dangerously non-conformist character of such attacks against certain 'sacred and inviolable rights'.

Finally, Verne was critical of two widely respected social conventions, on the one hand the fictitious value placed on gold as a metal, and, on the other hand, the conception of territorial sovereignty (which he considered artificial) and government-controlled colonization. Both of these appear so extensively in his writings that we can deal with them more effectively below, in the chapters (VIII and X) specifically devoted to them.

In place of established society with its constraints and artificialities, the French 'anti-authoritarians' of Verne's time and the anarchist intellectuals proposed to set up 'free environments' of small communities created by voluntary action and based on mutual help and interdependence, in the Proudhon* tradition.[82] Verne never uses that term, and perhaps he did not even know it. Nevertheless, communities of that kind are frequently to be found in his books. They are brought into being by chance, and unite the survivors of catastrophes or adventures: the inhabitants of *The Mysterious Island*, whose balloon had been destroyed by a storm and fallen on the island; the garrison of Fort Espérance, sent by the Hudson's Bay Company to open a sub-Polar trading station, who have installed themselves on an earth-covered ice-floe which starts to drift away without their being aware of the fact; Hatteras and his companions wintering close to the Pole in an ice fortress; Captain Servadac's little community carried away by the comet Gallia; the survivors of the shipwreck in *The Second Fatherland*, a pastiche sequel to the famous *Swiss Family Robinson*; the children of the Chairman boarding school, thrown ashore for two years on an island in the Magellan Strait after their vessel, without a single adult on board, drifted there from New Zealand (*Two Years' Holiday*); the crew of the *Nautilus*.

It is not by accident that these communities are so often placed on islands. Islands are of the sea and, like it, possess the essential characteristics of 'free environments': wide horizons, freedom from governmental restraint and the possibility of organizing social relationships with ease and flexibility.[83] There are, for instance, Hanover Island in *Two Years' Holiday*, the island of Antekirtta in *Mathias Sandorf*, Hoste Island where the survivors of the shipwreck of the *Jonathan* find refuge, and also the 'mysterious' island, the secret base of *Nautilus* long before the arrival

---

*Pierre Joseph Proudhon, 1809–1865, French socialist, opposed to Marxism.

Keraban the Inflexible.

of the five survivors of the air-crash, engineer Robur's X Island, and Back-Cup Island in Bermuda, the lair of the pirate Ker Karraje.

Certain of these 'free environments' born of adventure are in fact characterized by their natural harmony; conflicts of nationality do not exist, or are soon effaced; everyone is free to let his human qualities develop; such communities act as schools for initiative as well as interdependence. This applies to the communities described in *The Mysterious Island, The Fur Country, Captain Hatteras, Hector Servadac* and *Two Years' Holiday*. But in other cases, where these new communities derive from rebellion, not from misfortune, they are explicitly opposed to established society. 'We live a life of noble and proud independence,' declares one of the members of the pirate Bee Hive colony in the Bermudas (*For the Flag*), 'and we are not subordinate to any foreign Power; we are free from any outside authority, we are not a colony of any state in the Old or the New World ... which is worthy of consideration by anyone with a proud heart and soul.' The outlaw community which furrows the waves aboard *Nautilus* under Nemo's command obeys the same principles, while Nemo is one of the central figures in Verne's world. He defies society in a manner which could not have been imagined by an author without some affinity, even if only secret or semi-conscious, with the ideas of libertarian individualism. His guest, Professor Arronax, says of him:

> Not only had he outlawed himself from human society, but he had made himself independent, he was free in the strictest meaning of the word, beyond reach! ... No one in the whole of mankind was in a position to ask him to account for his actions.

Though a rebel, Nemo is not a misanthrope. He looks on himself as the defender of all the victims of society:

> I am the law, I am justice! It is I who am oppressed, and there is the oppressor.* By its action all that I have loved, respected and cherished, fatherland, wife, children, my father, my mother, all perished before my eyes. Everything I hate is there. Do not speak of it.

Certainly, in the end, Nemo retracts his libertarian principles. He dies in the arms of Cyrus Smith and his companions with the words, 'I am dying because I thought that man can live alone', and whispering, 'God and my country'. But there is nothing to prevent us interpreting this final scene as a concession by Verne to his public (or to his publisher?), and it is so conventional, anyway, that it can have no real significance.

20,000 Leagues under the Sea is the book in which Verne gives most evidence of secret libertarian sympathies – at any rate until the posthumous publication of *The Survivors of the 'Jonathan'*. This is perhaps the place to record the curious legend according to which the real author of the novel was the communist leader Louise Michel,* who sold it for a hundred francs one day when she was penniless. This story, in the form in which it is generally told,[84] is clearly without foundation. The manuscript of the novel was handed to Hetzel in December 1868,[85] which was much earlier than the date on which it is supposed to have been bought by Verne. In particular it is impossible that Louise Michel could have

---

*The *Nautilus* has arrived in view of an English ship.

*Louise Michel, 1830–1950, French communist who fought in the Commune and was deported to New Caledonia from 1871 to 1880.

Captain Nemo posed against the setting sun under his black flag bearing the letter 'N' (*20,000 Leagues under the Sea*).

dreamed up the name *Nautilus* by remembering the sea-shells ('nautiles') which she used to find on the beaches of New Caledonia during the period of her deportation.

Nevertheless it is worrying that this story should be told of the very novel which, of all Verne's works, carries the clearest indication of anarchist ideas. The anarchist writer Hem Day tried to prove that the Louise Michel story was false,[86] but why did he not think of obtaining his evidence from the novel itself, instead of confining his examination to indirect sources? It is no more than a hypothesis, but we may ask ourselves whether, at the end of the Empire, Verne may not have been in contact with members of the 'anti-authoritarian' intelligentsia of Paris; it is known that, later, he was very close to the Reclus brothers and their group,* and that his friend Nadar was to evolve towards anarchism.

Nemo's flag is black; it is this flag, carrying the letter N, which he plants at the South Pole as a sign that he has taken possession of a land free of all state colonization. It is also the flag which he hoists when he is attacking the English ship. The appearance of the black flag of anarchism and piracy is all the more remarkable because it is seen repeatedly in Verne's universe. It is the flag raised by the French Canadian peasants in their revolt against the English (*Family without a Name*), with mottoes such as: 'Fly, tyrants, the people awake ... A united people are the terror of the aristocrats ... Rather a bloody struggle than oppression by a corrupt power'; this flag carries the skull and cross-bones and the names of the hated Governors, Dalhousie and Craig. Engineer Robur flies a black flag with a yellow sun. And it is also a black flag, bearing the letter S, which is flown by the pirate Sacratif when he attacks the Greek ships fighting against the Turks (*Islands on Fire*), and a similar flag is hoisted by the pirates who attack the inhabitants of *The Mysterious Island*. All this means that the black flag in Verne's writings has a very significant double meaning, being the emblem both of despicable characters and of undoubted heroes.

Nemo is the most spectacular, but not the only embodiment of a solitary genius who hurls defiance against society. Thomas Roch, the inventor in *For the Flag*, scoffed at by his own and other governments, says: 'I no longer have a homeland! An inventor who has been rebuffed has no homeland. Wherever he finds refuge, there is his country.'

It is true that Thomas Roch experiences a reawakening of patriotism at the end of the novel, refuses to fire on a warship flying the French colours, and thereby leads to the destruction of the military base built by the pirates with whom he has thrown in his lot. This end, however, is fairly conventional and artificial, and carries little more conviction than Nemo's death.

Engineer Robur also, when he has been universally rejected, refuses to sell his polyvalent vehicle, combining the features of an airplane, an automobile and a ship, which has made him all-powerful:

> This invention will be neither French, nor German, nor Austrian, nor Russian, nor English, nor American. It will remain my own property and I will use it as I like. With it I can exercise power over the whole world, and there is no human power able to hold out against it.

---

*Elisée Reclus, 1830–1905, and Onésime Reclus, 1837–1916, prominent French anarchist intellectuals of the late nineteenth century.

A meeting of the British authorities – the Governor, the Commander-in-Chief and the Chief of Police – in Canada (*Family without a Name*).

The *Voyages extraordinaires* contain one other picture of a solitary rebel, but so discreet and deliberately unobtrusive, that so far as we know his name has never been mentioned in any study of Verne's works. It is Kamylk Pasha, the very rich Syrian recluse who leaves his fortune to a Breton sailor in return for saving his life during the siege of Acre by Napoleon; his unusual will is the basis of the romantic plot in *Master Antifer*. Fidelity to the Ottoman dynasty makes him refuse to support Mehmet Ali, and he dies in a Cairo gaol after eighteen years of imprisonment: 'forgotten by all those who had known him, he died aged 72, and neither threats nor bad treatment had ever dragged his secret from him.' Before his arrest, he had managed to bury his treasure; giving up the normal society of men, he withdrew into solitude. Sadly he looked on while the work of digging the hiding place proceeded:

> Kamylk Pasha stood a little to the side, lost in reverie and saddened by some painful thought. He wondered whether it would not be better for him to lie down beside his treasures and enter into eternal sleep. And in truth, where would he find a more certain shelter from injustice and the perfidy of men?

Kamylk Pasha was a lonely figure, even on the political level, because he had refused to support Syrian separatism:

> Of melancholy, even depressed appearance. . . . He was not a communicative character, preferring to live a life of retirement. . . . He left Egypt only to go on long journeys, . . . with haughty indifference to others, he travelled aimlessly over the seas of Asia, Africa and Europe.

Kamylk Pasha not only provides us with a moving self-portrait of Verne consistent with what we know of his character and tastes in the latter part of his life, but he gives us a key to Verne's secret thoughts on political matters, all the more valuable for being hidden in the pages of a novel which seemingly has nothing whatever to do with politics. Kamylk Pasha is the link between those two glamorous rebels, Nemo and the Kaw Djer of *The Survivors of the 'Jonathan'*, but he brings with him a certain note of discouragement, of 'disinterestedness', which was the word used by Roger Vailland* in describing Don Caesar, that other old recluse, who is the central character in *The Law*.

Solitary rebellion may express itself in extreme and dramatic ways, even going as far as a complete break with society, as in the case of Robur and Nemo. But it can also assume the less combative and more unobtrusive shape of eccentricity, a refusal to conform with commonly accepted customs and morals. The aristocrat Keraban is an eccentric, as are Professor Liddenbrock, Phileas Fogg, Paganel and the Indian Rajah who had the whim of ordering a steam elephant to pull along his travelling residence.

In the *Voyages extraordinaires* there is one basic image which conveys the exaltation of a man standing alone: the picture of a man with crossed arms. This has already been noted by Marcel Moré,[87] but in a psychoanalytical sense and not as an indication of an ideological attitude. That stance of a man with crossed arms, head thrown back, is that of Nemo on the deck of *Nautilus*, that of Ayrton (*The Children of Captain Grant*) forsaken on his island ('arms crossed, motionless as a statue on a rock'), that of the leader of the Sepoys in *The Steam House*, Nana-Sahib. The

---

*Roger Vailland, 1907–1965, French novelist.

illustrations in Hetzel's original edition, which were influenced or controlled by Verne, confirm and amplify this point. It is with arms crossed that Thomas Roch is shown in the garden of 'Healthful House', where he has been shut up against his will, despite the fact that the text has nothing to say on the point.

'Arms crossed, head proudly thrown back, motionless, as if refusing to become integrated with a society whose constraints are inacceptable.' The young Jules Verne had already had himself photographed in such a posture when he was twenty-five and secretary to the Théatre-Lyrique.

In *A Drama in Livonia*, the lawyer Dimitri Nicolef takes up the same attitude when he shows himself at his window, defying the threats of the crowd shouting 'Death to the murderer', while the funeral procession of the man he is wrongly accused of killing passes before his house: 'Arms crossed, head proudly lifted, motionless as a statue, a statue disdaining to utter a single word.' The loneliness of the person in question is here accentuated by contrast, since he is face to face with the crowd, a crowd carried away by the contagion of excitement and deceived by false rumours. In the same way, Robur stands up to his angry audience in the Weldon Club premises as they wax sarcastic over his theories on the possibility of 'heavier-than-air' flying machines.

In the same manner, the abolitionist Southern planter, James Burbank, faces the whites of Jacksonville when he is sentenced to death during the Civil War for having been in touch with the North. He 'remained calm and master of himself. All he had for the shouting populace was a look of disdain.' Disdain for the crowds, for the masses, is yet another link between Verne and the anarchists of his day.

These many signs, unobtrusively scattered throughout the *Voyages extraordinaires*, will suffice to suggest that the tendency towards libertarian individualism is deeply embedded in Verne's writings. This conclusion, however, is acceptable only on one condition: that we remember that it is the political 'interpretation' of Verne's novels which is in question, and not an analysis of the author's own political ideas as he himself defined them. All we can say about the latter is that the eclecticism of his way of life and his friendships *was in no way incompatible* with such individualist and libertarian trends.

We know, for example, that he was friendly with Elisée Reclus, one of the leaders of the anarchist intelligentsia around 1880–90. He may also have known Bakunin,* or have been informed of his ideas and activities through Hetzel who was in touch with Bakunin.[88] We also know that Verne was interested in Esperanto,[89] the supra-national

---

*Mikhail Alexandrovich Bakunin, 1814–1876, leading Russian anarchist who lived many years in western Europe.

character of which was very attractive to the libertarians of his day. His friend Nadar, who started out as a Saint-Simonian, later turned towards anarchism. To what degree did this change influence Verne?[90]

But we must not go too far; it would be just as easy to call to mind the audience he so respectfully requested of Pope Leo XIII, his bourgeois, conventional life, and his professed opposition to the partisans of the *Commune* and of Dreyfus. The clue to the political tendencies of the *Voyages extraordinaires* is not to be found in Verne's public life. The strength of the libertarian tendencies found throughout his writings is a fact in itself, which is not necessarily a reflection of his personal convictions (or what he thought were his personal convictions).

In a posthumous novel, *The Survivors of the 'Jonathan'*, published in 1909 (it is not certain when it was written), the cry 'No God, no Master' suddenly resounds in the *Voyages extraordinaires*. The individualist and libertarian tendencies which, until then, had found expression in passing references, episodes of secondary importance and marginal characters, are here replaced by a coherent and explicit analysis of all aspects of anarchism.

There is no reason to doubt the authenticity of this novel, as has been done by an Italian scholar.[91] On the contrary, the character of the book itself seems to us to confirm its authenticity, since in it is reassembled, clarified and systematically formulated everything which had earlier been only discreetly hinted at. Nobody other than the author could have effected such a change. It is a novel of exceptional power, and it is worth noting that, except for *Captain Grant* and *The Mysterious Island*, it is the only novel composed on a ternary plan, broader and more dramatic than the other 'long' novels with their bipartite structure.

On Hoste Island in the Magellan Strait there lives an outlaw whom the Fuegians have named the Kaw-Djer. He is an anarchist who has run away from the civilized world and who recognizes no social principle other than the freedom of each individual; he prefers the primitive life of that land to civilized society. But then an American ship, the *Jonathan*, is wrecked nearby. The passengers are emigrants recruited in California by a colonizing company and are on their way to Africa. This crowd of people comes ashore in complete confusion and disorder and the Kaw-Djer, against his will, finds himself obliged to direct, to supervise, and to organize their way of life. Thanks to the ship's cargo, intended to equip an establishment in Africa, the survivors of the shipwreck organize themselves to live through the winter. The Chilean government, owners of the island since the signature of a demarcation treaty with the Argentine, grants independence to the inhabitants of Hoste Island on condition that they agree to develop it. Thus a community is born, a new social experiment begins. A town, Liberia, is built; but the experiment is not a success. Socialist and communist politicians gather followers but prove incapable of running the community. By the second winter, famine appears, bands of robbers form and civil war breaks out between the followers of the socialist Beauval (who had managed to get himself elected Governor) and those of the communist Dorick.

For the second time the Kaw-Djer agrees to undertake what is to him a horror, the task of governing the community. He re-establishes law and order, reorganizes agriculture and commerce, fights off an invasion by Patagonians, but when gold deposits are found he is powerless to stop the 'gold rush' which brings to Hoste Island a crowd of adventurers from the five continents. There is disorder again, and the Kaw-Djer is forced to order his militia to open fire against the rebellious miners, killing more than a thousand people. Chile then revokes the concession, using the disorders as a pretext. The Kaw-Djer abdicates and takes refuge on Horn Island where he lives a solitary life. He climbs up to the lighthouse above the cape, kicks at a block of gold-bearing quartz, 'the accursed metal', and meditates:

> Standing upright as a lofty column on the top of the rock, lit up by the rays of the setting sun, his white hair and long white beard floating in the breeze, the Kaw-Djer was lost in thought, looking out over the immense horizon in front of him, where, far from everyone but useful to everyone, he would henceforth live free, alone – forever.

Several of the anarchist tendencies which can be found in Verne's other writings are once more apparent in this novel, but this time essential to the plot, which turns on such themes as gold, the ownership of property, territorial boundaries and national sovereignty. The artificial character of gold as a monetary standard is all the more strongly emphasized since what we are being shown is a new society, potentially free from all conventions:

> The Kaw-Djer was amazed at the continuing belief in the value of gold, a purely imaginary value since men cannot eat gold, cannot use it as protection against rain or cold; yet it is coveted as much as real property which does possess these advantages. How strange and wonderful that the whole of mankind bows down by common consent before an essentially useless material whose value derives from nothing more than a widespread convention! Are not men acting thus like children who, in the way of make believe, gravely sell to each other little pebbles transformed by their imagination into objects of value?

In this novel, gold-fever, already stigmatized in *The Brothers Kip* and *The Children of Captain Grant*, is shown up as a major social scourge and as the basic cause of the colony's failure. With the opening of the first placer, agricultural production ceases, morality declines, crews leave their ships, even the police desert and the island is given over to pillage. Only the Indians escape the contagion — an interesting reminder of the theme of the 'good savage':

> In a few weeks the town of Liberia, the villages and the farms were emptied of most of their inhabitants as a result of this irresistible mania. Men, women and children went to work at the placers. A few of them became wealthy by discovering one of those pockets of nuggets which had accumulated under the action of torrential rains. But hope never left those who, after many long days and at the cost of endless toil, found that their labours had been in vain. Everyone rushed to join in, from the capital, the villages, the fields, the fisheries, the factories and the trading posts along the shore. The gold seemed to have a magnetic power which human reason was not strong enough to resist.... Only the original inhabitants of Hoste Island, the Indians, refused to join in the general rush. They alone stood aloof from that mad lust. It is to the honour of these humble Fuegians that a few fisheries and several agricultural enterprises were not completely abandoned. They were saved from the contagion by their natural honesty.

The right to own property, also, is openly questioned. The Kaw-Djer is astonished to see the survivors of the shipwreck continue to think in terms of ownership:

> The Kaw-Djer was amazed at the imperfection of men, at their inability to break away from their accustomed routine, but even more... that the idea of property remained an article of faith. Not one of these people would not say, as the most natural thing in the world, 'this is mine', and none of them could see how vastly absurd it was — an absurdity so strikingly clear to a libertarian philosopher! — for a being so feeble and fragile to claim for himself, for himself alone, any part whatsoever of the universe.... The Kaw-Djer thought how astonishing such theories would appear to his friends the Fuegians, in their wandering bands traversing the Magellan territories, who had never possessed anything other than their own bodies.

The episode of the Irishman Patterson brings the problem of the private ownership of natural resources into the novel in an objective way, not just subjectively in the hero's mind. This survivor of the shipwreck is more cunning than the others and, when the plots of land are being distributed, he chooses one at the only point where the river is accessible. When the colony has settled down, he turns this to his profit by taking a fee from the women as they come to draw water each day.

We also find again in *Jonathan*, but this time clearly posed, some of the problems lightly touched upon in several other books, such as the seizure by governments of territories all over the planet, the artificial and conventional nature of national sovereignty and international frontiers. Early in the novel the Magellan territories are described as a land free from any government installation – just like the South Pole when Nemo plants his black flag there – and it is this which has brought the Kaw-Djer to the region:

> Up to 1881 this part of the New World was not linked with any civilized state, not even with its nearest neighbours, Chile and the Argentine Republic, which were then squabbling about the Patagonian pampas. The Magellan territories belonged to no one, and completely independent colonies could be started there....
>
> In such a country where no authority existed, who would have the right to question it? It was not one of those well-ordered states where the police are interested in people's past lives and where it is impossible to remain unknown for long. Here, nobody was authorized to exercise authority, and a man could live in complete liberty, free of all constraint of law and custom.

In 1881, however, a treaty signed between Chile and the Argentine placed the southern islands under Chilean sovereignty. It was a terrible blow for the Kaw-Djer when he heard the news: 'Not a word passed his lips, but his eyes flashed with hate and he stretched his hand northwards in a gesture full of menace...' It was 'the end of a free land' – the title of Chapter II.

In *Jonathan* Verne also takes up again the stupidity of declarations of war and the diplomatic formalities connected with them. The survivors of the shipwreck constitute a microcosm which proceeds to rewrite – in Verne's view, for the worse – the whole experience of human societies throughout history. A crisis arises between the socialist Governor, Beauval, and the group of the Kaw-Djer's friends over a young girl whose father wishes her to marry against her will. Tension mounts and the Kaw-Djer's friends break down the wooden bridge separating their houses from the area occupied by their adversaries. Jules Verne notes with wry humour:

> Thus, the pugnacious character of human beings became manifest again. By their tacit acceptance of the possibility of recourse to war, and by taking the preliminary step of breaking off diplomatic relations in accordance with recognized custom, the inhabitants of these two hamlets way out at the ends of the habitable world bore witness to the fact that the citizens of the great empires are not the only people who deserve to be called 'men'.

In *The Survivors of the 'Jonathan'* we thus find Verne repeating much more clearly and forcibly certain libertarian themes mentioned only in passing in earlier works. But the main interest of this novel for our present purpose lies in its systematic exposition of anarchist ideas through the character of the Kaw-Djer. Remarkable for its tone of intimacy and inside knowledge, this exposition is noteworthy, above all, for the fact that only on the subject of anarchism does Verne relax the rule of silence on political matters which he seems to have imposed on himself throughout the *Voyages extraordinaires*. The Kaw-Djer is the only character in the whole of Verne's writings to give systematic and coherent expression to a political philosophy; and this is done, not reticently at the end of a paragraph – a method pleasing to Verne, as all his commentators have noticed – but from the first chapter and in such a way as to hit the reader straight on:

> Arms crossed, upright on the rock he had climbed, the Kaw-Djer stood motionless as a statue; his face alight with rapture, eyelids quivering, eyes shining with a sort of holy ardour, he stood contemplating that prodigious stretch of land and sea, the last bit of the globe belonging to nobody, the last region unbowed beneath the yoke of law.
>
> A long while he stood there this way, bathed in light and whipped by wind; then, opening his arms, he stretched them towards the horizon and a deep sigh swelled his breast as if he wished to encompass all infinity in one look, breathe it in one breath. Then, when his eyes seemed to challenge the heavens and sweep proudly across the earth, his lips opened in a shout expressive of his savage desire for freedom, absolute and unfettered. It was the cry of all anarchists in all countries, a phrase which has become so famous, so characteristic, that it is currently used as a synonym of anarchism and which in four words embraces the whole doctrine of that redoubtable sect.
>
> 'No God, no Master,' he proclaimed in a loud voice; half bent over the waves, he seemed to sweep the immense horizon with a wild gesture.

Throughout the novel, numerous episodes underline the Kaw-Djer's deep attachment to anarchist ideas. His eyes 'flash ominously' when the word 'laws' is mentioned in his presence by one of his opponents. He teaches his Fuegian friends to worship freedom and independence: 'A master? There is no such thing, and there can be none for a man worthy of the name', he explains to them.

The Kaw-Djer is thus 'a wild character, untamable, intransigent, incapable of obedience, and rebellious against all forms of law.' And Verne is careful to distinguish between two kinds of anarchists: some 'eaten up by envy and hatred, ever ready for violence and murder'; the others 'true poets dreaming of a chimeric humanity from which evil would be forever banished'; the Kaw-Djer belonged 'to the dreamers, and not to the professionals of the bomb and the knife'.

Verne makes it clear that the Kaw-Djer is 'a member of the ruling family of a great empire, destined by birth to rule as a master'; he had pledged himself to 'a profound hatred' of all social institutions; 'without telling anyone, he went away one fine day, abandoning his rank and his property.' It has been supposed[92] that this character was suggested to the author by the 'depraved Archduke' Jean Orth, brother of the last Grand Duke of Tuscany, who disappeared in South America around 1890, and is mentioned in Verne's novel *Clovis Dardentor*.[93] Verne had met the other brother, the Archduke Louis Salvador, in person when the latter was living on his luxurious yacht in the Mediterranean.[94] But does not the combination of the Kaw-Djer's anarchist ideas and his aristocratic origins bring to mind, rather, the name of Kropotkin?* There is a tradition[95] that Jules Verne was introduced to the latter by Elisée Reclus. Is there not a Tolstoyan aspect to this old man with a white beard who, at the end of the novel, quits civilized life for the second time and escapes to solitude?

On the other hand, socialist ideas receive very rough treatment in *The Survivors of the 'Jonathan'*. The socialist lawyer, Beauval, 'bitten by the tarantula of politics', is turned into a sort of caricature: muddle-headed and conceited, he favours collective ownership of the means of production at a time when the primitive state of the island's economy deprives these words of any meaning at all; he has to fall back on the small fishing boat and the only gun in the colony. His rival Dorick, a history professor who favours total communism, is an embittered failure whose misfortunes all stem from 'his ulcerated soul'. These two are relentless rivals, and each tries to build up a following among the survivors of the shipwreck; they end up fighting pitched battles. Both are quite ridiculous. Beauval, nevertheless, manages to get himself elected Governor by 'a sham election'. With a large number of abstentions, and after two recounts, he obtains thirty votes out of a possible thousand; a 'conjuring trick', says Verne, thus expressing his opinion of universal suffrage in a way that the anarchists of his day would not have repudiated.[96] Like them, he had little respect for the masses, represented by the passengers:

> This hybrid group of people was a microcosm, a small cross-section of humanity, representing all social classes except the rich. . . . It was, in short, no better and no worse than any other crowd of people with their different natures, their virtues and their vices, a confused mass of contradictory desires and feelings, an anonymous crowd

---

*Peter Alekseivich, Prince Kropotkin, 1842–1921, Russian anarchist.

animated, occasionally, by a single common purpose like one of those currents which form in the sea and become separated from the amorphous mass of water around it.

The Kaw-Djer was to be troubled by the 'fecklessness' of that crowd who 'showed no desire to make nature serve their needs and had no wish to exert themselves in order to improve their living conditions.'

The crux of the plot is, in fact, the tragic confrontation between the Kaw-Djer's anarchist conception of life and the society which evolves on Hoste Island after the shipwreck. *Jonathan* is not just a simple adventure story for children, but a morality play of quite particular intensity. The Kaw-Djer sees his theories contradicted, or at least questioned, by the behaviour of the survivors, with their attachment to the idea of private property, their egoism, their readiness to submit to the authority of others, their disregard for the welfare of the community. This microcosm even goes to the length of tearing itself to pieces by civil war. The hero reaffirms his anarchist convictions, however:

> Once and for all, my friend, you must understand that I am irreconcilably opposed to all government, of whatever kind, ... All laws, ordinances and interdictions enacted in the so-called public interest to the detriment of the individual are nothing more than a trick.... This conviction is the basis of my life; and though I was unable, despite the great power I possessed, to make it prevail in the corrupt societies of the Old World, I have sacrificed a great deal, more than the majority of mankind – and for good reason – could possibly have done; and I have come here to the Magellan territories to live and die a free man on a free soil. My ideas have not changed since then, ... the events of recent months have saddened me, but they have not altered my way of thinking.

Nevertheless, the Kaw-Djer is forced by circumstances to set up himself the very mechanism of government controls which he abhors. After the shipwreck he finds himself obliged to organize an embryonic police force (recruited among the sailors from the ship) in order to protect the stores and, in particular, the supplies of alcohol; for him this decision is a most difficult matter of conscience:

> What? He, the believer in freedom, a man incapable of submitting to any constraint, here he was imposing constraints on others! And laws would have to be made by a man who rejected all laws! The supreme irony of it! The apostle of anarchism, the adherent of the famous creed, 'No God, no master', being turned into a master himself, becoming invested with authority, a principle which he regarded to the depths of his being with savage hatred!
>
> Did he have to accept this hateful task? Would it not be better to run far away from these people with the souls of slaves?... But

then, what would happen to them, left to their own devices? What responsibility for suffering would lie upon the conscience of the man who deserted them?

The Kaw-Djer is, in fact, obliged to take up the reins of power; the first time provisionally just after the shipwreck, the second time, when the members of the colony ask him to restore peace and order after the outbreak of civil war. He accepts the responsibility although 'his conscience is torn by painful debate'; to the agitated crowd he declares: 'Henceforth I myself will be your leader.'

He builds a prison, he promulgates laws, he starts a land register to regulate the ownership of private property, he even organizes the search for minerals. When the colony is attacked by the Patagonians, blood is shed by his order; the same thing happens when the miners rebel against him. Painful experience proves his ideals to be false:

> The fact that he had always acted with the best intentions and without a thought for his own advantage did not in any way save him from committing, in his turn, just those same inevitable crimes for which he had reproached so many other persons in authority. He, the believer in freedom, had given orders, the believer in equality had acted as judge of his fellow men, the believer in peace had made war, the altruist philosopher had decimated the crowd, and his hatred of shedding blood had only resulted in more blood being shed.
>
> Not one of his actions but was in contradiction of his theories, and at every point his former errors had been made clear.

Far from being a vindication of anarchism, therefore, *The Survivors of the 'Jonathan'* seems to be a critical summing-up, a statement of total failure, proving that the Kaw-Djer's theories ('his former errors') did not stand up to the test of social experiment. The political conclusion arrived at in the novel is reassuring and rational: 'Human nature does not change,' etc. Nevertheless, Verne shows extraordinary sympathy for his hero. The long quotations we have given were essential to establish the degree of intimacy, of inside knowledge, with which Verne relates his story. An author anxious only about his craft, or one who had not himself been long familiar with libertarian ideas, could never have made the Kaw-Djer speak so naturally and passionately, with so much elegance of thought and expression. Besides, the novel is constructed in such a way as to give the Kaw-Djer the last word. In the penultimate chapter he gives up his attempt to organize society along the lines of anarchist ideals, but he continues to regulate his own life upon them. The book finishes with his lonely climb to the top of Horn Island. The last view we have of him is identical with the first: he stands with arms crossed, defying the immensity of the sea.

CHAPTER VI

Colonial people: 'good savages' and 'bad savages'

The *Voyages extraordinaires* were written during the last third of the nineteenth century at a time when the great voyages of world discovery were coming to an end. The majority of the *Known and Unknown Worlds* were in the process of moving out of the latter category into the former. Like the French bourgeoisie of his time, Verne had a much fuller and more accurate idea of the other peoples of the world than had the men of preceding generations; nevertheless, when he tries to relate such faraway communities to the society in which he lived, he does so in terms of 'good savages' and 'bad savages'. On the one hand, the *Voyages extraordinaires* continue the tradition of the *Supplement to Bougainville's Travels** and are redolent of eighteenth-century idealist views about the superiority of 'a state of nature'; on the other hand, they somewhat naively reflect the racist and ethnocentric prejudices which at that time provided convenient justification for colonial expansion and the pillaging of colonial territories.

In Verne's writings, the prototype of the 'good savage' is Thalcave, the Araucanian guide in *The Children of Captain Grant*:

> Fifty paces away from the river, a very tall man was standing motionless upon one of the first steps of the mountain.... Dressed in the style of the frontier Patagonians, this native wore a splendid mantle made from the lower part of the neck and the legs of a guanaco, sewn with ostrich sinews, the silky wool outside. Beneath the mantle he had on a tightly fitting garment of fox-skin ending in a point in front.... His proud features expressed real intelligence despite the medley of colours with which his face was painted. Motionless, solemn and dignified, he stood waiting like a statue on his rocky pedestal, the personification of self-control.

Thalcave compels the admiration of Lord Glenarvan and his companions 'by his natural gracefulness, his ease of manner and his proud lack of

---

*Louis Antonine, Comte de Bougainville, 1729–1811, French navigator, founder of a short-lived colony in the Falkland Islands.

constraint', but also by his moral qualities of discretion, intelligence, devotion and generosity. No less noteworthy is his innate familiarity with the natural world; his intimate bond with his horse, Thaouka, 'a proud, courageous, lively and understanding animal'; his instinct which averts impending dangers whether floods or wandering packs of wolves. When he parts from those he has been protecting, he refuses all payment for his services, and refuses to follow them outside his own country; 'with a passionate gesture he seemed to embrace the whole immensity of the plains'.

Thalcave is far from being an isolated character in the *Voyages extraordinaires*; Verne returns frequently to the theme of the 'good savage' whom he places deliberately in a New World setting, doubtless remembering the novels of Fenimore Cooper which had delighted the people of his generation and which were read to him in his childhood by his father. One such native is Martin Paz (*The Chancellor*), of whom Verne praises 'the surprising physical strength, the insuperable strength of will and, above all, that power of self-control which is one of the privileges of the free Indians of the New World'. Such also is the young Indian girl, Cayatte, in *Caesar Cascabel*, as well as the Fuegians among whom the anarchist prince of *The Survivors of the 'Jonathan'* takes refuge.

In the same way, Verne writes of the innate innocence of the Tuareg tribes and their 'dignified way of walking' (*The Invasion of the Sea*), or the gentleness of the Kanakas and Tahitians when visited by the millionaires of *Propeller Island*. He even goes so far as to contrast the natural harmony of these primitive societies with the injustices and servitudes of modern life. 'The Eskimos are happier than the working people of our great cities,' declares Dr Clawbonny, one of the author's favourite mouthpieces, while meditating on civilization.

The Eskimos of northern Alaska also live in a state of nature (*Caesar Cascabel*): 'The most perfect equality reigns among them. . . . They are pagans in religion, worshipping as divinities their carved and red-painted totem poles. . . . They are of good moral character and they have a highly developed family feeling.'

Not surprisingly, praise for the perfections of the good savage turns in Nemo's mouth into criticism of civilization: '– Savages! And are you astonished, Professor, to meet savages when you travel in certain parts of the globe? Where does one not find savages? and in any case, are they any worse than those others whom you call savages?'

But such nostalgia for the state of nature is in fact fairly exceptional in Verne, the enthusiastic apostle of scientific and technical progress. Much more frequently, dependent and colonial peoples who figure in the novels are depicted as unpleasant and disturbing characters in a way which derives from the most blatant racism. However sincere Verne's faith may have been in democratic ideals, in the 1848 tradition and in freedom, however strong his belief in the value of human labour, progress and science, on this point we meet with an entirely negative aspect of his political thought which must not be glossed over.

The black people of Africa, for example, are described by him as 'miserable niggers', 'nasty creatures', 'horrible animals', 'beasts with human faces'. Quite as disdainful are the terms he uses to describe the natives of the Lykhovsky Islands, north of Siberia, in *Caesar Cascabel*, the Sioux Indians in *Around the World in Eighty Days*, and the Melanesians in several other novels. He constantly speaks of cannibalism and piracy in connection with all these peoples, purposely dwelling on revolting details. Nor does he fail to make use of every occasion to underline the animality which he believes these people betray: 'bestial faces', 'monkey-like agility', etc. The black king in *The Boy Captain* is called 'stupid nigger' or 'ape reaching the end of extreme old age.'

The same racism is easy to perceive in *Michael Strogoff*, but here it is associated with a fairly characteristic whiff of Yellow Peril since we are dealing with Tatars who attack Russian outposts in Siberia. The novel complacently enlarges on their ferocity, on the acts of arson, pillage, torture and depredation which they commit in the lands they overrun. Their chieftain, Feofar, is an evil being given to looting and destruction, forcing those who surrender to enrol in his army, and carrying into captivity those who resist; 'He moved from one town to another, . . . and all with the boldness of a modern Gengis Khan.' The same racial prejudice is clear in the description of the traitor Ivan Ogarev, who is denounced by the 'Tsar's courier':

> Ivan Ogarev had inherited some Mongol blood from his mother, who was of Asiatic origin; he enjoyed tricking people and setting traps for them; . . . deceitful by nature, he liked to disguise himself in the vilest way, . . . he was cruel and could at need have become a killer . . .

In short, we find in Verne's writings all those *clichés* which second-rate authors at the end of the nineteenth century were inspired to write on the themes of 'bad savages' and the Yellow Peril.[97] But an important difference of emphasis must be noted. Verne's racism and contempt are often discriminating: they apply to the tribal aristocracies and ruling classes rather than to the peoples of Africa and Oceania as a whole. What he most criticizes as typical of African 'barbarism' are such things as the ritual massacres carried out on the occasion of the burial of a ruler, as in the case of the petty king of the Congo in *The Boy Captain*, or the mass sacrifice of prisoners in honour of the enthronement of the new king of Dahomey (which is stopped by Robur, overhead in his flying machine). That is to say, Verne's racism is half-hidden beneath a certain feeling for democracy which, as we know, was skilfully utilized by the French colonialists of the Third Republic when they had to justify their intervention in the 'despotic' states of Asia and Africa.

Ivan Ogarev, the Siberian traitor, blinding Michael Strogoff.

More generally, it should be noted that Verne was interested in the problems presented by the social structure of such communities, and he frequently tried to interpret in terms of class distinction the facts he was writing about and which he had drawn from the tales of contemporary travellers. For example, he presents the Polynesian conception of tabu (*Propeller Island*) as 'a law invented by the strong for use against the weak, by the rich against the poor, in order to safeguard their privileges and property, . . . thus giving rise to a class which was tabu, including the priests, the sorcerers or Touas, the Akarkis or chieftains, and a class which was not tabu to which were relegated most women as well as the humbler people.'

It would be tempting to try to establish whether Verne's novels contain any sign of a chronological evolution reflecting an interesting ideological transition from the good savage to the bad savage; but the attempt would fail. His racism is already clearly to be seen in his first novel, *Five Weeks in a Balloon*, published in 1863; on the other hand, 'good savages', even if they figure less frequently, are to be found throughout his writings. There was clearly, therefore, an inherent contradiction in the author's own mind.

The period when Verne was writing, the last third of the nineteenth century, is the same during which the last stages took place in the division of the world into vast empires belonging to England, France and their rivals. The colonial wars of conquest and the resistance to them are given a not unimportant place in Verne's works, thereby confirming that this 'childrens' author' was remarkably sensitive to the political evolution of the world of his day. Here again, however, his description of colonial expansion and the national movements opposed to it is very contradictory.

One of his most original characters, the engineer Robur, in his aircraft *Albatross*, witnesses the English columns marching on Herat during the second Afghan War (1880–71). Robur is a man of progress who symbolizes Verne's faith in the unlimited possibilities of technology, and to him the spectacle of Anglo-Russian colonial rivalry in that area, as seen from the air, appears quite ludicrous:

> The engineer never meddled in the affairs of other people, except when it was for him a matter of honour or humanity. He took no notice. If Herat is, as has been said, the key to Central Asia, it was a matter of indifference to him whether that key landed in an English or a Russian pocket. The daring engineer who had made the air his private domain had no interest in what happened on the earth.

In another novel dealing with the future, *Upside Down*, Verne attacks even more directly the very principle of colonial conquest. An international conference is called to decide about the possible sale by auction of the Polar regions to a company wanting to exploit the coal deposits. Verne wonders whether the princples laid down at the Berlin Conference of 1885 are applicable (the novel was published in 1889):

> It is true that some years ago the Berlin Conference laid down special rules of conduct to be observed by the Great Powers whenever they wished to expropriate the property of other peoples on the pretext of colonizing it or of opening up markets for commerce. It does not seem, however, that such rules apply in the present circumstances.

In the case under consideration, as generally in all cases of 'colonial sharing-out', the decisions are taken without the slightest regard to the wishes of the populations concerned, and when the Polar regions are put up for auction, the inhabitants have no say in the matter.

> There they were, the Samoyeds of Asiatic Siberia, the Eskimos and natives of Greenland, and the people living in what used to be Russian Alaska; but these tribes, who are without doubt the true natives of the northern regions, were given no say in the matter. How could the poor devils have put in a bid anyway, however small? ... Nevertheless, as the original inhabitants, they must have some sort of rights in the land about to be auctioned. But, of course, they were not even consulted, these Eskimos, these Choukchis, these Samoyeds.

In this case Verne is logically following the '48 principle of sympathy for national liberation movements which inspired him to write *Mathias Sandorf*, *Foundling Mick* and *Islands on Fire*; but to what extent was he capable of extending to all colonial peoples the principle of liberty which he defends in the case of the Hungarians, the Irish and the Greeks, in those three books? To what extent did he recognize the 'right of self-determination' in the case of resistance to the colonial conquests of France, England and other Powers?

Such movements of national resistance to colonial expansion do, in fact, have an important place in his writings and provide him with opportunities for political and psychological analyses which are often both shrewd and subtle. It is clear that Verne has great respect for those who stand up to the West and that he wants to help his readers to understand them. Such is the case with the Indian Mutiny, which provides the key to the attractive personality of Captain Nemo, a nephew of the great Tippu Sahib, 'who united in his own person all the wild hatreds of the defeated for the victors' (*The Mysterious Island*). Nemo has acquired immense culture and learning in Europe but, 'scientist and artist though he was, he remained Indian at heart, Indian in his desire for vengeance, Indian in the hope he nourished of being able one day to assert his country's right to independence and to throw out the foreigners.'

When the Mutiny breaks out in 1857, Prince Dakkar becomes one of the leaders, but the revolt fails and his family is put to death by the English. Thereafter, 'filled with immense disgust for anything in the shape of man, hating and abhorring civilization', he becomes Captain Nemo and shuts himself up in the *Nautilus* with his crew. But this misanthrope never forgets his homeland: 'That Indian', he says, pointing to a poor Ceylonese pearl-fisher whom he has saved from a shark, 'belongs to a country of oppressed people; I still belong to that country, and will do so to my dying breath.'

The Indian Mutiny also provides the historical and social setting for another of Verne's novels, *The Steam House*. The hero, the Marhatta prince Dandou-Pant, or Nana-Sahib, one of the leaders of the Mutiny,

Brahmins inciting the Sepoys in the Indian Mutiny (*The Steam House*).

manages to escape from the repressive action to the Deccan where he tries, 'in place of a simple military mutiny, to organize a national movement in which Hindus of all castes would take part.'

Using material from a book published by a former French Consul in Calcutta, *New Studies about the English in India*, Verne takes the opportunity to enlarge upon the memories of the 1857 Mutiny and the ferocity with which it was suppressed by the British authorities, which he qualifies as 'downright human butchery'. In particular, he relates numerous cases of mutineers being bound alive to the mouths of guns and gives the figures of 120,000 Indian soldiers and 200,000 civilians killed at that time. In this novel, Verne develops the capacity of popular guerilla bands to continue resistance, even against troops with superior armament, by leaving a vacuum in front of the English troops and reforming elsewhere: 'The war-cry, so familiar to the ears of mountain peoples, becomes a cry of alarm ... we must run away ... let the agents of authority find nothing but ruins.' Nana-Sahib's efforts to continue guerilla warfare in the foothills of the Himalayas are no doubt doomed to fail, but he is nevertheless the central figure of the novel, impressive in his fierce determination and desire for revenge.

The great Maori rebellion of the 1860s also provided Verne with the setting for one of the episodes of *The Children of Captain Grant*, when the expedition searching for the captain is crossing New Zealand. Verne carefully makes it clear that this is a question of a 'national party', of a 'war of independence', and that the struggle is extended to the economic sphere as well by a league of Maori landowners opposed to the sale of land to the English. The Maoris are depicted as 'men of pride and courage ... who fight foot by foot against English encroachments.'

Similarly, the Peruvian Indians' struggle against the Spaniards offered Verne the theme for a short story written in his younger days.[98] Here again, the principal character is a young Indian, Martin Paz, who leads an unsuccessful rising in Lima in the eighteenth century and dies a romantic death.

Finally, in one of his last novels, *The Invasion of the Sea*, it is the French colonization of North Africa which is called in question. The Tuaregs of southern Tunisia and of the region south of Constantine rise up against the proposal to cut a waterway between the Gulf of Gabès and the Shotts of the regions in question; the policy of confining them to certain regions, the economic results of which are analyzed by Verne with some care, has already tried their patience, and this new plan would bring confusion to all the local agriculture, small-scale commerce and nomadic stock-breeding. Resistance to the French is headed by Hadjar, one more in the long series of fiercely rebellious characters who appear throughout the *Voyages extraordinaires*; he is beaten in the end by the French troops sent against him, but he is shown as being morally superior to the victors.

Verne's surprising political sensitivity to the reactions of colonial and dependent peoples can be illustrated yet again in a passage in *The Fur Country*. Soldiers of the Hudson's Bay Company, sent to set up a trading post on the shore of the Arctic Ocean, establish themselves on a piece of ice which for centuries has been linked with the coast, but comes adrift as the consequence of an earth tremor. The settlement only just manages to escape disaster. The interesting point is that the Eskimos who helped to build the fort knew by tradition that the site chosen was dangerous, but they said nothing 'because of the feelings every native experiences about foreigners who take possession of his land.'

On occasion, Verne goes even further in the way of expressing clearly anti-colonialist views, for example when he indicts British colonialism in Oceania. When the story is set in that region, as in *The Children of Captain Grant, Mistress Branican* and *Propeller Island*, he is critical of what he calls 'the English system' of colonization, meaning the complete elimination of the native populations. 'If the annihilation of a race of human beings is the last word in colonial progress, the English are right to boast that their task has been properly completed,' he declares à propos of Tasmania (*Mistress Branican*). And he thinks that the Fiji Islands are another example of systematic depopulation caused by the harsh conditions of labour imposed on the natives by the planters; the former are 'nothing better than serfs' and also the victims of disease (*Propeller Island*).

In the case of the commercial colonialism of the Hudson's Bay Company his indictment is no less precise: 'Turning the poverty of the Indians to their own advantage, maltreating them and robbing them after having tracked them down; defying Parliament's prohibition of the sale of alcoholic beverages in native territories...'

In *The Children of Captain Grant* a formal indictment of British colonialism is made by Paganel, a French geographer and one of Verne's favourite mouthpieces:

> The British system pushes primitive conquered peoples into annihilation and results in their elimination from those regions where their ancestors lived. This baneful tendency could be seen everywhere, and in Australia more than elsewhere. In earliest times, the deportees and even the colonists looked on the blacks as savage beasts and used to hunt them with guns and shoot them; they were massacred. Legal authorities were quoted as proof that the Australian was a natural outlaw and that the murder of these wretched people was no crime. Sydney newspapers even suggested that the most efficient way of getting rid of the Lake Hunter tribes was to poison the lot of them.
>
> At the beginning of their conquest, the English evidently used murder to assist their colonizing efforts. They indulged in atrocious cruelties. They behaved in Australia as they had done in India where five million Indians disappeared, as they had done at the Cape where the Hottentot population has fallen from a million to one hundred thousand; the aboriginal population in consequence, decimated by bad treatment and drunkenness, tends to disappear from the continent before a murderous civilization...

The same theme is taken up again in *Mistress Branican* when an expedition searching for the survivors of a shipwreck reaches Australia. Verne again mentions, but this time as a positive fact and not just a rumour, the tale of mass poisonings by strychnine. In order to explain more clearly 'the hate felt by the Australian aborigines for their murderers', Verne quotes the brutal words of an English colonist in Australia: 'I shoot all the men I find on my pasture-land because they kill my stock, and all the women because they give birth to men who become killers of stock, and all the children because they will turn into killers of stock.'

One could doubtless object that these anti-colonialist diatribes do not single out England by chance. Verne's anglophobic chauvinism was already latent in his earliest works: it increased in later novels and became particularly virulent after the period 1885–90. *Mistress Branican* (1891) and *Propeller Island* (1895) are in the same vein as those other anti-English broadsides: *Foundling Mick* (1893) dealing with Ireland, or *Family without a Name* (1889), about Canada. Colonial genocide becomes a matter for frontal attack only when it is perpetrated by the English, and national resistance movements in the colonies (Maoris, Sepoys, Peruvians) are only brought into the limelight when they are directed against the English or, at need, the Spaniards. (*The Invasion of the Sea* was a late novel and stands rather by itself.)

Yet one may wonder whether the anti-British slant in these works is not a cover for a more general disapproval of colonial conquest, or at least of some of its methods, just as the description in *The Begum's Fortune* of the giant steel complex of Stahlstadt, which seems to derive from the most elementary anti-German chauvinism, leads in the end to a much more general criticism of the evils of large-scale industrial capitalism.

Confirmation of such an interpretation is, paradoxically, to be found in the fact that Verne gives very little space in his writings to French colonial expansion. Now, at first sight this is all the more surprising because he was writing precisely in that third of the century during which, between the end of the Second Empire and the colonial agreements negotiated at the time of the *entente cordiale*, saw the building of the French colonial empire. It was a wonderful opportunity for an author, who is sometimes suspected of taking the line of least resistance in money matters, to cash in on the clichés then current about the 'French colonial epic'. If, for example, one looks up contemporary issues of the *Petit Français illustré*, one can find on almost every page references to the 'brave marines' fighting Tonkinese pirates, or the heroic deeds of the French army in Africa.... Verne never mentions Indochina, which is all the more remarkable because of his great interest in the civilizations of the Far East (*cf. The Tribulations of a Chinese Gentleman*). There is hardly any mention of French territories in Oceania apart from some fairly conventional paragraphs in *Propeller Island* describing the happy results of the French protectorate in Tahiti. Similarly there is very little about French Africa south of the Sahara, which is mentioned only in passing in Verne's very first novel, *Five Weeks in a Balloon*, and in the last, *The Astonishing Adventures of the Barsac Mission*; in the former it is a question merely of providing, in the form of a French administrative post in Senegal, somewhere for Dr Fergusson to bring his journey to an end; in the latter case, the law and order prevailing in French colonial territory are mentioned only indirectly for the purpose of contrast with the disorder in the pirate city of Blackland. The mission under the leadership of the French Deputies Barsac and Baudinière, two 'colonial experts' who have never been outside France before, has the task of studying the possibility of granting votes to the Blacks of French Africa; the circumstances in which they are given this task, and the means by which they carry it out, are described in a manner implying very little respect for 'France's colonial mission'. The incompetent pretentiousness of these two Deputies and future Ministers provides an opening for some rather wicked satire, and the discreet anti-colonialism of the novel here takes on a tinge of anti-parliamentarianism. Even the word despotism is used in the context of colonial administration:

> The fact that they have to live all the time in the company of people who are, after all, their inferiors, and over whom they have unlimited authority, often transforms such Europeans into brutal satraps; strength of character and goodness of heart are not proof against temptation. Despotism is an endemic disease in the colonies.

Verne is even cautiously critical about the French in Algeria: the tourist Clovis Dardentor is impressed by the natural riches of that country but puzzled that it should be so poorly developed:

> This led M. Dardentor to express the same thought which has come to so many intelligent people:
> —Why is it that Algeria with all its natural resources is not able to provide for its own needs?
> —There are too many civil servants there, replied Jean Taconnat, and not enough planters; the latter would in any case be stifled there. It is a question of clearing out the thistles.

In the end, however, it is French colonialism which wins out in Verne's novels as a whole. In more general terms, despite his efforts to understand the people struggling against a colonial Power, and despite his secret sympathy for those rebels who, like the Rao brothers, are stubbornly fighting in a hopeless cause, Verne nevertheless accepts colonial rule as an unavoidable and accomplished fact, or rather, as a necessary fact of history. The passages quoted from *Captain Grant* or *Mistress Branican* are critical of certain particularly hateful aspects of colonialism, rather than of colonialism as such. Verne's undoubtedly sincere dislike of slavery and his denunciation of the slave trade (*cf. The Boy Captain*) derive from the same humanitarian idealism, and would be quite appeased by a colonial rule that was limited to abolishing these evils. For him, colonization was not so much a question of certain peoples exercising

For supporting the cause of Hungarian freedom Mathias Sandorf is found guilty of treason.

authority over certain others, but rather one of the methods by which man can achieve mastery over the globe. Colonization is one of the aspects of progress, and it must be given precedence over 'those African barbarians who will necessarily be brought to order one day as the result of a civilizing war' (*The Fur Country*). However great his sympathy for the Maori nationalist movement in *The Children of Captain Grant*, Verne nevertheless believes that the Anglo-Maori wars must 'decide for long centuries to come between civilization or barbarism'. What this means is that despite his faith in the traditions of '48 and his ardent defence of the smaller peoples of Europe, he cannot bring himself in the

The friends Wang and Kin Fo strolling along a quay in Shanghai (*Tribulations of a Chinese Gentleman*).

end to decide that the principles of liberty should be extended systematically to all colonial peoples.

This 'threshold', which he cannot cross over when it comes to the application outside Europe of the right of self-determination, is very clear in *Mathias Sandorf*. The hero, condemned to death by the Austrian political police for supporting the cause of Hungarian freedom, takes the name of Dr Antekirtt and, in the hope of avenging his people, establishes a sort of secret base off the coast of Cyrenaica which becomes the target for unsuccessful attacks by the Senussi. Verne describes the latter in terms analogous to those used by the Austrian police in regard to the Hungarian hero: 'bloody associates', 'pirates' whose 'fanatical bravery' derives from 'their contempt of death, their hope of loot and their hatred of Europeans'. The Senussi movement, nevertheless, was the expression in Tripolitania of exactly the same fundamental aspiration as Sandorf's in Hungary, namely freedom from foreign domination.

Nemo, the character in whom the 1848 tradition and the theme of national liberation are most precisely focused, is defeated in the end. He dies in solitude confessing his failure to the colonists of the Mysterious Island. The leader of the colonists, the engineer Cyrus Smith, tells Nemo (that is, Verne talking to himself): 'Captain, your mistake was to think you could bring back the past, and you have been fighting against necessary progress'. The 'necessary progress' was the British domination of India; and Verne concludes, after having spoken of the efforts of Prince Dakkar: 'Right, once again, has been defeated by force. But civilization never retreats, and seems to borrow from necessity all the rights it needs.'

Verne sees here an inevitable and irreversible process (*The Great Raft*):

> It is the law of progress. The Indians will disappear. Australians and Tasmanians have faded away in face of the Anglo-Saxon race. The North American Indians are being made to vanish by the conquerors of the Far West. Perhaps, one day, the Arabs will be annihilated by French colonization.

That is why the French journalist, Jolivet, in *Michael Strogoff*, finally expresses his preference for the law and order imposed by the despotic rule of the Tsars, whatever its excesses, to the Tatar rebellion, however great its popular support:

> We must not become too much like the Tatars! The best part is still that of the character who wields his arms in the interests of civilization, and it is clear that the peoples of Central Asia have everything to lose and absolutely nothing to gain from this invasion. However, the Russians will be able to defeat it.

Even in China, it is 'progress' which has the last word in the *Voyages extraordinaires*. Two different versions of China come face to face in *The Tribulations of a Chinese Gentleman* through the friends, Wang and Kin Fo. Wang is a Confucian sage as well as a militant in the ranks of the Taiping rebels. He represents both the strength of a people's movement and the attachment to tradition. Kin Fo is a westernized Chinaman from Shanghai with a passionate interest in technological progress. The novel suggests that China's future will be fashioned according to the image and tastes of Kin Fo, and not those of Wang.

The conception of colonization as 'the exploitation of natural resources' derives directly from the 'colonism' of Saint-Simonian tradition. According to this view, the relations between the colonizers and the native populations are only of secondary importance; the conquest of colonial territories finds its justification on another level, as is evident from the quotations given above about the conflict between 'barbarism' and 'civilization'. Political domination by a Western Power is the commonest form of such 'colonial relationship', but it does not constitute the essential element. The essential thing is to take possession of nature, to exploit new territories in the interests of economic and technical progress.

The contradictions inherent in Verne's attitude towards colonial peoples become very clear in retrospect. His naive and shabby racism may be irritating, and it is regrettable that he failed to understand both 'the double role of British imperialism in India' (although he came close to doing so!) and the 'connection between the question of nationalism and the colonial question'.

Nevertheless, for a man of his time and *milieu*, he lacked neither shrewdness nor originality nor courage. To make a great hero out of an outlaw like Nemo, a rebel against British colonialism, and thus against colonialism in general, was to go directly counter to accepted ideas; and in this sense, Verne was responsible for turning many young readers into anticolonialists (as the author of this book can personally testify). Even if it is progress in the Saint-Simonian sense that triumphs in his writings, his sympathy towards colonial peoples in their fight for independence and their primitive reactions, Eskimos, and Maoris, Tuaregs and Indians, Fuegians and Blacks, is a far cry from the bourgeois façade behind which he liked to hide himself as an author.

CHAPTER VII

Chance and providence

[The *Voyages extraordinaires*] are charming, except for one omission which, though it may not spoil anything, is generally distorting and leaves the wonders of nature a riddle. That is what is wrong with your books, which are otherwise admirable.

They are fine, but they lack life. Someone has been left out. The landscape has no figures, man has no objective. Excuses must be made for a way of thought which has become general, because it has become necessary. Nevertheless, and forgive me for saying it, this way of thought is false and, because of it, the best and most praiseworthy work remains sterile. A tree with flowers, but no fruit...

These severe words were used by Louis Veuillot* to express his indignation in a letter to Hetzel about what appeared to him sacrilege by omission.[99] Indeed, Hetzel, despite his personal liberalism, was anxious not to attract the hostility of the Church and thereby put at risk the sale of his publications to young Catholics; he was certainly aware that this was one of his author's weak points, and that the treatment of religion in the *Voyages extraordinaires* is ambiguous, to say the least. He probably insisted that Verne should 'make an effort', and it was he, for example, who recommended that mention should be made of the existence of a church in the island of Antekirtta, the scientific colony established by Sandorf in the eastern Mediterranean.[100]

To the eyes of anyone less exigent than Louis Veuillot, no doubt Jules Verne and his novels contained nothing which was not reassuring to the respectable bourgeoisie of his day. His friend Nadar referred to him as 'most Catholic';[101] he was received in audience by Pope Leo XIII; and his family have always been very careful to speak of him as 'a good Catholic'.[102] It is possible to glean, throughout the novels, a fair number

---

*Louis Veuillot 1813–1883, French journalist and writer, was the leader of the most conservative group in the French Catholic Church in Verne's day.

of episodes and characters stemming directly from the most conventional Christian morality – for instance, Lord and Lady Glenarvan exhorting their companions to meditate while they are waiting to be executed by the Maoris:

> —Where is the man who does not think about God when he is facing death?
> —My dear friends, replied his Lordship, our lives and those of these poor women are in God's hands. If heaven has decreed that we shall die tomorrow, then I am sure we will all know how to die like sincere men and Christians, prepared to face the Supreme Judge without fear. God, to whom our souls are an open book, is aware that we are acting in a noble cause. Should we meet death in place of success, it is His will, and however hard his judgment may seem to us, I will not complain against it.

In the same way Mme Toronthal, a pious Catholic though married to an unscrupulous and criminal banker, rejoices in the love of her daughter for Pierre Bathory which 'is in accord with the designs of Providence' (*Mathias Sandorf*). Similarly, Axel, nephew of the intrepid geologist Liddenbrock, resorts to prayer when he thinks that he is about to die of thirst deep inside a volcano in Iceland (*Journey to the Centre of the Earth*): 'Beyond all human help and powerless to do anything to save myself, I thought Heaven might help me, . . . I started to pray; knowing that I had little right to expect any mercy from God, whom I had only approached at this late stage, I prayed fervently.'

Many such quotations could be listed. Nevertheless, while examples of religious sentiment can be found widespread in the various episodes of the *Mondes connus et inconnus*, religious institutions, churches, priests, figure much less frequently. In all the sixty-four novels there are hardly more than two priests with some human depths and imaginative importance: Abbé Johann and Father Espérante. The first is a leader of partisans, a kind of Camille Torrès before his time, who rekindles the will to fight in the French Canadian peasants (*Family without a Name*):

> A militant priest who joined the Sulpician Order with the intention of supporting the inalienable rights of his country, . . . he is a real champion of popular rights, compellingly eloquent, and restrained by no thought of his own interests; he would certainly be ready to sacrifice his life and liberty for the [French Canadian] cause.

The other, rather similar to Dr Schweitzer,* makes his home in the upper reaches of the Orinoco basin. A former French colonel, he

---

*Albert Schweitzer, 1875–1965, French doctor, pastor, organist, musicologist, devoted his life from 1913 to the hospital he founded at Lambaréné in Gabon, Africa.

organizes the Indian tribes of the region into a military colony. Reading between the lines in which Verne so admiringly describes this character, it is clear that the Saint-Simonian idea of 'progress' means more to this almost lay missionary than the conversion of souls (*The Superb Orinoco*):

> He was engaged in the noble task of bringing civilization to those territories, of developing unused land, of raising the intellectual level of tribes whose degeneracy and poverty would soon have led to their disappearance....
>
> This missionary then stood revealed as a man of action with a courage equal to his talents as an organizer. All adult Guaharibos were enrolled as soldiers, taught disciplines and how to handle arms....
>
> They were happy, their families prospered and their lives were easy.... Their standard of life continued to improve and they enjoyed ever greater well-being....
>
> It was an act of charity to convert these Indians, for they were the poorest of the poor; and it was also a civilising act because they were among the wildest Indians in Venezuela.

All this means that the 'Santa Juana Mission', as it was called, was much more preoccupied with social progress and military training than spiritual advancement towards Christ.

The world of the *Voyages extraordinaires* is thus a world without priests, without churches, without religious ceremonies; or rather, when these external forms of the religious life do figure, it is in terms more appropriate to straightforward anti-clerical satire or burlesque 'caricature'. Catholic, Protestant and Orthodox services are made fun of with equal verve. Thus, Clovis Dardentor, after a series of misadventures, is drawn into a church in the Balearic Islands during the service of benediction in a cart (*galera*) drawn by runaway mules.

> One can imagine the extraordinary effect when the mules stopped at the steps of the altar at the very moment when the priest pronounced the words '*et spiritu sancto*'. – '*Amen*', replied a loud voice.
>
> That this unexpected event should have been believed to be a miracle is not surprising in such a profoundly religious country;...
>
> It was thereafter celebrated as the Feast of the *Santa Galera de Salud*.

Just as irreverent is the description of a Protestant service on board the liner *Great Eastern*: the service takes place in the dining-room, the faithful are seated at the tables, and trays are handed round 'full of Bibles in place of sandwiches'. The clergyman Hunter is not treated any more respectfully: he is described as 'a great salesman of Bibles which are both antiseptic and anti-sceptic' (*An Eccentric's Will*). As for the Maoris during their rebellion against England, they used leaves of the Bible as wadding in their guns; this causes Paganel, a favourite mouthpiece of

Verne's, to say, 'If that is how they use the verses of the Scriptures, I am very sorry for the missionaries; they will find it difficult to establish libraries for the Maoris.'

The Orthodox Greek clergy are not given any better treatment: the Peloponnesian monks, the 'caloyers', are 'careless, naïve, familiar, and seem to have few qualifications to be the leaders of a naturally superstitious people.' The priest of the little town of Vitylo is 'a big, fat man with the fatness which comes from idleness, and a crafty face'; his job is to point out to the fishermen-pirates which ships they should try to lure onto the rocks – not a vocation of much spiritual significance (*Islands on Fire*).

The disrespect shown by Verne towards ecclesiastical institutions was carried to even greater lengths, if we accept the very plausible interpretation given by Marcel Moré to the last scene in *Village in the Tree Tops*.[103] The Wagdis, a tribe of beings halfway between man and ape (this 'anthropological' novel is one of the first of its kind, a strange precursor of Vercors' 'tropis', are ruled by a mysterious sovereign called Msélo-Tala-Tala.[104] An organ is brought into the village square as a mark of reverence towards him, and Verne is careful to point out that an organ is 'a sacred instrument'. This white sovereign is carried about on his *sedia gestatoria*, words which the former recipient of the honour of an audience with Leo XIII does not hesitate to use. Indeed, the satire is quite evident, although Moré, not well versed in student slang, failed to see the very explicit support for his argument provided by the words *Tala-Tala*.

The 'most Catholic' Jules Verne is thus shown in practice to have had little respect for religious institutions. His attitude, however, cannot be reduced to a simple antithesis between conventional piety and anticlerical caricature, since the problem of a higher force directing the destiny of human societies and putting limits to their activities receives much more serious treatment in the *Voyages extraordinaires*.

It is in *The Mysterious Island* that this problem seems to us to be presented most clearly. Michel Butor is right to use this novel as the starting point for his attempt to define Verne's conception of religion, although, for our part, it leads to a completely opposite conclusion.[105] For Butor, *The Mysterious Island* is first and foremost a religious parable, the island standing for Paradise and its inhabitants for the righteous, whereas we, on the contrary, have suggested that it should be regarded as a Saint-Simonian parable of faith in science and human effort. Butor writes: 'They are in the power of someone who knows them yet whom they are unable to get to know, ... this invisible power operates only for their good, and its manifestations are invariably veiled in secrecy.[106] There is 'someone' whose activities imply a power so to speak infinite. In short, 'Nemo is the image of God', and in fact it is just this mental attitude which the sailor Pencroff, a simple, dedicated soul, adopts towards the mysterious happenings on the island: 'The sailor had absolute confidence in the God of his island, and the hidden power which had so far manifested itself in so many inexplicable acts certainly seemed to be infinite.'

Pencroff has a mental image of the 'master of the island' similar to those religious images given to children with the object of inspiring respect for God the Father: 'He must be handsome, tall and strong with a long beard and hair like rays of light, reclining on a cloud, holding a large ball.'

But the author makes use of Pencroff's naïve religious conceptions only to bring into relief the much more complex thinking of the engineer Cyrus Smith, the leader of the colony to whose skill and scientific knowledge the survivors of the shipwreck owe their lives, and who is their real mouthpiece in philosophic matters. Cyrus Smith also invokes God, for example when he decides to try to save Ayrton abandoned on his island ('to save God's creature from degradation, ... to fulfil one's duty as a civilized man and a Christian'). Similarly, when he is comforting Nemo in his death agony, he says, 'God alone is the judge of our mistakes', and reminds Nemo that 'all noble actions belong to God'.

Cyrus Smith, however, adopts a much more subtle attitude in regard to the unknown power with which the five men, and through them all humanity, are confronted:

> Here we are, my friends, thrown by the hand of the Almighty onto this piece of land. This is to be our home, ... and perhaps for a long time. Maybe, on the other hand, unexpected help will arrive, if some ship or other should pass this way by chance.

Thus in one and the same sentence, and in particularly dramatic circumstances, Cyrus Smith refers simultaneously to two completely opposite versions of human destiny: the will of God and the vagaries of chance.

After making his first inventory of the biological and mineralogical resources of the island, he similarly says: 'This is what nature provides for us, this is nature's contribution to our common task.' That is to say that the survival of those on the island depends upon the physical resources of the world and not upon the will of an all-powerful being.

Again, in the long monologue in which he forecasts the geological future of the globe, the cooling of certain continents and the formation of new lands, Cyrus Smith refers impartially to 'the prescience of nature' and 'the secret of the creator of all things'. When he recapitulates for the benefit of his companions all the strange facts which they have learned since they came to the island, he describes them first as 'so to speak supernatural'. But he corrects himself at once to say that the facts in question 'cannot *yet* be explained' (italics mine). The lapse is significant. Verne could not have been unaware of the very precise meaning given to the word *supernatural* in Catholic theology, but for him the word meant events that would be explained later, when the survivors of the air-crash would become aware of Nemo's presence on the island. This is a very long way from the mysticism and super-rationalism which Michel Butor attributes to Verne.

We have dealt at some length with the example of *The Mysterious Island*, but throughout all Verne's writings there is a whole complex of ideas and words, apparently very diverse, but denoting the relation between man and the world, between man and the future: in alphabetical order

— Chance
— The Creator
— Destiny
— Fate
— God
— Nature
— Providence
— The Unknown.

Some of these, such as Destiny, Fate and the Unknown, are more descriptive of those forces and situations which impose themselves upon the individual will and over which the latter has no control:

'Are you sorry that *Destiny* has thrown you into the power of Captain Nemo?'

'Without trying to disentangle cause and effect, Hans followed blindly where *Destiny* led him.'

'*Fate* has thrown us into the path of this incandescent lava.'

'Accidents at sea, a collision, a shipwreck, explosions in the engine room, some twenty years like Robinson Crusoe on a desert island, so what! ... No, indeed! Although I am not really interested in it at the moment, the *Unknown* is the X factor of life, the secret of *Destiny* which, in olden days, men used to cut into the skin of the goat Amalthea, that which is written in the great books up there, illegible to us even with the help of the best spectacles, the ballot-box wherein life's votes are cast to be drawn out by the hand of *Chance*.'

Verne is particularly fascinated by Chance, as Marcel Moré has rightly noted.[107] It is a game of uncontrollable and unforeseeable factors to which one must know how to entrust oneself in case of need, as do Gilbert and Mars when they despair of regaining the trail of those who have kidnapped their sister and wife (*North against South*): 'It was possible that *Chance* might guide them to the central island of the Black Creek. ... Thus it was to that *unconscious guide* that Gilbert and Mars had to entrust themselves.'

Likewise Judge Jarriguez, convinced that his prisoner Dacosta is innocent, but incapable of deciphering the document which he thinks may reveal the name of the real criminal (*The Giant Raft*): '*Chance* must come to his assistance, he tried by every possible and impossible means to bring this about. ... He was reduced to asking his servant to act as "the interpreter of *Chance*" by mentioning the first figure that came to mind.'

The death of Captain Nemo (*The Mysterious Island*): Cyrus Smith is standing, with Gideon Spillett, Herbart, Pencroft and Ayrton; the servant Neb is on his knees.

Then there is the case in *Mathias Sandorf* of the adventurers Zirone and Sarcany (the latter 'born by *chance*, grown up by *chance*, destined to live by *chance*'), deprived of everything until chance comes to their assistance in the form of an exhausted homing pigeon; from the latter they learn about the plot which they reveal to the police for the reward. But this last example shows that chance does not confine man within a completely contingent future. The pigeon which falls by chance at the feet of Zirone and Sarcany may indeed, in the short term, cause Sandorf's conspiracy to fail, but in the long term ensures for him an altogether

133

Professor Liddenbrock and Axel discover the sixteenth-century runic characters that spell Arne Saknussem (*Journey to the Centre of the Earth*).

exceptional destiny as Dr Antekirtt. It is also chance which places in the hands of the geologist Liddenbrock the message left behind by the Icelandic alchemist, and induces him to undertake his subterranean expedition. It is the chance effect of a storm which throws the five survivors of the air-crash onto the mysterious island, thereby giving them the opportunity to develop their human qualities in a most exemplary manner. It is through the chance discovery of the message in a bottle that Captain Grant's children and their rich protectors travel over seas and continents along the 37th parallel of the southern hemisphere. It is the result of chance that Fort Providence, built on the shore of the icy Arctic Ocean, is located on an invisible ice island destined to drift away from the land, thereby exposing Hobson, Mrs Barnett and their companions to the most terrible tribulations. In other words, chance provides the man of character with an opportunity to show his capabilities, to reveal his hidden potentialities, to be truly himself.

Destiny, Fate and Chance are mysterious forces concerned principally with the development of each individual human being. Nature, also, so often mentioned by Verne, is predominantly a 'creative force' controlling the whole physical and biological world:

> A bed of pearl oysters, an inexhaustible mine of wealth, because '*the creative force of nature*' is stronger than the destructive impulses of mankind. (*20,000 Leagues under the Sea*).

> An enormous crab, to whom *nature* has granted the instinct and ability to feed on coconuts. (*Ibid.*)

> *Nature* has provided it [the ichthyosaurus] with an extremely powerful optical mechanism able to resist the pressure exerted by the water in the depths where it lives. (*Journey to the Centre of the Earth*)

> *Nature*, normally so prodigal, has not buried enough forests to allow us to go on extracting coal for thousands of years; it will be worked out one day, that is certain. (*Black Diamonds*)

Do these mysterious forces (Destiny, Fate, the Unknown, Chance, Nature) have any relation with traditional religious concepts? The little we know about Verne's personal religious beliefs would no doubt lead to a classic reply: that it is God, including all His different attributes (Creator, Providence), who determines everything in the last resort, and that the other things, Nature, Destiny, Chance, etc., are no more than relay-points in the transmission of His intervention. That, in any case, was the position taken up by Verne at a period (in his thirties and forties) when he still sometimes talked about himself: 'I am astonished', he wrote to his father in 1862, 'at the foolish satisfaction which many good people experience in giving the name of chance to the activity of a higher power which it would be just as simple, and more logical, to call Providence.'[108]

There is a similar statement of belief in his study of Edgar Allan Poe, published in 1864 in the *Musée des Familles*:

> Despite their extraterrestrial and superhuman beauty, the *Extraordinary Tales* remain, in the end, materialist. One is never aware in them of the intervention of Providence, whose existence Poe seems unable to admit; he tries to explain everything in terms of physical laws, which he even invents himself at need. One cannot find in him one atom of that faith which his incessant contemplation of the supernatural should arouse.

But this simple reply does not hold water when one reads the *Voyages extraordinaires*. Sometimes, no doubt, we can still find in them affirmations of the primacy of God's power and Divine providence – for example, when Lady Glenarvan tries to console Paganel, who had boarded the *Duncan* in the mistaken belief that she was bound for India: 'Believe me, it is better to trust to chance, or rather Providence.' (*The Children of Captain Grant*.) Similarly, Captain Len Guy, who is exploring the South Polar seas in search of his brother (a real person whom Edgar Allan Poe is supposed to have used as the basis for a romantic character in *Arthur Gordon Pym*):

> What is unreasonable about admitting the intervention of a supernatural power in the most ordinary circumstances of life?... Think a bit, Mr Jeorling, are these events not of a providential nature? I go even further and state that after giving us so much held in our search for our compatriots on board the *Jane* [the ship on which Pym embarked in Poe's novel], God will not abandon us.
>
> I do not think as you do, Captain. No indeed! His intervention cannot be denied and, in my opinion, it is not true that chance plays in human affairs the part which superficial minds attribute to it. All events are joined together by a mysterious link, a chain . . . (*An Antarctic Mystery*)

Yet another statement seems to lead in the same direction, this time expressed by the voice 'off', which sums up the futurist visions of *Propeller Island*:

> Would not the creation of an artificial island, an island moving on the surface of the sea, go beyond the limits assigned to human genius, and is it not forbidden to man, who controls neither the winds nor the waves, to try so rashly to usurp the functions of the Creator?

There are, however, equally numerous and important passages which give rise to doubts, and seem to contradict the above, namely those in which Verne treats the problem of the supernatural in a very different way. Very often, in fact, instead of suggesting that Chance, Destiny and Nature are no more than modes for the intervention of Almighty God in His capacity of Creator and Providence, Verne makes the former operate on the same level as the latter. The two series of ideas, those denoting mysterious forces, and those relating to Divine power on the other, seem to become interchangeable and are used almost indiscriminately in the same paragraph. For instance, 'nature' and 'the Creator' (*Black Diamonds*):

> Nature had already created the numerous galleries and tunnels of New Aberfoyle. Yes, nature alone. No ancient Egyptian hypogeum,

no Roman catacomb could be compared with them.... New Aberfoyle was not the work of men, but of the Creator.

The relationship between Providence and Chance is equally ambiguous, equally interchangeable. When the pious Lady Helens, in *The Children of Captain Grant*, uses the former word in preference to the latter, it is often the reverse that is suggested: 'Chance is the beggars' Providence,' Verne himself says at the beginning of *Mathias Sandorf*, and in *The Clipper of the Clouds* he is most ambiguous on the same subject: 'Providence – for those who believe in Divine intervention in human affairs, or chance, for those who are so stupid as not to believe in Providence – came to the aid of the survivors of the shipwreck.' The universal machinery on which mankind and the universe depend is thus deconsecrated, and everyone is free to choose his own system of explanation and his own scheme of ideas.

That Louis Veuillot's fears were fully justified in the end, and that Verne's views were very far removed from classical Christian theology is equally apparent from the presence in the *Voyages extraordinaires* of certain 'Godlike' characters, in the sense of Butor's interpretation of Captain Nemo. The latter does not stand alone; there are others, such as Dr Antekirtt or the engineer Camaret. But M. Moré seems to us to be quite right in pointing out that, far from being the image and reflection of the Divine power, these characters are its earthly and human antithesis, and constitute a challenge rather than an homage to God.

Dr Antekirtt, the figure into whom Mathias Sandorf transforms himself after his escape, has a face like God the Father, with 'an air of nobility and greatness', but he remains 'only a man, nothing more than a man'. Camaret, the founder of a marvellous city in the middle of the desert, claims almost Divine powers (*The Barsac Mission*):

> I have created all that exists here. It is I who have spread the beneficent rain on the parched and arid desert soil. It is I who have transformed it into fertile fields. It is I who have created this city from nothing, like God who created the universe out of nothingness.

When he goes mad and decides to destroy his own creation, he exclaims: 'God has pronounced sentence on Blackland,' and utters curses in the manner of the Old Testament prophets. As M. Moré has said, 'It is a kind of Apocalypse in which Christianity is replaced by the religion of science.'[109]

Several of the most remarkably human characters in the novels similarly challenge God, either implicitly or explicitly. The intrepid and obstinate Liddenbrock impiously penetrates into the interior of the terrestrial globe in order to measure himself directly against the forces of nature; heir to the cursed alchemist, Arne Saknussen, who had been burnt for heresy long ago, 'he seemed to defy the gods', shouting proudly: 'We are rushing like madmen to enjoy the sight of the unleashed forces of the elements.'

Robur finds no reason for the intervention of supernatural power since, for him, the relationship between man and nature through the mediation of science is sufficient unto itself: 'Just as he has mastered the sea by means of ships, oars and sails, paddlewheels and screws, man will master the air by means of machines heavier than air, because you must be heavier than air in order to be stronger than it. And finally Hatteras, abandoned by his crew and facing death in the middle of a wilderness of ice, sees no need to invoke Divine help, and thus relies upon his own powers: 'The cowards have run away! But we who are strong will attain our goal. Johnson, Bell, you are brave men; and you, doctor, have the necessary scientific knowledge, while I have the faith! The North Pole is that way; so let us get on with the job. The same Promethean doggedness shown by Liddenbrock, Robur and Hatteras can already be seen in the central character of one of the short stories Verne wrote in his youth, *Master Zacharius*; the latter is a watchmaker of genius who defies the watchmaker of the Universe: 'I can no more die than the Creator can die who has made this Universe obedient to His laws. I have become His equal and I have a share in His power! If God has created eternity, Master Zacharius has created time.'

This defiance of God is brought out even more strongly in a significant alteration in the text when this short story was reprinted in the series of *Voyages extraordinaires*; the first text in 1854 showed Zacharius yielding in the end to Divine grace, which could not but please the respectable readers of the *Musée des Familles*, while the alteration printed in the 1874 edition, clearly Verne's own work, shows Zacharius refusing to bow down, but 'staring directly at the consecrated Host'.[110]

In his religious thinking, therefore, Verne comes closer to a vague Deism, or rather pantheism (suggested by his obsessive preoccupation with the mysterious, creative forces of nature), than to official Christianity. Moré is reminded of Victor Hugo with his confused religious ideas,[111] but is it not also possible to see a parallel with the Deism of Freemasonry, since Verne must have met many of its initiates among Hetzel's circle of friends? His lively feeling for 'system in the Universe', particularly in the fields of geology and astronomy, naturally makes one think of the formulas of Freemasonry ('The Great Architect of the Universe,' etc.):

> To change the conditions governing the movements of the earth is to go beyond what is permitted to human activity; it is not for men to alter the arrangements made by the Creator for the functioning of the Universe. (*Upside Down*)

On the other hand, as we have seen, religious matters and clergymen figure hardly at all in these works. Religious services are important principally for their social and utilitarian results, for example in maintaining morale during Polar expeditions:

> In the course of these long expeditions, men of all persuasions should often come together for community prayers and Bible readings to revive their courage in times of discouragement; Shandon knew from experience how useful such meetings could be and their good influence upon the members of the ship's company. (*Captain Hatteras*)

As for the non-Christian religious, Verne describes them with tolerant objectivity – for example, Hinduism (*cf.* the description of Benares in *The Steam House*). The same respectful treatment is given to the character of the Confucian philosopher Wang, a former Taiping rebel converted to the philosophy of resignation.

Finally, can we not detect a note or ironic scepticism, of religious pessimism, in the following remark about the practice of the Catholic religion in Ireland and its meagre effectiveness (*Foundling Mick*): 'Poor Ireland! You do not fail to give praise to the Most High, but will the men of good will ever be able to ensure that you have social peace by giving you independence?'

CHAPTER VIII

Nationalism and Internationalism

> In order to achieve your common purpose, you have stopped bothering about this wretched question of nationality! You have said to yourselves that England and America have nothing to do with all this, and that we must be united in the closest harmony against the dangers of our expedition. If the North Pole is reached, does it matter who shall have discovered it? Why lower oneself to boasting about being English or American when one can take pride in being men?

It is Dr Clawbonny who utters these words as he congratulates the Englishman, Hatteras, and the American, Altamont, on their reconciliation after the accident from which they have just escaped. For months, their disagreement has been poisoning the atmosphere of the Polar expedition; they have been at loggerheads over everything – for instance, on the subject of previous Polar expeditions led by their compatriots respectively, or when it was a question of naming some geographical feature in the lands they discovered. Clawbonny's denunciation of the artificial character of international rivalries is a profession of faith, and he seems probably to be speaking for Verne.

The *Voyages extraordinaires*, however, are not always steeped in the spirit of humanitarian internationalism to which the good doctor bears witness. Quite often the prevailing tone is that of anti-British chauvinism, and it would be easy to put together from the novels an astonishing collection of anglophobe 'wisecracks' in the fashionable style of the nineteenth century:

> England has always been ahead of other nations (for it is a universal rule that nations are always ahead of each other).

> The English always feel at home, even when destiny takes them several thousand leagues away from their own country and, being excellent colonizers, they will colonize the moon on the day they manage to plant the British flag upon it.... very phlegmatic, very proud of being English and opposed to anything not English....

Their natural pride leads them to agree that the Anglo-Saxon race was moulded from a special clay which has so far evaded all chemical analysis.

If the world had any idea of the injustices which these English, so proud of their guineas and their naval power, have perpetrated throughout the world, there would not be enough insults in the human language to throw in their faces.

The United Kingdom was there with its territorial ambitions, its tendency to absorb everything, its too well-known obstinacy and its encroaching banknotes.

Sir Edward Turner, one of those men who think everything is permitted to them by the mere fact of being English.

The Anglo-Saxon pincers which will end by gibraltarizing all the straits of the world.

John Bull generally wears his hat firmly clamped on his head, and unclamping it requires a good deal of manipulation.

England does not easily give up her possessions. She is greedy and, as much by instinct as by interest, has a tendency to appropriate the conquests of others.

The list of such quotations could be made much longer,[112] and it would be just as easy to enumerate those episodes in the *Voyages extraordinaires* which make fun of England, criticize her imperial policy or caricature her people: there is the simple-minded little Australian aborigine to whom English missionaries have taught a fantastic system of geography according to which the five continents, including France, are directly or indirectly controlled by England (*Captain Grant*); there is the accusation of colonial genocide solemnly made against England in her dealings with the Australian and Tasmanian aborigines and the Hottentots (*Captain Grant, Mistress Branican*); the disagreeable and arrogant character of the shipwrecked English children on Chatham Island (*Two Years Holiday*); the nationalist struggles of the French Canadians and the Irish against English domination (*Family without a Name, Foundling Mick*); the rudeness and selfishness of the English crew of the whaler *Repton* who are saved against their will by French sailors on board the *Saint Enoch* (*The Tales of Jean-Marie Cabidoulin*), etc.

Is this anti-British tendency of Verne more or less permanent, or did it become progressively stronger? Some people have thought that during the period 1890–95 Verne was influenced by the wave of anglophobia in France which culminated with the Fashoda incident.* Indeed,

---

*Fashoda, Sudan, scene of an Anglo-French diplomatic incident in 1898, which brought anti-British feelings to a peak in France.

Family without a Name was published in 1889, *Mistress Branican* in 1891 and *Foundling Mick* in 1893. On the other hand, Hatteras (the novel bearing his name appeared in 1867) is a stereotype Englishman, but extremely dignified:

> As an Englishman I do not want, we do not want to see men more daring than ourselves going to places where we have not been.... If a human foot ever treads the region of the Pole, it must be an English foot.... I hate that American with a really English hatred.

Phileas Fogg and Dr Fergusson, who are other examples of positive characters in the earlier novels, are also men of eminence. Nevertheless, the anglophobia we find diffused throughout the *Voyages extraordinaires*, even if it was intensified by the political turn of events, goes far beyond that. As the examples quoted have shown, the tendency is an evident in the early books (*Captain Grant, Hector Servadac*, for example) as in those written much later (*Propeller Island, Travelling Scholarships, Thomson & Co.*). Verne is therefore clearly reflecting a permanent trait of French popular feeling, as A. Gramsci has shown, and it is precisely the example of Verne's anglophobia to which Gramsci refers when he explains what he means by 'a popular novel'.[113]

On the other hand, this hostility towards England hardly ever stems from simple national chauvinism; it is politically motivated. England is castigated as the oppressor of the Scottish, Irish and French Canadian nationalists, or for being a great colonial Power. Verne's anglophobia is directed towards a country regarded as typical of certain negative political tendencies, much more than towards an 'enemy' nation. Moreover, did not Verne at the outset of his career write to Hetzel, 'I adore London and the English'?[114]

In the same way, Verne's germanophobia, with the exception of one or two casual and ridiculous characters, is invariably linked with political criticism. Germany is attacked in *Flight to France* for its opposition to the French Revolution, in *The Secret of Wilhelm Storitz* or *A Drama in Livonia* for its oppression of Magyar or Slav nationalist movements. In *The Begum's Fortune*, the most brutally and grossly germanophobe of Verne's works, German pride is caricatured in the person of Herr Schultze:

> For him it was a question of proving to the Englishman, Sharp, that the German race must predominate over all the others. His insistence upon claiming the fortune was motivated principally by the wish to prevent its falling into the hands of a Frenchman who would inevitably put it to some inept use ... what he hated most in his opponent was his nationality. ... He would certainly not have pushed his claim against another German ... but at the very idea that a self-styled scientist, a Frenchman, might utilize that enormous fortune to advance French ideas, he was beside himself with rage.

But even in this case, symptomatic of the extreme vengeful chauvinism widespread in France in the 1880s, the 'eternal German' Schultze is indistinguishable from Schultze the armament industry magnate, the master of a gigantic totalitarian and, so to speak, proto-Hitlerian complex, a scientist who uses his knowledge in the service of destruction.

For the rest, Verne does not give much space to his own country. Doubtless, as G. de Diesbach has observed,[115] it was normal for such 'journeys' to take place abroad, thereby offering small opportunity for depicting France and her people. But is this entirely by chance? As we have noted above, is not a traveller setting out on a journey already making a kind of break with his social and national environment?

Very few expressions of real national self-esteem are to be found in Verne's books: for example, when Robur's flying machine plays the *Departure song* as it passes over Paris; when the unknown Frenchman in Nemo's crew is seized by a giant octopus, 'forgetful of the day-to-day language spoken on the ship, [he] reverts to the language of his country and mother, to make his supreme appeal for help.' There is also the very flattering description of Max Réal, a young American painter of French origin (*An Eccentric's Will*):

> Max Réal had just turned twenty-five. By birth he was a typical Frenchman with his gracefulness, distinction and elegance. Above medium height, he had brown hair and beard, dark blue eyes; he held his head high without arrogance or stiffness, and he had a smiling mouth; his movements were deliberate, a sign of that interior peace of mind of which the outward expression is an unfailing and happy confidence. There was in him a great expansion of that vital power, which is translated into the acts of existence by courage and generosity.

Even fewer are the novels in which French national self-esteem is the main factor in the plot. One of these is *Flight to France*, which describes the struggle between Revolutionary France and Prussia at the time of Valmy, in the style of Erckmann-Chatrian.* *For the Flag* shows us a misunderstood French engineer who has sold a new weapon of destruction, the Roch fulminator, to outlaws, but who changes his mind when the French fleet is about to be destroyed and he sees before him the French tricolour. The basis of *The Begum's Fortune* is the contrast between German megalomania and French generosity and idealism, the latter represented by the philanthropic Dr Sarrasin and particularly the young Alsatian, Marcel Bruckmann; the latter possesses 'a virile maturity, resulting from the defeat of France [1870]. . . . It is for youth to make good the errors of the previous generation.

---

*Erckmann-Chatrian, the name under which Emile Erckmann, 1822–1899, and Alexandre Chatrian, 1826–1890, published their novels, in a style of rustic realism.

Thus French national feeling has only a small place in the world of the *Voyages extraordinaires*, and Verne, as we have seen, treated 'the French colonial epic' very discreetly. He expressed hardly any emotion at the time of the French defeat in 1870, and he showed real independence of mind in connection with Bonaparte, denouncing his 'duplicity' and 'ferocity' at the time of the surrender of Jaffa and the capture of 4,000 Turks in 1798:

> And so, showing that he was one of those conquerors who will stop at nothing, he gave the order for them to be shot. . . . They were condemned to die. They were shot down on the beach; those whom the bullets had missed thought they were being spared, but they were killed as they tried to walk ashore. . . . It was a terrible massacre, and at least some Frenchmen were sickened by it, let it be remembered to their honour. [One of the latter saves the life of the Syrian, Kamylk Pasha, and this is the starting-point of the plot of *Master Antifer*.]

Instead of patriotic feelings towards France, do we not rather perceive in the *Voyages extraordinaires* signs of a curious Celtic patriotism? 'My dear man, you have a fund of Celtic ideas' – this is the worst fault Herr Schultze finds in Marcel Bruckmann (who has passed himself off as Swiss in order to get into Schultze's factory). The young Erik Durieu in *The Wreck of the 'Cynthia'*, is 'a solemn and serious child'; he presents 'the Celtic type in all its beauty and purity.' The description of Antifer, citizen of St Malo, is a lyrical eulogy to the Celtic type:

> A stocky man of medium height with a thick neck. Here are the details of his appearance: Celtic head; a rough mane of hair standing up like porcupine quills; face bronzed, tanned, burnt and burnt again by the sea air and the hot sun of the southern latitudes, and round his neck a scrubby beard like lichen on a rock. . . . The whole effect was one of uncommon strength, with bundles of muscles like the fasces of a Roman lictor, the iron constitution of a man who eats and drinks well and who can look forward to having a clean bill of health for a long time to come. But how irritable, highly-strung and passionate was this moral and physical human composite which, forty-six years earlier, had been entered in the parish register under the suggestive names of Pierre-Servan-Malo-Antifer!

The lively sympathy which Jules Verne, a Breton, so often expressed for the Irish (*Foundling Mick, The Brothers Kip*) and the Scots (*The Green Ray, Black Diamonds, The Children of Captain Grant, The Steam House*, etc.) could also be regarded as reflecting a certain Celtic solidarity. M. H. Huet declares that 'Jules Verne uses the word Celt not only in a racial, linguistic or literary sense, but also in a political, even an ideological sense.'[116] The Celts have political qualities which are lacking in the Teutonic races – the English and the Germans – who are authoritarian and dominating. The demonstration of the 'political' contrast between two temperaments is no doubt made easier if one is content to compare the great Anglo-Saxon powers, irresponsibly lampooned, with two small Celtic nationalities, and if one passes over certain rather un-Celtic aspects of French expansion. But Verne has not altogether got around this difficulty: it is a pure 'Celt', Antifer, who saves the life of the noble Syrian so ferociously treated by the Corsican general at Acre.

Much more unconventional than such occasional echos of pro-French, anti-British and anti-German nationalism is the criticism of national rivalries, militarism and war suggested by so many passages in Verne's work. It is, for example, 'because of a stupid question of nationality' that three Frenchmen and two Englishmen fight each other while exiled all alone on Amsterdam Island at the edge of the Antarctic Ocean (*The Children of Captain Grant*). Declarations of war are equally absurd, especially when, as in *Measuring a Meridian*, they put an end to the scientific co-operation, the mutual esteem, and even friendship between teams of men engaged together on a difficult geodesic operation in South Africa. All that is forgotten in a moment when the Russo-British expedition learns that their two countries are on opposite sides in the Crimean War:

> They stood up quickly. Nothing more was needed than the words, 'war is declared'. They were no longer companions, colleagues, scientists working together on a scientific job, but enemies taking each other's measure, thus proving how strongly such duels between nation and nation can influence men's hearts.

The youngest of the astronomers, William Emery, shakes hands with his Russian colleague, Michael Zorn, 'formerly his friend but now his enemy, by the will of Their Majesties the Queen and the Tsar.'

War and militarism are frequently denounced in *The Begum's Fortune*, and this aspect in the end assumes greater importance than the anti-German and pro-French chauvinism which can be found in the book; Schultze, as we have already suggested, is someone who sells guns and could just as well be an Englishman or a Frenchman. This same problem of militarism is the starting-point for the novel *From the Earth to the Moon*, a fact which should not be forgotten even if the recent exploits of American astronauts, which have repeated the imaginary journey of Barbicane, Nicholls and Ardan, cause us to attach greater importance to that aspect of the novel which may be called scientific forecasting. Its basic theme is the reconversion of a highly militarized industry to the cause of peace and progress, a problem which is by no means of less contemporary interest than that of interplanetary travel. The Gun Club of Baltimore has made a lot of money out of the American Civil War, which the Yankees won 'by their prodigal expenditure of bullets, millions of dollars and men.' But peace weighs heavily upon 'this group of exterminating angels, in other respects the best chaps in the world.' Barbicane addresses the members of the Club: 'For far too long already the members of the Gun Club have been regrettably idle as the result of an unproductive peace.... We have had to give up our work and have come to a standstill on the road of progress.' The Frenchman Ardan, that is to say Nadar, Verne's Saint-Simonian and somewhat Anarchist friend, openly accuses the Gun Club of militaristic tendencies, and appeals for the reconversion of American war industries to peaceful uses. This is the essence of the alteration he proposes to Barbicane's plan: instead of sending a cannon ball to the moon, i.e. a warlike object, *men* should be sent there inside a capsule:

> If we are to believe certain people of limited intelligence – that is the best way to describe them – mankind will always be shut up inside a circle of Popilius,[117] unable to escape, condemned to vegetate on this globe without ever being able to rise into interplanetary space. Nothing of the sort! We will reach the moon, we will reach the planets, we will reach the stars with the same ease, speed and security with which we now travel from Liverpool to New York.

Government-controlled colonization and the apportioning of colonial territories are just as stupid and artificial as declarations of war and war industries. Verne seems to have been literally obsessed by this idea, and to have felt deeply the fragility and contingency of frontiers and territorial sovereignty. In *Caesar Cascabel* this provides the romantic plot. The treaty ceding Alaska to the United States and the transfer of sovereignty come into force on the very day when an outlawed Russian arrives at the frontier and fears that he may fall once more into the hands of the Tsarist police; Verne also points out that the boundaries of Alaska were 'capriciously fixed to follow the coastal mountain chain'.

The artificial and conventional character of the frontiers between European states is clearly underlined in a fine lesson in political geography given by the temporary inhabitants of the comet Gallia when they return sufficiently close to the Earth to be able to distinguish details (*Hector Servadac*):

> Yes indeed, it was Europe they could see laid out under their eyes. They could make out the different states with the odd shapes they had been given by nature or international conventions.
>
> There was England, a lady walking towards the east in an over-elaborate pleated dress with a hat of islets and islands.

Norway and Sweden, a magnificent lion with a backbone of mountains hurling itself upon Europe from the hyperborean regions.

Russia, an enormous polar bear, head turned towards Asia, the left hind paw leaning against Turkey and the right on the Caucasus.

Austria, a fat cat doubled up on itself and sleeping fitfully.

Spain, unfurled like a flag at the end of Europe with Portugal looking like the yacht on which it flies.

Turkey, a cock with its feathers on end, one foot clutching the Asian shore and the other grasping Greece.

Italy, a thin, elegant boot appearing to juggle with Sicily, Sardinia and Corsica.

Prussia, a fearsome hatchet deeply embedded into the German Empire with its cutting edge touching France.

Finally France, a vigorous tree trunk with Paris at its heart.

At the other end of the world, the splitting-up of the Magellan region between Argentine and Chile is described as equally artificial, and provides one factor of the plot of *The Survivors of the 'Jonathan'*. Similarly, the division of the Papuan Islands between England and Germany by the Convention of 1884, leaving all islands to the west of 141° Meridian to England and the rest to Germany, is a conventional act far removed from geographical realities, and brings in its train the immediate necessity for renaming the islands. 'English or Melanesian names were replaced by German ones', New-Ireland became Neu-Mecklenburg, Birara Island or New-Britain became Neu-Pommern, and the whole became the Bismarck Archipelago (*The Brothers Kip*).

Verne's demonstration of the artificial, ephemeral and unstable character of territorial sovereignty is carried to its extreme in the case of the Lesser Antilles (and all the more forcibly because here it is a question of colonial sovereignty and therefore doubly questionable). This novel, *Travelling Scholarships*, is normally regarded as one of Verne's weaker works – at least by those who do not take the trouble to seek the key to his political thinking. In point of fact the demonstration is both vigorous and unconventional. A group of children from the various islands of the Antilles, pupils at the Antilia School in London, are due to visit their home islands during a cruise. But the crew of their ship are murdered by a band of criminals who have escaped from an Irish prison, and the pleasure cruise turns into a tragedy as they go from island to island. The principal point here is the objective, physical importance of the region and the way it has been broken up into colonial micro-sovereignties, a theme of astonishingly contemporary interest as we were reminded in 1970 by the British government's despatch of a marine detachment to the island of Anguilla. In order to stress its unity, Verne gives the name of Antilia to the whole archipelago, which is a condensed microcosm of all the international conflicts of modern times and their absurdity:

> Various European nations have fought each other for possession of these islands at the cost of bloody wars, horrible massacres and never-ending disputes, and it is not even yet certain that any definite solution has been achieved.[118] ... European navies have fought in these regions, capturing, recapturing and tearing apart the islands of Antilia, as wild beasts do with a prey that excites their greed.

In an almost playful way, Verne lists the many changes in sovereignty which make the history of Antilia since the seventeenth century a real political merry-go-round. The island of St Bartholomew had been in turn under French and Swedish control (to be bought back by France just as it is visited by the ship carrying the schoolchildren); St Martin had been subject to France and then to Holland; St Croix belonged in turn to England, Spain, France and Denmark; Dominica was successively French, British, Dutch and French. The record is held, as Verne ironically points out, by Santa Lucia which was nine times subjected to changes of sovereignty between France and England.

The artificial nature of these crumbling sovereignties in the Antilles is finally underlined by Verne, in his own futuristic and naturalistic manner, by conjuring up a geological upheaval which will lift the whole region and thus create a new continent: 'What will then be the position, with England, France, Holland and Denmark struggling to extend the region over which their flags fly? – a perfectly logical *reductio ad absurdum*.

The internationalist leanings scattered throughout the whole of *Known and Unknown Worlds* are apparent, too, in the imaginary cosmopolitan and polyglot communities which Verne describes, with manifest sympathy, on several occasions. Indeed, the Antilian School where the young pupils of *Travelling Scholarships* are being educated already has this character of an international community, a result of deliberate school policy: 'The headmaster was doing his best to fuse together the various temperaments and differing characters presented by the group of young boys of different national origins, and as far as possible to turn his changes into Antilians.' It is for this reason that, during school recreation times, it was obligatory to use the different colonial languages in turn: English for one week, then Dutch, Danish, French, Swedish and Spanish each for a week. In the case of the shipwrecked children on Chatham Island, it is a question of a cosmopolitan community resulting from a natural calamity, but the dominant note is the same (*Two Years' Holiday*).

At the other extreme of the social scale, it is a matter not of innocent scholastic activities, but of rebel communities such as Ker Karraje's band (*For the Flag*) or the army of Harry Killer (*The Barsac Mission*);

they also display the same cosmopolitan character. When speaking to each other, the raiders who have carried off the members of the French Parliamentary mission led by Barsac use French, English, Spanish and German indiscriminately. In the case of *Nautilus*' crew, the linguistic cosmopolitanism is carried still further since 'between themselves they use only a queer sort of language, of which I could not even guess the origin.' Verne gives us an illustration of this when a sailor approaches Nemo and says: *Nautron respoc lorni virch*, which is not a simple parody of synthetic modern language but an interesting forecast of linguistic development: *20,000 Leagues under the Sea* was in fact published in 1868, whereas Volapuk and Esperanto were created respectively in 1879 and 1887.

By another path, therefore, we are led back to the tendency towards libertarian individualism which lies hidden behind so many episodes and characters of the *Voyages extraordinaires*, even if Robur at the end has to follow his solitary path, declaring that 'the nations are not yet ready to come together'; even if Nemo in the end, on his death bed, comes round to the conception of classical patriotism ('The Fatherland, that is where we have to return! That is where one must die! You should therefore make every effort to leave Lincoln Island and go back again to live on the soil where you were born').

CHAPTER IX

The American mirage and the American peril

The picture which emerges from the analysis we have attempted in the preceding chapters is so far a fairly static one. There is nevertheless a progression within the *Voyages extraordinaires*, though it is in the direction of pessimism. This becomes apparent when we consider Verne's thinking about the United States, but it is also clear in the context of defining the social power of money.

Verne was fascinated by the nineteenth-century United States, by the American character and by American society. For him it was as if the United States stood on the frontier between the 'known worlds' and the 'unknown worlds'. It was part of the political society of his time and, young liberal bourgeois that he was, born in 1828, he was deeply affected by the American Civil War. At the same time, however, the United States with hardly any ties to the past and its rapid demographic, technical and economic development, constituted a futurist theme in itself. In the world of the mid-nineteenth century it was the United States which came closest to the 'model for development' of which Verne dreamed in the interests of humanity. It provided a perfect setting for his scientific and social forecasts. It inserted itself quite naturally into his project, and it is not by chance that in twenty-three of his novels, out of a total of sixty-four, the action takes place on American soil, either wholly or in part, or that American characters play an important role.

For Verne, the United States was the country of born mechanics and born engineers: 'The Yankees, who lead the world in mechanical matters, are engineers as the Italians are musicians and the Germans are metaphysicians – by birth', a statement made with the object of explaining why the idea of sending a cannon ball to the moon arose perfectly naturally in the United States (*From the Earth to the Moon*). It was a country in which modern industrial techniques had full freedom to develop and which provided favourable conditions for launching the most daring plans. In the case of the trip to the moon, all that was needed was to calculate the dimensions of the gun to be used and, above all, to decide how it is to be cast. The operation takes place in Florida for astronomical reasons and it is described by Verne in a chapter ('Festive

Casting Day') which is nothing less than a lyric hymn to the glory of the American metallurgical industry and, more generally, to the prowess of mankind.

In Verne's eyes, American society was one in which scientific and technical problems were dealt with publicly and thoroughly discussed by all shades of opinion, rather than being hidden away, as in old Europe, in the dusty offices of academic bodies and learned societies. The session of the Weldon Institute of Philadelphia devoted to the merits and demerits of 'lighter-than-air' and 'heavier-than-air' flying machines is as lively and turbulent as a political meeting (*The Clipper of the Clouds*); it is attended by the engineer Robur, that prototype of the American of the future, who has come to demonstrate that his flying machines are superior to balloons. Robur's futuristic machines are thus American creations: the *Albatross* is a sort of helicopter with multiple air-screws on top of vertical poles, and the *Terror* is capable of moving in the air, on land and in the water. Verne also used the United States as the setting for several other of his scientific forecasts: for example, the construction of *Propeller Island* which was to carry a number of American millionaires back and forth over the Pacific Ocean; or that amusing fancy, *The Boston to Liverpool Pneumatic Tubes Company*, which sends its passengers through the depths of the Atlantic Ocean at 1,800 kilometres an hour as though they were ordinary express letters.[119]

For Verne, the United States was also, above all others, the country of railways, those living footprints made by man on the face of the globe, the initials by which he stamped his superiority on the face of entire continents. The vast spaces of America were particularly favourable to the establishment of a railway network which Phileas Fogg, for example, takes advantage of to win his bet in *Around the World in Eighty Days*. He takes seven days to travel from San Francisco to New York, by way of Omaha and Chicago, using the Pacific Railroad and the Middle Western Lines. It is only an attack by Sioux Indians which delays him and causes him to miss his steamer.

There is also the fact that in America the confrontation between man and nature takes place on a vaster scale, and is much harsher than in Europe. Like many young Frenchmen of his generation, Verne had been brought up on the tales of Fenimore Cooper, the traditions of Leatherstocking and the prairies, the exploits of the earliest pioneers. Indeed, in 1867 he visited the United States for a short time as a tourist, doing all the usual things, such as travelling up the Hudson on a paddle steamer – the idea of covering over the river to make an aerodrome had not then been mooted – and going to see Niagara Falls. This trip, which gave him physical experience of the grandiose scale of natural phenomena in America, is described by him almost exactly as it happened in his novel *A Floating City* (dealing with the giant liner *Great Eastern*, in which he had travelled from Le Havre to New York). Niagara Falls made a permanent impression on him as a symbol of the powerful forces of nature which the young American republic had to cope with. ('A Niagara of molten metal', is how he describes the casting of the gun aimed towards the moon.) In the novels belonging to the American cycle of his works, *The Begum's Fortune, From the Earth to the Moon, Around the World in Eighty Days, North against South, An Eccentric's Will, The Master of the World*, Verne lingers with evident pleasure upon the immensity of America, the vigour of its vegetation and the wealth contained in its subsoil – in short, upon everything which gives value to man's fight against nature.

This vision of the United States as the country of technical and economic progress is in direct line of descent from French nineteenth-century utopian socialism. The United States was of great interest to the Saint-Simonians, who saw in it the prototype of a new kind of society founded upon technology and free of the political stagnation of Europe. René Rémond,* the historian of the American image in nineteenth-century France, wrote that 'A new chapter of history begins with the United States. Man ceases to submit and starts to impose himself on things, taming the forces of nature, exploiting its wealth and changing the world. His attitude of resigned submission has been replaced by an attitude of creative will.'[120]

One of the most brilliant of the Saint-Simonians, Michel Chevalier, published several very flattering books about American society after he had travelled to the US in 1835 to carry out an investigation into the railways. A utopian socialist who, during the Second Empire, became an active businessman and theoretician of economic liberalism, he was 'Admirably trained to understand a society with no past, in which there is no place for idlers, where everything is directed towards work, efficiency and the production of wealth, and where economics takes the place of politics.' René Rémond goes on to say:

> It is basically the Saint-Simonian aspect of the United States that Michel Chevalier admired: the freedom of industry, the general activity, the development of means of communication, the ease with which credit was sought and obtained, in short everything which would today be called economic expansion.

Rémond's study stops in the middle of the nineteenth century, long before the publication of Verne's earliest novels. But that only makes the similarity all the more striking between the way a man like Michel Chevalier envisaged America and such thoughts of Verne's about that country as can be gleaned by reading his novels. The experimental character of society in the United States makes it possible to place Verne's picture of America also in the tradition of utopian socialism.

*René Rémond, b. 1918, French professor of political science and history.

The deck of Captain Robur's flying machine, the *Albatross* (*The Clipper of the Clouds*).

We know that throughout the nineteenth century men of progressive ideas in the old continent dreamed of realizing experimentally on American soil embryos of the perfect society, prototypes which, if successful, would set the whole of humanity on the path of progress. The Englishman Robert Owen's attempt to found his ideal colony of New Harmony, or those of the French communist Etienne Cabet (*Journey in Icaria*, 1848), were followed by many others. Verne, too, can be placed in this line of 'the imaginary continent', to use René Rémond's apt expression. It is in Iowa that the colonists of *The Mysterious Island* establish their model community, making use of the gold left them by Captain Nemo, after the cataclysm which engulfs the colony they had planned to 'offer to the Government of the Union'. Similarly, it is in Oregon that the two inimical heirs of the Begum's fabulous fortune build their rival cities of Franceville and Stahlstadt, both intended to serve in exploring the future direction of human development, one towards works of peace, the other towards works of war. The site chosen is not fortuitous; Verne notes that Franceville was 'advantageously placed in a federal republic and in a state which was still new, thus temporarily ensuring its independence on condition that it join the Union after a certain number of years.'

For Verne, the United States was thus the country of progress. Of the California city of San Diego he says (*Mistress Branican*):

> If progress in all its forms is not to be found in a modern city, especially when that city is an American one, where else is one to look for it? Railway station, telephone, telegraph, the inhabitants have only to lift a finger for light, to correspond with each other or to speak with each other ear to ear.

He describes San Diego as 'a young city, stubbornly solicitous of its moral and material interests ... benefiting from the various institutions in which the vital movement of large agglomerations is attended to: a customs house, two banks, a chamber of commerce, an emigration association, vast office premises and many business agencies where enormous deals in wood and flour are carried on.'

All these positive aspects of American society, the big industrial undertakings, the taming of nature, the spirit of initiative and enterprise, the economic activity, are indissolubly linked with a certain type of man, certain Yankee national characteristics (because in Verne's eyes – and we will be returning to this point – the United States is the United States of the North, the victors in the recent Civil War). This Yankee character stems from the atmosphere of progress and success to be found all over the country (*From the Earth to the Moon*): 'Nothing can astonish an American, ... In America everything is simple, everything is easy, and as for mechanical difficulties, they are resolved before they arise.'

A Yankee is a man who does things and who makes a success of them; he does not beat about the bush but decides quickly on the road which, in most cases, takes him to his objective.' (*The Clipper of the Clouds*)

A Yankee knows nothing of the stupid personal rivalries and egotisms prevalent among the people of old Europe (*From the Earth to the Moon*):

> When an American has an idea, he looks for a second American to share it. If there are three of them, they elect a president and two secretaries. If four, they appoint an archivist. If five, they call a general meeting and the club is constituted.

This Yankee character finds expression not only in attitudes of mind, but also in physical traits. To Verne it appears that the new social and political conditions which evolved during the expansion of North America in the nineteenth century gave rise to a really new race, in the biological sense of the word. This is an idea to which he returns frequently in the *Voyages extraordinaires*. Take, for example, Cyrus Smith, the first-class engineer from Massachusetts to whose knowledge and skill the survivors of the air-crash in *The Mysterious Island* owe their lives:

> A true North American, thin, bony, lean and about forty-five years old.... He had one of those handsome, 'numismatic' faces which seem made to be reproduced on medals.... In addition to possessing quick wits, he was supremely competent in the use of his hands.... In him were fulfilled to the highest degree the three conditions which, between them, determine human action: an active body and mind, intensity of purpose, and great strength of will.

Another example of this physical Yankee type is Captain Altamont, that daring sailor who is for a time ahead of Hatteras on the road to the North Pole: 'One of those full-blooded, sturdy types from the United States, energetic, intelligent and resolute, an enterprising and audacious American, ready for anything'. Then there is the rich businessman, Seth Stanford, in *The Hunt for the Meteor*:

> a pure Yankee type not lacking a certain unconventional distinction, ... his handsome and robust constitution, his whole attitude, indicated the man of action, the man of resolution, the man of impulse. He was not one to waver between eagerness and fear, for that is the mark of a hesitant character...

Hipperbone, the eccentric millionaire, is another of 'those superb North American types, tall, broad-shouldered, deep-chested, somewhat unbending in character, very cool, very positive and master of himself in all circumstances.' Even a hardened criminal like Len Burker, whose plotting and greed are the cause of the misfortunes of the Branican family, has 'the abrupt and somewhat brutal manner which is the prerogative or the old race of Americans.... This Yankee from New

England with his cold, hard face and vigorous body was a man of great determination, great activity and great powers of concentration.'

In *Two Years' Holiday* the young American, Gordon, shows even at the age of fourteen 'a certain Yankee ruggedness, a taste for serious matters, an observing character and a cool temperament,' which implies that these characteristics are imprinted, as it were, at birth. The young Gordon is chosen as leader by the small community of shipwrecked children on Chatham Island because of these qualities of the Yankee temperament.

The United States as seen by Verne is not only the country of economic expansion and of progress; it is also the land of freedom. And this brings Verne into line with the great French americanophils of the mid-nineteenth century such as Tocqueville and Michel Chevalier. In Verne's opinion (*The Begum's Fortune*) it is that freedom 'which is the basis of the power of the Republic of the United States.' It was towards the United States that progressive men of that time, the opponents of conservative and authoritarian governments, turned their eyes. In *Family without a Name*, that shrewd prophecy of the 'Free Quebec' movement (written in 1889), the French Canadian insurgents in rebellion against the British Viceroy at Ottawa look upon the United States, on the other side of the St Lawrence River, as a land of hope and a base from which they can draw support. The action of the novel takes place during the anti-British troubles in Quebec in 1837. Among the leaders of the French Canadian nationalists are to be found Americans, who invoke the spirit of Jefferson and the Monroe Doctrine, and wish to see England driven out of her remaining possessions in the New World. The insurgents receive help from American territory and get arms from Vermont. Their flag is white in homage to old France, but it also shows the American and Canadian eagles.

That the hope and future of the whole of America lay in the United States is brought out also in the statements of the French Canadian trapper working for the St Louis Fur Company, who is critical of the commercial privileges enjoyed by the (British) Hudson's Bay Company (*The Fur Country*): 'The expression 'Old Europe' does not go down well in America. . . . Sooner or later the English claims will be defeated. . . . America will be American from the Straits of Magellan to the North Pole.'

Even more than the Quebec insurrection of 1837, the American Civil War provided an opportunity for Verne to express his sympathy with the United States as the land of freedom. For him the war between the States was 'the war which resulted in the victory of justice and right.' He was on the side of the 'Northerners, the anti-slavers, the abolitionists, the federalists' against 'the Southerners, the slave owners, the secessionists, the confederates.' (*North against South*) The five survivors of the shipwreck in *The Mysterious Island* are opponents of slavery, and one of them is a black, the servant of Cyrus Smith; he is treated as an equal by all the others. In this case Verne's sympathy for the United States stems from the '48 tradition rather than from Saint-Simonism, and there is no room to go into it in detail; abundant proof is to be found in the *Voyages extraordinaires*: Max Réal's admiration for John Brown, Captain Nemo's portrait gallery, support for the North in *North against South*.

Being the land of freedom, the United States is consequently the country with the minimum of government control and social constraint. Verne's sympathy is obvious when he says (*An Eccentric's Will*), 'In America people have the excellent habit of looking after their own interests without expecting the administration to give the help of which it is incapable.' In *From the Earth to the Moon*, when describing the free and easy way the Baltimore crowd surrounds the cosmonauts as they are about to set off, he speaks of 'that freedom of action shown by the masses only when they have been brought up in the tradition of self-government'. One of his novels provides an opportunity for highlighting the liberalism of the American government machinery in contrast to the vexatious bureaucracy of the Tsarist administration; the novel is *Caesar Cascabel*, set in 1867, when Alaska was ceded by Russia to the United States. A touring company of clowns, the Cascabel family, try to return to Europe from California by way of the Bering Straits. On the first attempt they are thrown out of Alaska by the Russian police because they have no passports. On the second attempt, however, they have to deal with the American authorities:

> The treaty of cession had been signed just in time. . . . On that soil which had just become American territory there were no longer any obstinate civil servants to deal with, nor was it necessary to go through all those formalities which the Muscovite administration had insisted upon so firmly.

On one particular point Verne frequently expressed his admiration for 'a government which does not weigh down on one', to use René Rémond's phrase: this was in connection with marriage and divorce. As Marcel Moré has shown,[121] Verne was somewhat misogynous, and did not hesitate in his novels to make fun of the state of bondage resulting from the ties of marriage. Marriage and divorce in the United States of his day seemed to him formalities which could be effected most expeditiously, and that was something he admired very much.

In *Claudius Bombarnac*, the American stockbroker, Ephrinell, unexpectedly gets married to a compatriot he has met on the 'great Transasian' railway travelling between Russia and China; the ceremony is performed right there in the train by a clergyman who happens to be among the passengers, 'just as these things are done in America, without any of the tedious preliminary formalities which are required in France and other conventional countries.... A Yankee has no time to waste.' The same absence of formality marks the wedding of Seth Stanford to Miss Arcadia Walker in a little town in Virginia (*The Hunt for the Meteor*); the bride and bridegroom do not even get down off their horses, and the Judge conducts the ceremony from the steps of his house.... A few chapters later, however, they divorce each other with an equal lack of ceremony in the middle of the street. Verne remarks admiringly, almost enviously, one might say:

> In some of the States of the Union, all one needs to do to get a divorce is to establish an imaginary domicile, and it is not necessary to be present in person; there are special agencies which will undertake the job of producing the witnesses and the stand-ins.

Thus the image of the United States which Verne built up for himself is like an epitome of his political sympathies. That country, in the full flood of economic expansion, crossed by railways from end to end, as the whole world would be one day, was dear to the heart of this heir of utopian socialism and Saint-Simonism; and this old '48er was pleased with that land of freedom whose one great political crisis, the question of the emancipation of the slaves, was (at least in *his* view) already over. Verne, the individualist with his secret libertarian sympathies, was fascinated by the American political machine and the discreet way it administered the country.

Verne's ideological outlook, however, began to change as the nineteenth century passed, as the development of large-scale industry increased the total of human wretchedness instead of alleviating it, as the humanitarian dreams of 1848 faded away, giving place to the implacable rivalries of the imperialist Powers. Verne gave up his Saint-Simonian vision of progress through science, became disappointed and bitter, and sank into a state of pessimism which also changed the picture he had formed of the United States. His enthusiasm for Jefferson and Lincoln, his admiration for that young and dynamic society, deserted him as the expansionist trends of the 'big stick' policy took shape (Verne died in 1905), as the power of the dollar grew stronger and as a materialist technology increased its hold over mankind.

At first the theme of the power of money is only lightly touched upon, for example in 1879 in *The Tribulations of a Chinese Gentleman* when the hero, the rich Chinaman Kin-Fo, insures his life with a firm in Chicago, 'the Centenarian', which has a branch in Shanghai. Two of the firm's men are permanently in attendance on Kin-Fo because the sum insured is considerable, but they abandon him in a desert in the middle of the

The touring group being turned back from Alaska by Russian officials (*Caesar Cascabel*).

night, when he is in great danger and his life threatened by pirates, because the monthly premium has not been paid and the policy has consequently terminated. 'Very practical people, these Americans', Verne remarks. 'They were devoted to Kin Fo so long as he was worth 200,000 dollars, but they were quite indifferent to his fate when he would no longer be worth a penny'. In *Robinson Island* (1882), criticism of the power of money is still expressed in a reserved and amusing way Kolderup and Taskinar, two San Francisco millionaires, bid against each other for a desert island in the Pacific which the American government is selling by auction; with dollars used as weapons, a heroic and ridiculous

159

battle ensues 'between two safes'. The satiric intention here is still expressed with some gentleness.

In *Propeller Island* (1895), on the contrary, the criticism of an American society based upon money is much more vigorous. This artificial island moves about the Pacific endowed with all the latest improvements of technology. It has been built by a private American company which allows only the greatest multi-millionaires to live on it. At that time (in the fairly close, but not very precisely indicated, future), the dollar is all-powerful and can buy everything, including art and talent.

> By buying the paintings of ancient and modern masters at enormous prices for their private or public picture galleries, by engaging at very large salaries well-known singers and actors together with instrumentalists of the highest talent, the encroaching Americans have managed to infuse themselves with a feeling for beautiful and noble things which they lacked for so long.

Thus the authorities of the island have no compunctions about kidnapping four French musicians, 'the Concert Quartet', in order to monopolize their music, paying each of them the fabulous salary of one million gold francs a year.

Two extremely rich families are the leaders of the island society, the Coverleys and the Tankerdons, and they vie with each other for control of the municipal government of 'Milliard City', the capital of the island. Tankerdon, a big merchant from the Middle West, is a boorish upstart, while his rival Coverley, a banker from New Orleans, retains something of the more refined civilization of the great Southern families of the past. Here, for the first time, Verne breaks with his attitude of political solidarity with the Yankees of the North, a solidarity which is evident, for example, in his novel *North against South*. The anxiety he feels at the trend the United States is following towards a purely material conception of progress takes precedence over his liberal sympathy for the anti-slavery North. The cultural level of the island, incidentally, does not match its financial power. If in the schools 'the teachers are paid ministerial salaries', the pupils on the other hand 'do not flock to attend the public lectures, and if the present generation still retains a smattering of knowledge acquired in the colleges of New England, the generation following it will have less education than income.'

Indeed there is little likelihood that the nabobs of the island will spend their leisure time in intellectual activities; the island's librarian, with a salary of $25,000, 'is perhaps the least occupied of the island's employees, . . . one no longer takes the trouble to read anything, one just presses a button and one hears an excellent voice reading the passage', since all the books are recorded. As for newspapers and magazines,

> their only purpose is to provide a moment's entertainment for the mind, and even for the stomach. Yes indeed! Some of them are

printed on sheets of edible dough with chocolate-flavoured ink; after reading them one eats them for breakfast. Some are astringent and others are purgative, and the human body puts up with them very well.

The island comes to a tragic end. The rivalry between the Tankerdons and the Coverleys reaches the point where each clan seizes one of the two power stations, situated on the port and starboard sides of the island respectively. Since the adversaries refuse to coordinate the machines, the resulting torsion finally breaks the metal framework of the island into pieces. May we not legitimately claim, without misuse of ready-made formulas, that Verne makes capitalist society destroy itself by its own contradictions?

In the second part of Verne's work, starting from about 1885–90, the United States thus progressively ceases to be a privileged land of scientific progress, a model for the future development of mankind, a field of application for Verne's ideas. In *The Clipper of the Clouds*, published in 1886, the engineer Robur was the symbol of a society at the height of expansion, full of confidence in the future of science ('Robur is the future science', Verne says at the end of the novel). But Robur returns in a second novel, *The Master of the World*, published in 1904, nearly twenty years later (which is all the more remarkable since characters do not often make a comeback in the *Voyages extraordinaires*); but he is now an embittered misanthrope, at loggerheads with mankind and hunted by the American police. Similarly, in *For the Flag* (1896), the United States government tries to seize the military inventions of the scientist, Thomas Roch, for the sole purpose of increasing its own military powers of destruction, and Roch is shut up in a mental asylum. Science has passed into the service of military power.

Indeed, Verne becomes more and more aware of the expansionist and dominating character of American policy. In one of his first novels, *From the Earth to the Moon*, in which he was still expressing his admiration for the United States as the privileged centre of technical and industrial progress, he had nevertheless already taken note of the progress of militarism during the American Civil War:

> The speed with which the military instinct developed among this nation of shipowners, merchants and tradesmen is well known.... That learned society [the Baltimore Gun Club] had only one interest: the destruction of mankind for philanthropic purposes, and the improvement of armaments, which they looked upon as instruments of civilization.[122]

This tendency towards militarism and expansion is underlined more and more clearly as Verne adjusts his mental picture of the United States. *Upside Down* was published in 1889, and in it we meet again the characters who figured in the first journey to the moon. This time, however, their purpose is no longer a scientific one, but territorial and financial gain, nothing less in fact than the appropriation of the North Polar regions with a view to the exploitation of the coal deposits. The firing of a gun, big enough for its recoil to displace the axis of the Poles, is supposed to result in the melting of the ice and thus ensure colossal profits for the North Polar Practical Association. The scheme fails, but not before an international conference had given legal sanction to American ambitions in the Polar regions, once again after an auction conducted in huge dollar bids.

In *Propeller Island* the United States flag has 67 stars.

> They [the United States] are in the full expansion of their industrial and commercial power, after having annexed the Dominion of Canada right up to the ultimate limits of the Polar sea, the provinces of Mexico, Guatemala, Honduras, Nicaragua and Costa Rica right down to the Panama Canal.

The Village in the Tree Tops (1901) starts with a discussion about a future American Congo: 'The Federal Government will one day claim its share of the African cake', declares one of the speakers, more than half a century before the American move which resulted in the blue helmets of the United Nations being sent to the Congo.

Verne was worried by what we would today call *the American way of life* as much as by American expansion. Already when Phileas Fogg's train passes through Salt Lake City, Verne expresses certain reservations about American cities, 'vast checkerboards with long, cold, straight lines and lugubrious right angles, to use Victor Hugo's phrase.... In this extraordinary country, where the people are certainly no match for their institutions, everything is straightforward and regular: their cities, their houses, their follies.'

In *An Eccentric's Will* (1889), an ingenious trick allows Verne to take the reader through the whole territory of the United States. The millionaire Hipperbone makes a will leaving his fortune to the winner of a game called 'goose', to be played by six people chosen by lot. The squares of the game are formed by the States of the Union with Illinois as 'goose', and that State consequently figures thirteen times (Chicago was Hipperbone's home). At regular intervals a 'solicitor' throws a set of dice and tells the players their next move, which they must make within certain time limits at their own expense and by their own choice of transportation. The novel is typically in Verne's style: the different episodes, as they take place in succession, according to the fall of the dice, provide the opportunity for an amusing descriptive geography lesson of the United States, in the manner so often favoured by Verne in his novels. But does the novel not hide a deeper symbolism? It concerns a children's game, and there is something rather disrespectful in thus

The excitement of the Chicago crowds watching the game of 'Goose' arranged by William J. Hipperbone (*An Eccentric's Will*).

assimilating the powerful United States with a board of sixty-one squares! Does this assimilation not also suggest certain conventional characteristics (as in all social games) in the American body politic, since many of the States have been 'drawn' with a ruler on the map of a still almost empty country?

Verne's satire on the American way of life, already strong in *Propeller Island*, is pressed further in *A Day in the Life of an American Journalist in the Year 2889*. This short tale was written in 1889 for an American magazine, *Forum*, but the editor was not at all pleased with such sharp criticism and insisted upon changes. The original text was not published until after Verne's death in the posthumous anthology entitled *Yesterday and Tomorrow* (*Hier et Demain*). In the period about which he was writing, Verne pictures a United States which has become powerful beyond measure. Not only has the whole of the New World been annexed, but England has also become its colony. The Federal capital has been moved from Washington, D.C., to Centropolis – quite an undertaking. The *New York Herald* has turned into the *Earth Herald*.

The mechanization of daily life has been immensely increased, thanks to the use of electricity and radiation. It has become possible to communicate across thousands of kilometres by 'phonotelephote', a machine which permits one to see and talk at the same time. A pneumatic tube has brought Europe to within 295 minutes' travel from the United States. Food is distributed automatically to each house. The countryside has lost all rustic character and is 'covered with a network of electric cables like an immense spider web'.

On the other hand, 'painting has fallen to such a low level that Millet's *Angelus* had just changed hands at 15 Francs, thanks to the progress in colour photography'. Publicity, however, is bringing in three million dollars a day to the *Earth Herald*, 'thanks to a patent bought for $3 from a poor devil who died of hunger. The system creates immense advertisements reflected from the clouds, which are so huge that they can be seen by a whole country.'

The principal character of this fanciful story, Francis Bennett, a direct descendant of Gordon Bennett (founder of the *New York Herald*), is one of the masters of the country. He owns gigantic plants, such as the power-houses at Niagara Falls, and lives in a palace of marble and gold.

> The plenipotentiaries of all nations and even government ministers flock to his door, ask his advice, seek his approval and implore the support of his omnipotent newspaper. Add to these the scientists he encourages, the artists he maintains, the inventors he assists financially.'

Indeed, the reader is present at the audiences Bennett grants to foreign ambassadors and at the requests for subsidies made to him by scientists. All this adds up to the fact that large-scale American capital has become the master of politics and culture.

The basis of Francis Bennett's power is a radical change in journalistic techniques: he is the inaugurator of 'telephonic journalism'.

> Instead of being printed, as in olden times, the *Earth Herald* is 'spoken' each morning. Subscribers are given the news that interests them in quick conversations with a reporter, a political correspondent or a scientist.

By this means Bennett has increased the readership to 85 million, his daily earnings to $250,000, and his personal fortune to 30 billion dollars.

CHAPTER X

Gold and silver

At first sight there is nothing more bourgeois than the respect for money, trade and profits, which is reflected in almost every book of the *Voyages extraordinaires*. The profits of capitalism are respectable and legitimate, and it is in pursuit of them that a little, ragged, Irish beggar eventually becomes a man of dignity (*Foundling Mick*). Merchants are honourable people; their business 'imperiously requires their full attention' (*The Boy Captain*) and they devote to it all their skill and moral energy. One of these types is the British trader, Hawkins, operating in Oceania (*The Brothers Kip*),

> Very alert, very active, very competent at his job, very venturesome in business matters. . . . It was known in Hobartstown that his financial position was perfectly secure and that, having made a fortune, he could already have retired. It would not have suited him, however, to live in idleness after working so hard all his life.

These traders all have big fortunes 'honestly gained', like that of the Catalan, Clovis Dardentor;

> If his fortune reached the figure of a good two millions, it had not come to him as a legacy or by inheritance. No! He had well and truly worked for it. Thanks to his great acumen, his many investments in commercial and industrial firms, in tanneries, marble workshops, cork factories and the Rivesaltes vineyards had invariably brought him considerable profits.

Verne, in short, seems to indulge himself in all the stock phrases accumulated by nineteenth-century bourgeois literature since Guizot's famous ringing cry 'Make yourselves rich!'* Even China becomes bourgeois in the person of young Kin Fo who lives a bourgeois existence in Shanghai, makes bourgeois investments abroad and treats his servant, Sun, in a thoroughly bourgeois manner. His bourgeois comfort comes

---

*The slogan of Louis-Philippe's prime minister, François Guizot, in the early 1840s, intended to distract French public opinion away from political opposition.

The Jewish moneylender, Isaac Hakhabut (*Hector Servadac*).

to an end with the news of a bank failure in San Francisco, and in true bourgeois style he tries to turn his bankruptcy to profit by taking out a huge life insurance policy in favour of his fiancée, covering even the suicide on which he is resolved (*The Tribulations of a Chinese Gentleman*).

This praise of the bourgeois virtues of commerce and financial enterprise, however, has a counter-tendency, more delicately sketched, but nevertheless widespread throughout the *Voyages extraordinaires*: towards anti-commercialism. This leads Verne to criticize with some zest such things as trade, the spirit of lucre, greed and narrow-mindedness. In the railway carriage taking Michael Strogoff and the young Naida to Siberia there is a group of merchants who are incapable of talking about anything other than the price of tea or carpets, at a time when the country is being ravaged by civil war. 'These selfish people were unable to think about the war, that is to say, the suppression of the rebellion and the struggle against invaders, except from the point of view of their own interests.'

The Anglo-Saxon traders on board the *Chancellor* are equally unpleasant. The American Kear is

> a *nouveau riche* rather than rich; ... coins are forever clinking in his pockets; ... Conceited, vain, forever thinking about himself and speculating about others; ... a fool and an egoist in one ...

The Englishman Ruby, for his part, appears as

> a vulgar shopkeeper, petty and lacking all originality. For twenty years this man did nothing but buy and sell and, as he usually sold at a higher price than he gave, he made a fortune. ... Ruby, his mind deadened by a whole life spent in retail trading, is incapable of thought or reflection; his brain is closed to all impressions.

It is, indeed, Ruby's sly greed which provokes the catastrophe in which the ship sinks. He has secretly placed on board a carboy of picric acid which threatens to explode in the hold when the cargo of cotton is set on fire by spontaneous combustion.

The money-dealers so despised by Verne are sometimes Anglo-Saxons, but more often Levantines or Orientals, and this is where Verne's anti-commercialism becomes tinged with a basic racism which was not rare in the provincial bourgeois nationalist circles he frequented in Nantes or Amiens. The traders whose selfish views shock Michael Strogoff are Jews and Persians. The bankers Toronthal (*Mathias Sandorf*), Elizundo (*Islands on Fire*), and Zambuco (*Master Antifer*), living respectively in Trieste, Corfu and Tunis, are all Levantines. Of Zambuco Verne says:

> He had amassed a large fortune in every kind of shady operation on the stock exchange – the kind for which one needs glue on one's fingers ... – thanks to his prodigious parsimony, to his miserly instincts, he had been able to pile up sack upon sack of coins, to monopolize silver, to make a corner in gold and possess himself of everything of the slightest value. His whole life had been dedicated to shady dealings of this kind.

The attack against profiteers becomes openly anti-semitic in the treatment of Isaac Hakhabut, the Prussian moneylender who is carried away into interplanetary space together with the other temporary inhabitants of the comet Gallia (*Hector Servadac*):

> Small, puny, with lively but treacherous eyes, a hooked nose, unbrushed hair, big feet, long, crooked hands, he was of that well-known German-Jewish type which is instantly recognizable. A

Professor Hog examining the winning ticket in Verne's novel about Norwegian nationalism (*A Lottery Ticket*).

typical moneylender with a supple back and cold heart, a money-grubber, a real skinflint.

Isaac Hakhabut lives off petty peddling aboard his boat; he tries to continue his trade at the expense of the small space community headed by Captain Servadac. He sells coffee and other provisions at exorbitant prices, uses false scales, and proves to be completely anti-social. But he is finally exposed and his goods requisitioned. This is an exceptionally gross case of anti-semitic caricature, but it is nevertheless very symptomatic of a political tendency which Verne hardly sought to conceal.[123]

Taking it all in all, Verne's anti-commercialism is thus as commonplace and conventional as the bourgeois admiration he expresses for the virtues of trade and profit. On the other hand, Verne introduces a much more original corrective to these platitudes; and this might be called a certain fortuitous and artificial aspect of wealth. This emerges in many of Verne's novels, not only in terms of the enormous size of the fortunes in question, but also by the suddenness with which they appear, and even more by the pure chance which decides to whom they should go.

These enormous sums of money, often the stake and the crux of a novel's plot, may be the fruits of speculation as, for instance, when the banker Lecœur learns that a meteorite of pure gold is going to fall on the earth (*The Hunt for the Meteor*), or when the ingenious Kin Fo hopes to make his fiancée rich by taking out an insurance policy on his life. These fortunes may also spring from the whim of an eccentric benefactor such as the fabulously rich Mrs Kathleen Seymour of the Antilles, who bestows a small fortune on each of the best pupils of the Antilia School in London (*Travelling Scholarships*). For the most part, however, they derive from unexpected legacies: that of the Begum Gokool of Ragganahra, widow of one of Napoleon's former soldiers who had made a fortune in India, and whose distant relatives in France and Germany had completely forgotten about her (*The Begum's Fortune*); the one left by the wealthy Syrian, Kamylk Pasha, which is desperately searched for from island to island by Master Antifer, whose father had once saved the testator's life. Then there is Uncle Starter, an unconventional Yankee who always refused to meet his niece, Dolly, but who leaves her his whole fortune, even when she is undergoing treatment at a mental asylum (*Mistress Branican*); and the rich merchant Dardentor who has promised his fortune to whoever contrives to be adopted by him. In the case of *A Lottery Ticket*, chance does not even need to express itself through a will and the ties of kinship since it is through the drawing of lots that a poor sailor gets the enormous first prize of the Norwegian national lottery. In *An Eccentric's Will*, the vagaries of a game of chance are added to the fortuitous effects of a bequest.

Seeing that such considerable sums of money may come to people of modest means by pure chance, it is natural that the money should be spent equally casually and off-handedly. The heroes of the *Known and Unknown Worlds* are spontaneously prodigal. If they spend money without stint, it is of course because many of them are rich, but much more because for many of them money is not an end in itself but a means of attaining the scientific or humanitarian purpose they have set themselves. Hatteras promises a bonus to the members of the crew of the *Forward* for each degree of latitude crossed in the direction of the North Pole, and the same takes place on board the schooner *Halbrane* when the crew are hesitant to undertake a difficult exploration in the Antarctic (*An Antarctic Mystery*). Liddenbrock has a similar sort of contract with the

Icelander who acts as his guide into the depths of the earth. These characters hardly give a thought to expense, any more than Lord Glenarvan does when he fits out, at his own expense, an expedition to search for Captain Grant, or Colonel Munro when he buys the luxury steam elephant built for the whim of an Indian Rajah; Munro's purpose is to search Northern India for his wife who disappeared during the Indian Mutiny (*The Steam House*). With even more prodigality, Phileas Fogg distributes his banknotes during his journey, buying indiscriminately an elephant or a ship when their owners refuse to hire them out. The same disregard for money is shown by Keraban who decides at all costs – literally – to travel all the way round the Black Sea rather than cross the Bosphorus for a fee which he considered iniquitous. The American millionaire Kolderup buys a Pacific island for his nephew with the sole object of educating him (*Robinson Island School*). Hadjine Elizondo and Dolly Branican spend their money like water for nobler purposes: in the first case, in order to buy the freedom of the captives held by Turkish slave-traders, and in the second, to fit out an expedition to search for her missing husband.

Fortune thus arrives unexpectedly, and one spends it without concern. In this respect Verne is very far from the morality of thrift taught in the primary schools of the Third Republic (see, for instance, the famous manual, *Two Children travelling round France*; or the story of the young Laffitte picking up a needle,* etc.). Except for a novel like *Foundling Mick*, in which a laboriously acquired fortune is finally a *political* solution to the problem of the national liberation of Ireland, the lesson to be drawn from the *Voyages extraordinaires* hardly encourages the practice of those virtues of frugality and saving so dear to the heart of the French *petite bourgeoisie* of the period.

Thus one is finally led to an attitude rather different from the initial banality of Verne's views on wealth, trade, gold and silver. When the *Voyages extraordinaires* are read more attentively, these bourgeois values are seen to be eminently artificial and conventional.

On many occasions in the novels Verne expresses lively disapproval of gold as an artificial medium conferring power and wealth.[124] He uses the geographer Paganel to accuse gold openly of corrupting men and bringing nations to ruin (*The Children of Captain Grant*):

> He a miner?[125] Never! To dig the soil, turn it over, plant seed in it and expect a good harvest for one's trouble, fine! But to ransack the

---

*Jacques Laffitte, 1767–1804, prominent French banker who was said, as a destitute young boy, to have attracted the attention of a director because, after having been refused a job, he was meticulous enough to pick a needle off the ground after he had trodden on it.

earth blindly like a mole in the hope of extracting a little gold, that's a sad kind of job....

—On the very spot where we are standing, below our feet, there may be a lot of gold?

—Yes, my son, it could be worth millions! We are walking over it! But if we are walking over it, it is because we despise it!

—Australia is a privileged country, then?

—No, Robert, said the geographer. Gold-bearing countries are not privileged. They produce only idle people, and never strong, hard-working races. Look at Brazil, California, Australia. Where are they in this nineteenth century? The most privileged lands, my child, are not those where gold is found, but those where there is iron.

For Verne, 'gold rushes' are nothing but social calamities. In New Zealand around 1885, for instance, there was a sudden increase in crime; crews deserted from ships calling at the ports, and this provides the starting-point for the plot of *The Brothers Kip*, who are two passengers falsely charged instead of certain criminals whom the captain of their ship had to take on to replace the members of his crew that had left for the gold mines. The Australian gold rush of 1851 produced equally unpleasant results (*Captain Grant*):

A whole horde of adventurers rushed there, thieves and honest men, those who send men to the gallows and those who get themselves hanged. Townsfolk, squatters and sailors abandoned their cities, their fields and their ships. Gold fever infected everyone, as contagious as the plague, and many died just as they thought they had made their fortune!...

During the last four months of 1852, no fewer than 54,000 immigrants passed through Melbourne alone; it was an army, but an army without leaders, without discipline, like an army on the day following a military victory which had not yet been won, in a word 54,000 looters of the worst possible kind.

The same awareness of the maleficent power of gold can be seen when the 'Swiss Robinsons' discover nuggets of free gold on their island (*Second Fatherland*):

This is a secret we must think over before telling others, said father Zermatt.
—What is there to fear, father?
—Nothing at present, but we have to think of the colony's future! ... When it becomes known that there are gold deposits here, that there is a wealth of gold nuggets in New Switzerland, crowds of gold seekers will come here bringing with them all the evils, the

disorders and the crimes which invariably accompany the acquisition of this metal.

Gold does more than corrupt men, it makes them mad, as happens to the inventor Thomas Roch (*For the Flag*); unable to find a government willing to buy his invention, he entrusts the secret to the pirate Ker Karraje; 'in a state of true frenzy' he recounts his misfortunes, while gold coins from every country supplied by his new partner roll out of his pockets onto the ground.

Even in the first of the *Voyages extraordinaires, Five Weeks in a Balloon*, Verne had suggested that gold represented no more than a conventional and completely relative value. When Dr Fergusson's balloon comes down in the middle of the African desert, he ballasts with huge blocks of gold-bearing quartz. This potential fortune causes his servant, Joe, to lose his mind:

> The worthy Joe was not the same person after his eyes had examined that ocean of gold; he stopped talking and looked greedily at the rocks piled up in the nacelle, rocks without value at the moment, but of inestimable worth in future.

But the blocks of ore will have to be thrown overboard as the journey continues and it becomes necessary to lighten the balloon.

Throughout his writings Verne systematically reverts to the idea that gold has no more than an arbitrary value; for this purpose he describes the consequences which would ensure from a massive increase in the amount of gold caused by astronomical or geological upheavals. This argument, all the more daring for being put forward during the nineteenth century when the gold-standard was unchallenged and immutable, is developed in three novels which might be called the gold trilogy of the *Voyages extraordinaires*. In *Hector Servadac* a handful of men are carried away, together with a piece of the earth's crust, by a comet of gold telluride, its contemporary value being 71 quintillions. On the day when the comet falls on the earth, 'the price of gold will fall to nothing, and it will more than ever deserve the name of "vile metal".' In *The Hunt for the Meteor*, a meteor of pure gold, representing the prodigious sum of 5,788 milliard gold Francs, is intercepted by a scientist who projects a sort of laser beam into space. Gold-mining shares fall at once and are bought up by an ingenious speculator, who becomes rich when the inventor causes his meteor to come down in the sea and explode into infinitesimal particles. It is in this novel that Verne invents the neologism '*emmilliarder*'; the word has a clear pejorative connotation, and it may be thought that Verne used it to suggest a somewhat coarse pun.

Finally, in *The Volcano of Gold*, a short and symbolic dramatic passage once again shows the preposterous character of gold. Men struggle and die to reach the gold. They have crossed the famous Chilkoot Pass and are smitten with a sort of 'collective madness', . . . all these visionaries, to whom the mirage of the Klondike imparted supernatural energy and tenacity.'

Having arrived at Golden Mount in Alaska, on the shore of the frozen Arctic Ocean, they find

> the richest deposits on earth, . . . no need to dig, . . . the earth itself throws out the gold from its entrails, . . . it is a volcano containing an immense quantity of gold, a volcano of gold, the Golden Mount.

The men engaged in this gigantic enterprise hate and murder each other. But when a group of them reaches the crater, the volcano suddenly starts erupting again, hurling huge nuggets of gold into the sea, where they are lost forever. The biggest block of gold crushes the criminal, Hunter, as he is trying to murder the hero of the novel:

> Below the scratches caused by the shocks, a yellow substance shone with a metallic gleam, . . . the retributive rock was composed wholly of pure gold, . . . the very gold which Hunter was so greedily seeking had put an end to his criminal dreams.

Published after Verne's death, this novel clearly shows the influence of Jack London and the romance of the Canadian Far North, but, at a deeper level of inspiration, it ties up with the theme that appears throughout Verne's writings, starting with the first novel of all, *Five Weeks in a Balloon*.

The only case in which gold appears in another guise is the episode of the galleons in Vigo Bay discovered by Nemo, thanks to his *Nautilus*, and which supply him with unlimited resources. But here the owner of the gold is a man who has broken with society and who at the same time helps oppressed people when needed; he donates a considerable sum to an emissary of the Cretan insurgents of 1868.

An echo of the denunciation of gold is to be found in *The Southern Star Mystery*, where the precious stone industry is also denounced. Man is corrupted by precious stones; for instance, the farmer Watkins, owner of diamond-bearing lands, loses all his human qualities and lets his greed come before the happiness of his daughter, Alice. But this greed is the cause of his own death when his giant diamond, the Southern Star, suddenly disintegrates:

> Had John Watkins been less attached to lucre, had he not attributed an exaggerated, an almost criminal, importance to those little carbon crystals known as diamonds, the discovery and the disappearance of the Southern Star would have left him indifferent. His physical and moral health would not have been at the mercy of an accident. He had given his whole heart to the diamonds, and it was the diamonds which had to cause his death.

Thus precious stones have no more than a conventional value, and Verne illustrates this idea in the same novel when he describes the cave where the Kaffir king, Tonaia, immures his prisoners and buries his dead. Inside the cave, an accident of geology has caused a concentration of fabulous quantities of different kinds of crystalline rocks:

> Diamond, rubies and sapphires were hidden inside that immense cavern, and in such extraordinary quantities that their value, as men assess these bits of mineral, must be beyond all calculation.... There, buried under the ground, undiscovered and unproductive, was material worth trillions and quadrillions of milliards! The Negro king thought of himself simply as the owner and guardian of a particularly strange cave, the secret of which an oracle, or some superstitious tradition, forbade him to reveal.

Since gold, silver and precious stones have no more than a factitious, artificial and illusory value, such 'external signs of wealth' cannot provide the answer to the real needs of human societies (*Propeller Island*):

> What is the use of being a multi-millionaire, to be rich like a Rothschild, a Mackay, an Astor, a Vanderbilt, a Gould, when no amount of wealth can avert a famine? ... Who knows that the day is not near when, with all their millions, they will be unable to buy a pound of meat or bread?

Verne, the former stockbroker and estate agent of the brilliant and easy years of the Second Empire, had thus become a radical critic of those economic values which formed the very basis of the society of his time. No doubt he had never read Marx, and was not well versed in economic theory; nevertheless, his systematic attacks on 'the worship of gold' are in their own way worthy of being placed alongside the criticism of 'commodity fetishism' to be found in *Das Kapital*.

Verne's indifference to money, fortune and financial matters is carried to its logical end in the early books of the *Voyages extraordinaires*, which deal with the taming of nature, the conquest of time and space, and getting difficult jobs done through will-power, skill and scientific competence. Provision of the necessary financial means could not be allowed to obstruct the accomplishment of the ambitious projects of Fergusson, Liddenbrock, Cyrus Smith, Nemo and Michel Ardan. That is why, in this first cycle of Verne's novels, supplies of money are 'given', almost in the mathematical meaning of the word; the real difficulties and achievements come later.

There are no money problems for Dr Fergusson as he sets out to cross Africa from West to East in his balloon. The son of an army officer, he no doubt has a private income; the cost of the expedition and of equipping the balloon is not even mentioned. Fergusson is not interested in money. He disdains the tusks of the elephant which tows the balloon along as the result of an accident: 'Are we dealers in ivory? Did we come here to make our fortunes?' The geologist Liddenbrock, who daringly follows in the tracks of the Icelandic alchemist, Arne Saknussen, in his journey into the depths of the earth, also has a considerable private income: 'For a German professor, he was quite wealthy'; and we are given no details about the cost of his expedition (apart from the allowance paid to the Icelandic guide).

The organizers of the expedition towards the moon, being Americans, show a little more interest in these financial problems (*From the Earth to the Moon*): 'To put the project into execution an enormous sum of money was needed. No private individual, no government even, could have provided the millions which were required.' That is why Barbicane, as President of the Gun Club, opens a general subscription and appeals to 'all men of good will on earth'. Four million dollars are subscribed in the United States within three days, and a million and a half are subscribed in foreign countries.

Hatteras was the only son of a London brewer 'who died in 1852 six times a millionaire', and he simply makes use of his father's fortune to pay for his Polar projects.

Money is no problem for Captain Nemo either. At the outset he enjoys the use of his princely family's treasures which had escaped confiscation during the repression following the Indian Mutiny. His jewels and precious stones enable him to meet with no difficulty the cost of building the *Nautilus*: 1,687,000 Francs, or four to five millions if we include the works of art he has placed in the ship. At a later date, the discovery of the treasure in Vigo Bay relieves him forever from all financial worry:

> Then you are a wealthy man, Captain? Infinitely wealthy, Sir; it would be nothing to me to pay off the ten milliards of the French national debt.

Neither have the Russian and English astronomers, who go into the South African deserts with the proud motto of 'triangulate or die', any problems about money. Their expedition is financed by the two governments in question, and it is backed by 'considerable credits'. Phileas Fogg is equally uninterested in money since he has a considerable private fortune – though Verne does not take the trouble to tell us how he obtained it:

> He was never seen at the Stock Exchange nor the Bank, nor in any of the big City agencies. Neither the Pool nor the docks of London had ever been visited by a ship owned by Phileas Fogg. . . . He was

not an industrial magnate, nor a wholesaler, nor a trader, nor an agriculturalist. . . .

He was well known to Baring Brothers, with whom he had an open credit, and this gave him a certain financial standing since his cheques were invariably paid on sight and debited to his current account, which was always in credit.

Phileas Fogg was incontestably a wealthy man, but should you ask how he made his fortune, not even the most knowledgeable person could tell.

Nevertheless, it is this fortune that enables him on a whim to risk £20,000 on a single bet, arising out of an argument at his club.

The proud attitude of financial and, especially, moral independence which Verne's earlier heroes adopt in the matter of monetary requirements comes to an end about 1880, or more precisely in 1879 with the publication of *The Begum's Fortune*, a novel which is interesting as being a turning-point in the series of Verne's novel cycles. A fabulous inheritance, deriving from the princely treasure of an ancient line of Bengali rajahs, happens to be divided between two cousins, a French doctor and a German professor. The former builds the 'happy city' of Franceville, with its very Saint-Simonian character (*cf.* Chapter 4), while the latter uses his share of the fortune in the service of evil by building Stahlstadt, a 'city of perdition' symbolizing the perversion of science, a theme which becomes more and more of a preoccupation with Verne (*cf.* Chapter XI). The important point here is that in both cases, i.e. from both the optimistic and the pessimistic aspects of Verne's political thinking, science is dependent upon money, or rather, falls into such dependence. Dr Sarrasin and Professor Schultze can act as they do only because they have the necessary financial means; they owe these to pure chance, personified by the English solicitor who comes to inform them of the extent of their good fortune. That the solicitor is supposed to represent destiny is obvious even from his physical characteristics; his funereal and corpse-like appearance resembles the description of one of those symbolic characters favoured by Ingmar Bergman in his films:

> A man still youthful, whom the doctor at first sight placed in the numerous category of 'death's heads'. His lips were thin, or rather dried up, he had long white teeth, almost fleshless temporal cavities beneath a skin like parchment, mummy-coloured complexion and little, grey, gimlet eyes, all of which entitled him without question to the doctor's classification.

As soon as Dr Sarrasin learns of his inheritance, he hails it as the means of accomplishing some great scientific task:

> It so happens that I have legally become the possessor of a considerable sum of money, to the extent of several hundred millions,

The grim city of Stahlstadt, which Verne contrasts with Franceville in *The Begum's Fortune* (see p. 71).

which is at present deposited in the Bank of England. In the circumstances, I do not need to tell you that I look upon myself as a trustee of science.... It is not to me that this money rightly belongs, it belongs to mankind, to progress!... The five hundred millions which chance has put into my hands is not mine, it is the property of science. Are you prepared to be the parliament which shall distribute this budget?

As for Schultze, he uses his share of the inheritance in order to build a gigantic gun factory which allows him not only to experiment with a whole series of arms of wholesale destruction, but also to produce them in industrial quantities:

> That mass of buildings is Stahlstadt, the city of steel, a German town which is the personal property of Herr Schultze, the former professor of chemistry at Jena, who, through the millions left to him by the Begum, has become the biggest producer of iron, and especially of guns, in both the Old World and the New. . . .
>
> Thanks to the power of enormous quantities of money, a monster establishment, a veritable town, which is also a model of what a factory should be, has risen out of the ground as if at the stroke of a magic wand.

Thus in both cases, the scientists derive their power from money. The factor which figured only fortuitously and by implication in the achievements of Hatteras and Nemo, Fergusson and Liddenbrock, has become the deciding factor in the success of a great scientific project, whether for good or evil. It would be difficult to overlook the fact that this sudden irruption of the importance of money into the world of the *Voyages extraordinaires*, which corresponds, incidentally, with a general change in Verne's outlook (*cf.* Chapter XI), coincides with a general turning-point in European society during the last quarter of the nineteenth century. The fusion of banking capital with industrial capital to form 'financial capital', together with the expansionist policies of the great European powers, the armaments race and the 'transition to imperialism', necessarily resulted in the increasing subordination of science to the power of money. The radiant da Vinci dream of the intellectual domination of nature, still so vivid to a man like Enfantin, was fading in the distance. The exploitation of the possibilities of science now lay in the hands of captains of industry such as Eiffel, who were successful and efficient engineers because they were also active in the field of big finance. Throughout the subsequent *Voyages extraordinaires*, this subordination of science to the power of money is clearly expressed.

The power of money has become manifest in *Mathias Sandorf* (1885). It is because Sandorf is the owner of an 'immense' fortune that Sarcany decides to hand him over to the Austrian police and to denounce the Hungarian nationalist plot which he has learned about by chance. And it is not until he has managed to build up his private fortune again that Sandorf, escaped from prison, is able to transform himself into the all-powerful Doctor Antekirtt and thus avenge Sandorf. He inherits the enormous sum of fifty million florins 'left to him by a wealthy Syrian who had formerly been his patient'.[126]

Similarly, the embittered and unsuccessful engineer Orfanik is enabled to find fulfilment and make use of his capacities as a scientist only after meeting the rich Rodolphe de Gortz who, in order to satisfy his own neuroses, furnishes the money to pay for all of Orfanik's strange experiments (*Carpathian Castle*, 1892). The engineers who work on *Propeller Island* (1895) are directly subordinate to the authority of the capitalist group which has built the floating Standard Island for the Yankee millionaires to travel about the Pacific in leisurely comfort. In *The Master of the World* (1904), the engineer Robur's wonderful flying machine gives rise to fierce financial competition among various countries vying with each other to buy it:

> It goes without saying that America will be free with her money and that, if necessary, the multi-millionaires of America will open their bottomless purses to the widest extent....
>
> The whole world became a public auction room in which the bidding reached unbelievable heights....
>
> In the end it was the United States which was able to win the auction, following a memorable session of Congress when the sum of 20 million dollars was voted.

Robur nevertheless refuses to sell his invention at that price; the da Vinci dream is still withstanding men of Eiffel's type. In two of Verne's last novels, however, *The Invasion of the Sea* and *The Hunt for the Meteor*, the captains of industry have definitely established their control over science. In the first case, the plan for the creation of a 'Saharan Sea' is carried to a successful conclusion by an engineer trained in the Central School for Arts and Manufactures, M. de Schaller, who is at the same time an active businessman and the representative of certain large banking interests; science and finance are thus united in his person. They are also united in the persons of Zéphirin Xirdal and Lecœur when a golden meteor is in danger of falling on the earth. The first of this pair is a physicist of genius but completely lacking in practical sense; the second, his sponsor, is a banker who supplies the money required for the construction of his laser-like machine and for the purchase of the area where he will make the meteor fall. Science has thus been annexed by the bank, to the considerable profit of the latter:

> Zéphirin Xirdal, it is true, was no stranger to the increase of this colossal power. M. Lecœur, who had now taken the measure of his capabilities, made full use of him; all the inventions conceived by that fertile brain were put into practical application by the bank, and the latter had no reason to complain of the results.

At this stage, indeed, science can with equal ease become the servant of such 'respectable' financial entities as banks, limited liability companies, and wealthy eccentrics, or of the leaders of pirate bands sufficiently intelligent to utilize, for the purpose of increasing their gains, the inventions of those scientists whom they had been able to attract to their service. Thomas Roch, the embittered and misunderstood inventor of a super-powerful explosive, after being scoffed at by the governments of various states and being shut up in a mental asylum, ends up by confiding his secret to the pirate Ker Karraje (*For the Flag*). Marcel Camaret, an even more brilliant inventor, works without knowing it for the bloody Harry Killer who has used his marvellous discoveries to build Blackland in the middle of a desert, the most terrible of all Verne's 'cities of perdition'. Lost in his dreams, Camaret is indifferent as to where the money comes from that allows him to realize those dreams (*The Barsac Mission*):

> As though it was the simplest thing in the world, Camaret had asked for a workshop to be built, and hundreds of Negroes immediately started to build it. He then asked for such and such machine tools, dynamos and a steam engine, and, if not immediately, at least within a few months the machine tools, the dynamos and the engine arrived miraculously in the desert. Finally, he asked for labourers, and one after the other labourers arrived until the number he had stipulated was complete. Marcel Camaret was not in the least interested in the way all these astonishing things were accomplished. He had asked for them and he had got them; to him it was as simple as that.
>
> He had never given a thought, either, to the amount of money required for the realization of his dreams, and he had never once asked himself the very natural question: 'Where does all the money come from?'

The 'legal' and 'illegal' aspects of financial power are thus assimilated in a very Brechtian, very modern manner. In both cases science has entered the widening reproduction cycle of large-scale finance, instead of depending only, as was the case in the earlier *Voyages extraordinaires*, upon the activity of the human intellect in pursuit of an ideal.

CHAPTER XI

Progress or pessimism: the future of mankind

The novels comprising the first stage of the cycle of the *Voyages extraordinaires* were imbued with a basic optimism, an unbounded confidence in progress, which we have interpreted as deriving from the Saint-Simonian tradition. Captain Holt's courageous shout in *The Steam House*, 'Everything will be accomplished', is an instance of this confidence.

Verne's utopian 'project' was based upon the idea that science and human character alone were sufficient to ensure the conquest of nature, without the help of any particular social system. Verne's earliest imaginary machines were of the da Vinci type, designed to enlarge man's natural powers and increase his comforts, not to serve the interests and needs of industrial production for the sake of society: for example, the flying machines of Dr Fergusson and Robur, *Nautilus*, the steel elephant, railways, giant ocean liners and lunar cannon balls. The earliest of the *Voyages extraordinaires* recorded individual exploits carried out by men of outstanding character, scientific competence and skill, exploits accomplished without reference to the kind of society from which these men sprang (and with which they had often broken, either of their own will or by accident); such men as Hatteras and Liddenbrock, Barbicane and Ardan, Nemo and Phileas Fogg, Cyrus Smith and Jasper Hobson.

Between about 1880 and 1890, the *Known and Unknown Worlds* alter their character. Man's efforts, his Promethean challenge to nature, are from then on expressed through well-defined social entities, clearly analyzed as such. Verne comes face to face with social realities. His scientific forecasts now give place to the problems of social organization, social conditions and the responsibility of scientists towards society; in each case, as we shall see, he reaches a pessimistic conclusion.

This confrontation with social realities is sketched out for the first time in *The Begum's Fortune*, published in 1879; with *Propeller Island*, published in 1895, it is complete and definitive. It is impossible not to notice that this basic change of direction in Verne's writings corresponds perceptibly with what the historians call the transition to imperialism. The years 1880–90 are those which were marked by the great development in Western Europe of large-scale finance capitalist enterprise.

Colonial rivalries became sharper; temporary agreements like that of Berlin (1885) concerning the apportionment of Africa, gave place more and more to implacable struggles for the redistribution of imperialist spheres of influence in Africa, Asia and America, to the benefit of the most grasping Powers. The armaments race reflected the growth of war technology, and the increase both in military budgets and in the political influence of the large-scale steel industry ('the cannon merchants'). Governments became more and more repressive in character at the very moment when they were openly defied by the working-class movements or the outrages committed by anarchists and nihilists.

These were also the years of an economic crisis which caused many bankruptcies, the closing of factories, decreases in pay and the adoption of a protectionist agrarian policy which isolated France. We may ask to what extent this crisis, the worst years of which are put by the historians between 1882 and 1895, affected Jules Verne and his friends morally and perhaps even economically. We lack the documentation which would provide an answer to this question. It should be noted, however, that this was the period when Verne sat on the town council of Amiens; there can be no doubt that the effects of the crisis on the economy of Picardy were discussed in his presence, and this must also have been true of the citizens of Amiens whom he used to meet socially and in the local Academy.

The Begum's Fortune, published in 1879, which we have frequently referred to in this book, is the starting-point for Verne's doubts about progress and his evolution towards pessimism. We know today that the novel is the result of a booksellers' deal: the former *communard* Pascal Grousset, living in penniless exile in London, had sold to Hetzel a somewhat mediocre manuscript entitled *The Heir of Langévol*; Hetzel handed it over to Verne, for him to write a new version to be published under his name. Grousset had signed a contract in which he renounced all claim to authorship of the book.[127] But it seems to us that this somewhat peculiar origin does not in any way reduce the political significance of the novel within the ambit of the *Voyages extraordinaires*. Traces of optimism and faith in science are still to be found; for example, Dr Sarrasin speaks of his fabulous inheritance as belonging 'to mankind, to progress'. Nevertheless, it is in this novel that Verne for the first time tackles the problems of social organization and tries to resolve it by opposing two rival cities: Franceville, the 'radiant city' of hygiene and harmony, with strongly Saint-Simonian traits; and Stahlstadt, which becomes the world capital of heavy steel industry. Of course, Franceville triumphs in the end, but it is impossible not to see how artificial and false the chapters devoted to Franceville are, even from a literary point of view, whereas the description of Stahlstadt is powerful and glaring with truth. This steel city of the future already foreshadows Le Creusot, the Ruhr, Pittsburgh; Verne confronts the inhuman character of modern, large-

Herr Schultze's formidable guards at Stahlstadt (*The Begum's Fortune*).

scale industrial production and scientific technology, the workers' death rate, the military surveillance of the foremen and the brutality of working conditions; and he does not hesitate to pass judgment on the lot by means of an imaginary model.

In this second phase of his work, Verne expands his novels of forecast to take in social problems, and not only technology; but this leads him to offer us a pessimistic and frightful picture of his 'cities of perdition'. These are the complete antithesis of the values of hard work, kindliness, human brotherhood and progress which imbue all the novels of his first period. Such a city is Stahlstadt. Its totalitarian character goes far beyond the satirical, anti-German chauvinism which is all that certain critics have been able to see in it.[128] It is a militarized, proto-Nazi society, in which the workers are arranged in a military hierarchy, are under military discipline and have to go through the motions of their jobs with military precision; they undertake to live in the quarters assigned to them, swear not to tell anyone what their duties are, and agree to their letters being read. The town is surrounded by ditches and high walls. It is separated into sections and divisions cut off from each other by watertight bulkheads; all movement is controlled by a system of sentries and double gates, 'as in convents'. In the middle there is the 'Central Block', to which only the initiates have access:

> It was said that anyone incautious enough to penetrate those private precincts was never seen again; that labourers and employees, before they were allowed in, had to undergo a whole series of Masonic ceremonies and take the most solemn oaths not to reveal what went on there, and that they were pitilessly put to death by the order of a secret tribunal, should they break their oath. ... The holy of holies was linked to the outer walls by an underground railway, ... during the hours of the night, the trains brought in unknown visitors. ... Sometimes the Supreme Council met there, and mysterious characters attended the meetings and took part in the discussions.

Indeed, that is where Herr Schultze has his secret laboratory, surrounded by a beautiful garden in the purest Wagner-Hitlerian style: rare flowers, waterfalls, rock-work, groves and hot-houses. The whole set-up is so centralized that everything stops when the dictator dies as the result of a sudden accident.

The same is true of Milliard City (*Propeller Island*), the capital of Standard Island, floating around the Pacific. It is a place of incredible luxury (moving pavements, air-conditioning, electric automobiles in the streets, etc.), and everything can be bought there. It is the triumph of idle money. As we have already noted, it is not by chance that this artificial society is a Yankee society. The debasement of social values described by Verne is symbolically directed towards the very country which, in his earlier period, had been for him the incarnation of his hopes of future social improvement. Standard Island is eventually destroyed as the result of the conflicts between two rival groups of multi-millionaires.

Finally, there is Blackland, the artificial city that rises out of the desert thanks to the inventions of the engineer Camaret: artificial rain to make the desert fertile, gliders to 'rake' the Negro villages for cheap labour, radar to watch over the city walls and to prevent any attempts at escape (*The Barsac Mission*). It is a society based on political terrorism and organized into strictly divided castes. At the top is the despot, Harry Killer, living in his palace with his nine counsellors, his black guard of fifty men, and his servants. Around him, there is the caste of the Merry Fellows, criminals recruited in Europe, who live by looting; their number are limited by statute to 566, and every vacancy is filled at once by promoting a member of the 'Civil Body', who are also criminals and outlaws from Europe. This white ruling caste is responsible for police and disciplinary matters, and all profits are reserved for its members; it rules over several thousand black slaves whose mortality rate is very high (through privation, punitive sanctions, and even murder by whim). A third social stratum exists between these SS or SA and their black transported labour, namely the 'free workers' who are serving under contract, are well paid and have agreed to live almost like prisoners inside their factory for the period stipulated in the contract. They think that they will then be free to leave, not realizing that they are to be killed in the desert and their savings returned to the dictator's treasury. Blackland is one of the clearest of Verne's social forecasts; it is possible that the idea was suggested to him by the adventures of the Frenchman Lebaudy* who dreamed of turning the land within the bend of the Niger into fertile country and building an ultra-modern town there named Troja, but the story in its essence is Verne's own creation and opens up political perspectives far beyond those of Stahlstadt: the latter leads to a Hitlerian nightmare, but Blackland goes a good deal further with its massive exploitation of black labour, and its picture of a political reign of terror founded upon racism.

It is worth noting that Verne took the trouble to give a careful description of the urban planning of these three 'cities of perdition'. In each case the plan is the expression of a political situation, of *a power system*. Stahlstadt is characterized by its absolute centralization. Everything is organized around the Central Block, the 'dragon's cave'. Divisions and sections are grouped according to a rigorously concentric plan, while the whole is surrounded by impassable walls. Standard Island, on the other hand, is based on a bi-partite plan which corresponds with the rivalry between the two clans of Yankee multi-millionaires, the 'Port-siders' and the 'Starboard-siders': the one clan are Catholics and the other Protestants, and a representative of each acts as deputy to the Governor of the island. As for Blackland, its city plan is more complex, as is its political power structure. On the left bank of the river, the quarters of the Merry Fellows and those of the Civil Body flank the areas in which the black slaves are penned up. On the right bank, the Palace, with its high cement tower, the centre of political power (Harry Killer, his counsellors and his black guard), faces the Factory, the centre of technical and economic power which is also dominated by Camaret's high tower. This city is therefore planned to accord with the strict

---

*Paul Lebaudy, 1858–1937, French industrialist who pioneered the construction of dirigibles.

politico-social 'zoning', and this is emphasized by the interior walls. It is a vision worthy of that in Fritz Lang's film *Metropolis*.

The theme of the perversion of science thus makes its appearance, through these men and these maleficent cities. Almost a century before the United States Air Force started dropping its monstrous 'fragmentation bombs' upon Vietnam, Herr Schultze conceived analogous weapons of destruction:

> These shells enclose a hundred small guns symmetrically distributed inside, sliding into each other like the tubes of a telescope, which, after having been shot through the air like projectiles, become guns again and in their turn vomit forth small shells filled with incendiary material. 'It is as if I were firing into space a whole battery of guns,' Herr Schultze declared, 'a battery capable of covering a whole town with a rain of unquenchable flames and death.'

Other shells made at Stahlstadt contain frozen carbonic gas which is released when they explode. Like Schultze, Thomas Roch uses his scientific imagination to make weapons of destruction, and his 'fulgurator' can cause the most terrible devastation at a distance. The men who run Blackland use automatically piloted electric gliders, monitoring radar screens, and torture by electricity.

From this point onwards, Verne was to become more and more preoccupied with the risk of modern science being perverted, and mankind becoming incapable of pursuing the path of progress. There is a striking contrast, for example, between the two books dealing with the exploits of the engineer Robur. The first of these, *The Clipper of the Clouds*, still ends, as we have said, with an act of faith in 'the science of the future', although the engineer is already a misunderstood man. In the second, *The Master of the World*, he has turned into a misanthrope who has declared war on mankind and is being hunted down.

At this later stage, the scientists whom Verne brings onto the scene are no longer men of high attainments and character, but figures of ridicule, anti-social, even madmen: Palmyrin Rosette (*Hector Servadac*) or Aristobulus Ursiclos (*The Green Ray*) are queer, unsympathetic characters without any warmth, and their intellect is purely mechanical. Zéphirin Xirdal (*The Hunt for the Meteor*) is an advanced case of schizophrenia with 'his two protruding eyes expressing, according to the time of day, or the passing minute, either the most wonderful intelligence or the densest stupidity.' The engineer Serkö (*For the Flag*) is misunderstood and embittered, as is Orfanik (*Carpathian Castle*). Of the latter Verne says:

> Scientific circles could see in him nothing more than a madman, rather than a genius in his own line, and this was the motive for the unquenchable hatred which this inventor, rejected and rebuffed as he had been, had sworn against his own kind.

The ridiculous scientist, Aristobulus Ursiclos, measuring metres by pacing (*The Green Ray*).

Thomas Roch (*For the Flag*), for his part, has completely lost his reason, as a result of being misunderstood and insulted, and this is true also of the alchemist Wilhelm Storitz. And this gallery of damned scientists, the antithesis of the tranquil Cyrus Smiths and Clawbonnys, ends with the culminating figure of Marcel Camaret. 'His head is too heavy', his eyes gleam with 'an uncertain, dim light', and it is in connection with him that the question arises: 'how short is the distance between a man of genius and a madman?' For the rest, as we have already said, such scientists become subservient to the power of money, represented indifferently by respectable bankers or by the leaders of pirate bands.

As our analysis of Verne's thoughts about the American mirage has shown, his pessimism extends to include the only country which symbolized progress in the first cycle of the *Voyages extraordinaires*, the country which stood at the historical frontier between the 'known worlds' and the 'unknown worlds'. American technology is now shown to have alarming negative aspects, American expansionism threatens the whole world, the American way of life and the American appetite for the power of money become the object of bitter satire. The characters in both *Propeller Island* and *The Mysterious Island* are Americans, but there is a difference of values: the serene absorption of a Cyrus Smith degenerates into an idle opulence, destructive in the end, since the rivalry between the multi-millionaire families of Tankerdon and Coverley leads to the annihilation of their capital, Milliard City.

In fact, all these 'damned' scientists and these cities of perdition come to a tragic end; Robur is struck by lightning during a storm and is swallowed up by the waves; Schultze is killed by the unexpected explosion of one of his carbonic gas shells and Stahlstadt dies with him; Milliard City breaks into pieces when the two rival capitalist clans order the port and starboard engines to work against each other. Blackland has an apocalyptic end, when Camaret becomes completely mad and himself scientifically carries out the explosions which destroy the town section by section.

It is thus the whole of Verne's project which disintegrates and goes off the rails, as Marie-Hélène Huet has shown,[129] through the check of those daring men who challenged the forces of nature. The present no longer opens into the future. Whereas the scientific forecasts in the earlier novels were invariably the result of exact deduction from objective reality, and even sometimes heavily pedantic (*From the Earth to the Moon, Black Diamonds, 20,000 Leagues under the Sea*), we now see even completely irrational entities appearing: the block of magnetic iron at the South Pole (*An Antarctic Mystery*), or the great sea-serpent (*The Tales of Jean-Marie Cabidoulin*), these two being respectively non-scientific replicas of Hatteras' Polar volcano and of the scrupulously careful descriptions of submarine zoology seen through the portholes of *Nautilus*.

The theme of *An Eccentric's Will* is equally significant as a pointer to this deterioration. The characters are no longer anything but pawns in a game, objects tossed through life and space according to the chance fall of the dice.

But this deterioration does not in any way affect the literary value of the *Voyages extraordinaires* nor their creative power. To claim, as some critics too often do, that Verne's later novels are 'boring', that 'he repeats himself' and that his talent is exhausted, is to accept without question the over-simple equation of the *Voyages extraordinaires* with science fiction, for such works as *Carpathian Castle, Propeller Island, For the Flag, The Shipwreck of the 'Jonathan', Yesterday and Tomorrow* and *The Barsac*

Mission have a creative and literary power in no way inferior to Verne's earlier triumphs.

What we see, then, is a state of pessimism concerning the organization of society, the relationship between man and his fellows, in which Verne questions mankind's chances of being able to confront and conquer the forces of nature. This late pessimism, however, converges with another pessimistic current which is already evident in the very first novels, and which thus forms a much more permanent element in Verne's vision of the world: anxiety and nervousness about the future potentialities of the forces of nature.

Cyrus Smith, in a long, philosophical discourse to his friends, wonders about the the problem of the 'thermic death' of the Universe:

> One day our earth will come to an end, or rather it will no longer be able to support animal or vegetable life because of intense cold. . . . In a more or less distant period, the temperate zones will be no more habitable than the Polar regions are today. . . . An immense migration will take place, . . . plants will follow the movement of people. Flora will retreat towards the Equator at the same time as fauna. Now, why should prudent nature not already be preparing in the equatorial regions the foundations of a new continent to serve as a refuge for all the migrating animal and vegetable species? . . . Centuries hence there will be Columbuses who will set out to discover the Islands of Chimborozo, of the Himalayas and of Mont Blanc, the vestiges of a submerged America, or Asia, or Europe. Then at last the new continents will become uninhabitable; their heat will be extinguished like that of a corpse from which the soul has just departed, and all life will disappear from the globe, if not for ever, at least temporarily.

James Starr, the engineer who specializes in the geology of the Carboniferous period, also deals with the problem of the end of the world, but in a rather more light-hearted way (*Black Diamonds*):

> Nature was very farseeing when she made out spheroid principally of sandstone, limestone and granite, which are incombustible. . . . Otherwise the whole earth, up to the last bit, would have been used up in the boilers of steam engines and locomobiles, steamships and gasworks, and certainly our world would have come to an end.

Nemo expresses himself on the same point with his usual bitter incisiveness: 'The earth will one day be a cold corpse. It will become as uninhabitable and as uninhabited as the moon.'

Verne had thus been deeply preoccupied with the future of the natural world even before he became dismayed by that of human society;

invariably, however, he posed the question of the end of the universe in terms of science and nature, without recourse to the intervention of any kind of Divine providence or religious eschatology. On the contrary, he suggests a naturalist eschatology, thereby again emphasizing how far removed he is from Christian religious orthodoxy.

In conjuring up, as Cyrus Smith does, the prospect of climatic changes and geological cataclysms resulting in a radical redistribution of the habitable zones of the earth, one cannot fail to run into the question of lost civilizations, those swallowed up through the play of natural forces. The myth of Atlantis reappears with obsessive regularity throughout the *Voyages extraordinaires*, from *Captain Hatteras* to *The Eternal Adam*. Verne's fascination with this theme may betray an even deeper pessimism than the foregoing analysis has indicated.[130] Dr Clawbonny, philosophizing during the long winter season of *Captain Hatteras* about extinct communities and Polar cosmography, quotes the French astronomer, Bailly,* who held that it was 'precisely here [at the North Pole] that the Atlantides used to live, that well regulated, lost nation of whom Plato speaks.'

In *20,000 Leagues under the Sea*, as Nemo conducts Arronax round the ruins of Atlantis, the scene is set thus:

> ... There, before my eyes ... a ruined city appeared – destroyed, broken up, demolished; despite its broken roofs, its ruined temples, its fallen triumphal arches and its columns lying on the ground, it was still possible to sense the solidity and symmetry of a sort of Tuscan architecture. Further on, some remains of a gigantic aqueduct; here, the raised foundations of an acropolis, with the flowing shape of the Parthenon; there, the remains of quays, as if some ancient port, at the edge of a lost ocean, had once provided haven for merchant shipping as well as for war triremes; further away still, long lines of ruined walls, of wide, deserted streets, a whole Pompeii drowned beneath the waters, and Captain Nemo was bringing it to life again before my eyes! ...
>
> Captain Nemo came towards me and stopped me with a gesture. Then, picking up a piece of chalk-like stone, he walked to a rock of black basalt and traced a single word:
>
> ATLANTIS
>
> What thoughts flashed through my mind! Atlantis, the ancient Meropidos of Theopompus,* the Atlantis of Plato, the continent

---

*Jean Sylvain Bailly, 1736–1793, French astronomer and politician.

*Theopompus, c. 378–323 BC, Greek historian.

'There, before my eyes, a ruined city appeared': Atlantis discovered in *20,000 Leagues under the Sea*.

denied by Origen, Porphyrius, Iamblicus, d'Anville, Malte-Brun, Humboldt,* who considered the story of its disappearance to be nothing but a legendary myth; accepted by Posidonius, Pliny, Ammianus Marcellinus, Tertullian, Engel, Sherer, Tournefort, Buffon, d'Avezac.* It was there in front of my eyes, still showing the unmistakable proofs of its catastrophic end! This, then, was the drowned land which once existed beyond Europe, beyond Lybia, beyond the Pillars of Hercules; this was the home of the powerful nation of the Atlantides with whom the ancient Greeks fought their first wars....

And thus, led by the strangest of destinies, I was treading on one of the mountains of that continent. My hand could touch those ruins, millennia old, contemporary with the geological ages. I was walking where the contemporaries of the first men had walked. I was crushing under the heavy soles of my boots the bones of animals which had lives in time immemorial and had sought shade beneath these trees, now turned into fossils!

Oh, how I wished I had more time! I would have liked to walk down the steep sides of that mountain, to explore the whole of that immense continent which must once have been a bridge between Africa and America, and to visit its great antediluvian cities. There, perhaps, under my very eyes, lay the warlike Makhimos, and the pious city of Eusebius, whose gigantic inhabitants lived for whole centuries, and certainly had strength enough to pile up those blocks of stone which still stand despite the action of the waters. One day, perhaps, some volcanic phenomenon will raise these drowned ruins once again above the water....

While I stood thus dreaming and trying to fix in my memory all the details of that grandiose landscape, Captain Nemo, his elbow propped against a mossy stele, stood motionless and as if petrified in a silent ecstasy. Was he thinking about those lost generations, and seeking from them the secret of human destiny? Was it here that this strange man came to reinvigorate himself in memories of

---

*Origen, c. 183–c. 253, Alexandrian theologian and scientist; Porphyrius, 234–305, Syrian neo-Platonic philosopher; Iamblicus, c. 250–330, Greek neo-Platonic philosopher who taught at Apamea; Jean-Baptiste Bourguigon d'Anville, 1697–1782, French geographer; Konrat Malte-Brun, 1775–1826, Danish geographer; Alexander von Humboldt, 1769–1859, German explorer.

*Posidonius, c. 135–c. 50 BC, Greek writer; Pliny the Elder, 23–79, Roman naturalist and writer; Ammianus Marcellinus, c. 330–c. 400, Latin historian of Greek origin; Tertullian, c. 155–c. 220, Carthage-born theologian and apologist; Joseph Pitton de Tournefort, 1656–1708, French botanist; Georges Louis Leclerc, Comte de Buffon, 1707–88, French naturalist and author of *Histoire naturelle* in 36 volumes; Marie-Armand-Pascal d'Avezac de Castera-Macaya, 1800–75, French geographer, head of the archives of the Ministère de la Marine.

history, and to relive that ancient civilization, he who had rejected modern life?

When the ridiculous Thomson Agency cruise ship passes close to the Balearic Islands and the Azores this is the opportunity for Verne's 'off stage' voice to remark, on a serious and romantic note which contrasts with the facile, playful nature of the rest of *Thomson & Co.*:

> Ships have replaced ploughs. Except for the highest mountain tops, everything has collapsed into unfathomable abysses, everything has disappeared under the waves, towns, buildings, people, and none ever returned to tell his brothers about the frightful catastrophe.
>
> On that mystery of life, of passion and of suffering, the sea now extends its impenetrable shroud as if over an immense tomb.

It is Atlantis again which provides the clue of the philosophical tale, *The Eternal Adam*, a posthumous work which has often been regarded as Verne's political testament. A scientist and statesman, the *zartog* Sofr Aï-Sr, is the leader of a highly civilized human society very far in the future. He is haunted by the problem of progress, and orders archaeological digs to prove the continuity and the irreversible character of the evolution of the natural and biological world. The excavations finally reach what is thought to be primordial mud, and reveal the remains of a very ancient civilization. His theory is proved wrong:

> There were bits of human bones together with fragments of weapons or machines, shards of pottery, scraps of inscriptions in an unknown language, delicately cut hard stones, sometimes carved in the form of statues that were almost intact. . . . The logical implication of all these objects is that about 40,000 years earlier, that is to say 20,000 years before the moment when the first representatives of the contemporary race of men arose, we know not where nor how, people were already living in this same region and had achieved a very advanced state of civilization.

For a long time the *zartog* refuses to believe the evidence, until he happens by chance upon a record left by the survivors of a planetary cataclysm in the twenty-first century. Having escaped a tidal wave that submerged all inhabited land, they had taken refuge on a continent which rose where the Atlantic Ocean had been:

> Half hidden in lava, at the latitude of the Azores, we found the evidence of human activity – but not the work of the inhabitants of the Azores, our recent contemporaries. There was the debris of pillars and pottery such as we had never seen. Doctor Moreno suggested that there ruins must come from ancient Atlantis, and that the flow of volcanic lava had brought them back to light.

> Doctor Moreno may be right. The legendary Atlantis, if in fact it ever existed, would have occupied more or less the area of the new continent. In that case, we would be faced with the extraordinary fact that three human societies, not linked by descent, had succeeded each other in the same region.

Forty thousand years thus separate the Atlantides from the civilization of the Andart Iten-Schu, the enlightened people of whom the *zartog* is the leader:

> It was doubtless the Atlantides of whose civilization Sofr's excavation had enabled the recovery of some barely perceptible vestiges from underneath the marine deposits. To what knowledge of the truth had that ancient nation attained when it was swept off the earth by the invading waters?

Sofr's comfortable convictions cannot stand up to this setback. He had been convinced that the irreversible evolution towards ever greater progress was the law both for the world of nature and for human society. All the animal and vegetable species known to the Andart Iten-Schu and studied by them, apart from some inexplicable exceptions, seemed to have developed from certain very simple marine animals and plants. The Andart themselves, after thousands of years of tribal wars and primitive life, and gradually evolved into three nations, and these in their turn had coalesced into one harmonious human community, mistress of its own destiny:

> Man had learnt to live by his brain, and no longer by his body alone; instead of wearing himself out in stupid wars, he had begun to think – and that is why, during the two last centuries, mankind had moved with ever-increasing speed towards the acquisition of knowledge and the domestication of matter.

But the manuscript left by the survivors of the tidal wave relates a totally different process, namely an almost animal regression which they were powerless to withstand:

> Our thinking life is gone.... At the beginning of our stay here, some of us started to build houses. These unfinished buildings are now falling in ruins. We all sleep on the ground at all seasons.... For a long time now, none of us has had any clothes to cover us. For some years we did what we could to replace them, using seaweed cleverly woven together, but then they became rougher, and finally we got tired of this effort which the mildness of the climate made unnecessary; now we live naked like those whom we used to call savages.
>
> Food, food, that is our perpetual object, we think about nothing else.... I think I can see them, those men of the future: articulate

language forgotten, intellect dead, bodies covered with rough hair, wandering around in this ghastly desert.

The Saint-Simonian theme of the 'domestication of nature', which had dominated the early books of the *Voyages extraordinaires*, thus returns for the last time in Verne's universe. But it is through an admission of failure. Whether or not he was consciously influenced by Nietzsche, as some have supposed,[131] it is clear that Verne had arrived at the idea of an 'eternal return':

> Would the day ever come when man, having finished climbing the slope, could rest on the conquered summit? . . . Bloody with the innumerable wounds endured before him by all that had lived, crushed under the accumulated weight of those fruitless struggles during infinities of time, the *zartog* Sofr Aï-Sr was slowly and painfully coming to the intimate conviction that all things are eternally renewed.

CHAPTER XII

A political interpretation of Jules Verne

The series of the *Voyages extraordinaires* covers an astonishingly wide field of historico-geography. From the mercantilism of the British Hudson's Bay Company to the Moslem rebellion in Kashgaria or the British expedition against Herat, from the Portuguese slave trade in the Congo to the anti-German movement in Livonia, from the Taiping rebellion to the struggles of the Hungarian, Transylvanian and Bulgarian nationalists, from the sale of Russian America to the Indian Mutiny, from the Maori insurrection to the Irish nationalist movement, from the Greek war of independence to the American Civil War, from the Senussi troubles to the division of the Magellan territories, the whole history of nineteenth-century people's movements and political crises lives again in the pages of *Known and Unknown Worlds*. The table of historical events that figure in Verne's novels (*cf.* p. 8–10) shows in fact very few lacunae in relation to the actualities of nineteenth-century history taken as a whole. There is nothing about the Maiji restoration in Japan, about the partition of South-East Asia, or the American penetration into Hawaii; nothing about the British invasion of Egypt and Black Africa; nothing about German and Italian unification, or about the Mexican War.

Jules Verne the Celt was not much interested in the Latin countries, and the ambiguity of his attitudes about colonial peoples (*cf.* Chapter VI) made him too uneasy to set his novels in the framework of colonial conquest or colonial régimes properly so called (with the one exception of India where the Mutiny provided him with a fascinating counterpoint). But the brevity of the list given above serves only to emphasize Verne's remarkable familiarity with all areas of political tension upon the planet, especially during the second half of the nineteenth century.

The second sub-title of Verne's cycle, *Mondes connus et inconnus*, is just as significant as the first, *Voyages extraordinaires*; it puts the accent not so much upon travel, adventure and unusual happenings, but upon man's desires to escape from the reality surrounding him, or rather, to go beyond it by means of the potentialities within it. For there is no rigid frontier between the known and unknown worlds, and in many books of the series this point is skilfully and intentionally left vague. In some cases this passing beyond reality is achieved through scientific anticipation, and Verne fully deserves his reputation as a science-fiction author. But, like H. G. Wells, for example, he is just as much a writer of 'political-fiction'. He is quite as ready to invent political and social perspectives opening before mankind, as the future developments of science and technology. Even if this aspect of his writings is much less frequently noted than their 'science-fiction' character, they belong actually to that very modern type of writing which Karel Capek,* for instance, has made famous with *The Salamander War*, or Robert Merle with his *An Animal endowed with Reason*.

The last of Verne's novels, *The Barsac Mission*, is the richest and most polished of his political-fiction writings, with its analysis of the power structure in a rebel society and its strict hierarchy of Counsellors, Merry Fellows and the Civil Body, the confrontation of the Palace and the Factory, the pitiless exploitation of both the white labourers and the black workers by a futurist despot with immense scientific powers. The rebellion which eventually sweeps Blackland away is based upon a political and military alliance between the coloured people (the Negro slaves organized by Sergeant Tongané) and the Western industrial proletariat (the labourers who remain faithful to Camaret), an extremely modern vision foreshadowing a political problem which is of capital importance to the whole political future of the twentieth century.

Long before *Barsac*, however, this 'political-fiction' character was sketched in many others of Verne's novels. In *Upside Down*, which was composed towards the end of his life, at the time when the Hague peace conferences were seeking to slow down the armaments race, it is an international conference which strives to allot the Polar regions by adjudication; in the end the winner is a big capitalist American company, the North Polar Practical Association. In *The Hunt for the Meteor*, another international conference has the task of deciding the ownership of a meteor of pure gold which has fallen on the earth. In *Propeller Island*, the whole book, and not just an individual episode, is a political-fiction. The artificial society of very wealthy passengers on Standard Island and in its capital, Milliard City, appears like an imaginary extension of the political and social structures characteristic of large-scale American capitalism at the end of the nineteenth century, not only in regard to the way of life of the ruling classes, but also in respect of the 'big stick' policy of expansion: the star-spangled banner is imagined by Verne as flying at that time over Canada, Mexico and the countries of Central America. Thus the book deals with an imaginary future, but nevertheless very

---

*Karel Capek, 1890–1938, Czech dramatist and novelist.

close, very possible, and of which Verne himself declared in a letter to his brother Paul that it was a continuation of *present customs and facts*:

> I think that the second volume of *Propeller Island* will be much more interesting than the first because of its humorous character! Everything in it will be related to existing customs and facts, but I am a novelist first and foremost, and my books will always have *the appearance* [the italics are mine – J.C.] of being fiction.¹³²

These political-fiction novels belong to Verne's late period, and this is not fortuitous. As his work developed, Verne showed himself to be more and more sensitive to political problems, but *The Begum's Fortune* which has already been mentioned so often that there is no need for another description, is eminently a novel of political-fiction, perhaps the best ever produced in the nineteenth century. *Black Diamonds*, with its community living in gigantic caverns and exploiting the subterranean coal deposits in an atmosphere of social harmony and joy in work, is also an exercise in political-fiction. The same can be said of an early novel, *The Children of Captain Grant*, the political setting of which is the Scottish nationalist movement, the yearning of the Scots to be separated from England. This aspiration is to be realized through the founding of an independent Scottish colony somewhere in the world – a dodge very typical of Verne's planetary outlook and his Saint-Simonian ideas about colonization; Captain Grant hopes that the old Scotland will be reborn by this expedient:

> He resolved to found a vast Scottish colony in one of the continents of Oceania. Did he dream of a future independence after the example of the United States, an independence which India and Australia could not fail to achieve one day? . . .

Captain Grant talks about the same plan when, at the end of the novel, he is found on the island of Tabor. He expresses regret that the latter is too small

> for the founding of the colony in the Pacific which I would like to present to Scotland. Our brothers in old Caledonia, all those who are suffering, must have a refuge against poverty, a new land. Our dear Fatherland must have a colony in these seas which belongs to her, to her alone, where she may find that freedom and well-being which she lacks in Europe.

The 'identi-kit' picture we have tried to draw of Verne's political ideas – or rather, of the ideas objectively underlying the whole series of the

Voyages extraordinaires – namely the 1848 tradition, the echo of utopian socialism, and libertarian individualism, has been built up with the help of indications dispersed throughout his works, from the earliest novels to those published after his death. Our study of his view of colonial peoples, or of the relations he establishes between nationalism and internationalism, has led us to recognize a consistency in both cases. The coexistence of the conceptions of the 'good savage' and the 'bad savage' is proved by a comparison between *Captain Grant* and *Five Weeks in a Balloon*, written in 1863 and 1868 respectively, and it is to be found more or less unchanged in Verne's late novels. The signs of anti-British or anti-German chauvinism are just as clear from one end of the Verne series to the other, while appeals to internationalism appear from the earliest novels (Michael Zorn, Dr Clawbonny), to be repeated with equal clarity in late works like *Travelling Scholarships*. The worship of gold, first arraigned in *Five Weeks in a Balloon*, is still being denounced in *The Volcano of Gold, The Hunt for the Meteor* and '*Jonathan*'. Long before *The Eternal Adam* and the *zartog* Sofr Aï-Sr, Captain Nemo meditated over the ruins of Atlantis.

There are some themes, however, which make their appearance progressively, or even at a late stage in the cycle of the *Known and Unknown Worlds*, such as the subordination of science to money (*cf.* Chapter X), the American peril (*cf.* Chapter IX), the debasement of human societies and the perversion of science (*cf.* Chapter XI). It is the Vernean 'project' as a whole that goes off the rails, the Saint-Simonian dream of the direct domination of nature. From the years 1880–90 Verne is face to face with the hard political realities of his time, whereas he had largely excluded them from the earlier *Voyages extraordinaires*. 'His work was invaded by the present,' declares Mlle Huet in her thesis on Verne;[133] she also notes as an example that it was at this time that Verne showed increasing sensitivity to the struggles for national independence (the Irish, the Indians, etc.). Nevertheless, it seems insufficient to attribute this development to the war of 1870, as has sometimes been done. Verne does not appear to have suffered particularly traumatic effects as the result of the war,[134] and it would be wrong to speak of an awakening of national consciousness in him under the effect of the defeat of France at the hands of Prussia. We prefer to relate this change to a change in the world itself.

The transition to imperialism (the armaments race and the struggles over partition of the world, the increasing subordination of large-scale industry, itself in rapid evolution, to the power of finance) seems to us to provide a much richer frame of reference for explaining the debasement of Verne's initial project, especially if we add to it the reactions provoked by the economic crisis.

In an attempt to define more clearly the deeper meaning of the *Voyages extraordinaires*, some critics have suggested recourse to 'archetypes':

> Verne's fantastic conceptions have roots reaching far back into the most distant mythologies. . . . Just as M. Jourdain used prose without knowing he was doing so, as we breathe the air without thinking about it, so do archetypes polarize the currents of imagination without one's being in the least conscious of it. . . . Verne's genius lay in the fact that he was able, instinctively and without volition, to conjure up some of the greatest archetypes. . . . The great modern adventure stories are transpositions into the secular mode of the ancient religious epics.[135]

That is to say that Verne, without always being aware of the fact, was able to tap such traditional literary themes as the journey of initiation, the blessed city, the lone rebel defying society, the chthonian powers, which are all quasi-timeless and mystical elements of universal literature. The presence of these 'archetypes' is probably not directly conditioned by his particular personality, by his social ego, although it is their presence which permits his work to transcend the facile achievements of science-fiction and stories for children. These ideas have been developed principally by Michel Carrouges (the vulcanian archetypes, the search for a father, etc.), by M. Cellier and S. Vierne (journeys of initiation); they serve more generally as a working hypothesis in the comprehensive research by S. Vierne into Verne's great romantic themes. Must we equally use the theory of archetypes to explain the recurrence, throughout the *Voyages extraordinaires*, of a certain number of very characteristic political themes which we have tried to identify in our present study?

Research into the archetypes that exist in Verne's writings has the unquestionable merit of placing the discussion at once on a high level of literary criticism – a treatment which the *Known and Unknown Worlds* assuredly deserve. At that level of generality and comparative thought, there is no doubt that some of Verne's favourite political themes can be related to myths which are common to the literature of all ages: the image of the demiurge as man, the dream of a perfect society, the rejection of social constraints and conventions, the hope of universal peace, the fascination of riches and the acute consciousness of their worthlessness. It would clearly be possible to place Cyrus Smith in the line of descent from Gilgamesh or Hercules, to recall Plato or Thomas More in relation to Franceville, to link Axel and Liddenbrock with the Arthurian tradition of the initiatory quest for the Holy Grail, to compare Nemo to the outlaws of Sherwood Forest or those in the marshes of Liangshanpo. One might link Verne's images of gold (we have noted above how rich and varied they are) with a whole series of impressive ancestors: Jason and the Golden Fleece, the Golden Calf of the

Israelites, the Rhinegold and the Nibelungen, the treasures of Ophir and Golconda in Arab tradition, Marco Polo and the inexhaustible wealth of Cathay, the vision of Eldorado which sustained the rough, unlettered soldiers of Pizarro.

Even the theme of the 'extraordinary journey' through 'known and unknown worlds' lends itself admirably to this kind of literary comparison: Ulysses, Sinbad the Sailor and the pilgrim-monkey (*Xiyouji*), Robinson Crusoe, Gulliver, Goethe's *Wanderjahre*, etc. Verne's particular political sensitivity, to the extent that it gave birth to a literary creation of huge dimension, could not fail to rediscover many of the great social themes cultivated by earlier generations. But isn't Verne's political thinking finally nothing more than a reflection of that 'collective subconscious' which Jung described in his theory of archetypes? Is it only a new formulation of a timeless tradition to which mankind tirelessly seeks to return, through a series of archetypes almost as immutable as the combination of the genes which give biological shape to each individual once and for all?

Just as disconcerting, and just as inadequate to the singular reality of Verne's work, are certain recent attempts to give it a structuralist interpretation inspired by linguistic experience and favouring the facts of language, an interpretation which claims nevertheless from the outset to deal with *pluralities*. According to this, Verne's writings become a system of signs and ciphers lacking any specific character. In his analysis of *The Mysterious Island*, Roland Barthes[136] declares that 'the engineer's power to effect changes is a verbal power', that an engineer is 'a singer of labour', a reader of signs and an interpreter provided with a very efficient 'transformation code'. What matters is what he says and 'the function of science is only to keep him on the right lines'. This interpretation of *The Mysterious Island* by Barthes fails even to take into account (except for a vague reference to 'contemporary metaphors') the extraordinary 'leap forward' that the industrial revolution in the west signified. We, on the contrary, have sought to establish that Verne's engineers are an integral part of the Saint-Simonian utopian cycle, of which *The Mysterious Island* is the direct expression, in the tradition of Saint-Simon's 'parables'.

There is indeed a relationship between language and society, but it is the inverse of what Barthes suggests. Barthes has recognized the importance of colonization in this novel, but he treats it as no more than a 'sub-code of the adamic theme'. Colonization, contrary to that which gives it real meaning in the Vernean universe, is here cut off from all links with its historico-political background. It becomes no more than a variant, among so many others, of mankind's eternal 'adamic' and 'edenic' quest for a perfect society. Barthes' indifference to the realities of politics and history is to be seen, however, not only in relation to Verne; his 'adamic' interpretation of *Robinson Crusoe* runs quite counter to recent work which seeks on the contrary to link the *Robinson* image to the economic and ideological debates in England during the seventeenth and eighteenth centuries: the transition from mercantilism to capitalism, the questioning of the source of economic values, etc.

Michel Serres, more systematically still, has sought to reduce to their 'basic structure' novels like *Black Diamonds* or *Michael Strogoff*, thus once again denying them any historical or political relevance.[137] In the one case, everything is supposed to stem from the idea of 'depth', and in the other from that of the courier-messenger. Around such central themes is woven a composite series of cultural references: *Exodus* and the *Odyssey* when it is a question of travel, Plato's cave whenever a cavern is found, while Carmel and Saint John of the Cross form the echo to any mystic events. But why leave out the Scandinavian sagas, the caverns of the *Arabian Nights*, or Swedenborg* and Blake! Michel Serres enjoys this game of intellectual interpretation, which is after all quite amusing. In fact, he says so himself:

> There is a fantastic formalism, an imaginary abstraction, an oneiric mathematics, into which the unreason of so-called rationalists can slip, the latent obsessions of minds overburdened by theory can insinuate themselves and logic gone mad can slink.

Thus, the oneiric reading, through the world of Jules Verne, is shamelessly substituted for the actual interpretation of Verne's works.

This oneiric reading fails once again to take into account the links binding Verne to his own times. To take the literary links first: the fact that Verne was attracted by 'secret and accursed things' (the title of a fine chapter in Jean Cassou's* *1848*) is neither fortuitous nor casual. It stems from the neo-mystic and neo-gnostic current of the 'second romanticism' (from Swedenborg and Ballanche* to Villiers de L'Isle-Adam* by way of Victor Hugo and George Sand).

Then, particularly, the historical links: the gigantic coal mine worked by the cavern-dwelling miners of New Aberfoyle is in fact much closer to the Saint-Simonian idea of a bee-hive than to Plato's myth; it is a centre of economic production. Serres, indeed, came very close to making this comparison when he read the name of the coal mine, New ABErfoYLE, as the word 'abeille' [bee] slightly deformed and interrupted by the anagram of the name of the Ford family who live in the

---

*Emanuel Swedenborg, 1688–1772, Swedish scientist and philosopher, as well as investigator of the supernatural.

*Jean Cassou, b. 1897, French writer and art critic.

*Pierre Simon Ballanche, 1773–1847, French writer, and precursor of Romanticism.

*Auguste, Comte de Villiers de L'Isle-Adam, 1838–1889, French romantic and mystical writer.

mine. For him, however, this explanation is no more than an echo of a society organized on traditional Platonic lines, whereas Saint-Simon's parable of the bees and the hornets cannot, in this context, fail to cross the mind of anyone who has not decided systematically to ignore the links that bind Verne to his own times.

Another example will illustrate our protest against so many attempts to mutilate Verne by isolating him from his times, under the pretext of lifting him into the more sublimated world of archetypes and structures. Serres, himself an eminent specialist in the history of science and technology, declares that *Black Diamonds* is 'an alchemy of four elements': the earth and the subsoil, lakes and lochs, the air-space of caves, fire produced from coal. At the end of the novel, the industrious cave community just escapes a catastrophe, an explosion resulting from that 'tetragon of elements'. For Verne, however, the combination of the four elements is not static, as, for instance, in Greek mythology or the Bible, but dynamic in the nineteenth century, energy was transformed by the laws of thermodynamics. Verne's 'tetragon of elements' may have its roots in the timeless depths of the unconscious, but only in order to emerge in the shape of the chemistry of coal, i.e., in response to the concrete needs of the industrial revolution – to which we always return.

Our political analysis of the *Voyages extraordinaires* has in fact led us constantly to dwell on the presence, the omnipresence of the nineteenth century in Verne's writings – they are a product of their times. They pose the problems of the times and they attempt to provide a solution. It is a fairly contradictory solution, however, since Verne, as a man of the nineteenth century, was in the end incapable of deciding between Destiny and Providence, anti-Negro racism and sympathy for colonial peoples, nationalism and internationalism, the American mirage and the American danger, the fascination of gold and the awareness of its worthlessness. It is no doubt tempting – and Verne is worthy of the effort – to link his work with some of the great myths of the literature of all ages. But it is no less important to recognize in his work some of the powerful lines of thought in the nineteenth century: sensitivity to popular movements, the Saint-Simonian ideal of the control of nature, admiration for independence, faith in science, acute awareness of the futility of many social conventions. That is the Verne an 'project', even if, after 1880–90, it progressively loses its force and finally breaks up altogether.

Historians of the modern epoch may well find it banal of us to insist upon placing a work of literature in the framework of its own times. It is rather a truism to define the works of Stendhal or Balzac, of Dickens or Zola as links with the great problems of Western society in the nineteenth century, but recent studies of Verne's works tend in so different a direction, that this reminder has seemed necessary.

Does the reading of the *Voyages extraordinaires* which has been outlined in this book enables us to penetrate the personal political thinking of Jules Verne, to decipher his 'political secrets'? That was our point of departure some years ago.[138] Now that we are approaching the end of our own journey, this seems to have become somewhat difficult. His political thinking, or at least what we know of it from his letters, the statements of his contemporaries and the activities of his public life, is rather vague, if not contradictory. He was aware of this. He was fond of saying that he was 'the most unknown of men' (letter to Turiello of 10 April 1895). Moreover, his intentionally ambiguous position in politics is made clear in a cautious declaration he puts into the mouth of a soldier from Picardy during the wars of the French Revolution (*Flight to France*):

> My friends understand me not at all, or at least so little as to amount to nothing. First one stated that I had belonged to the Right, when it was the Left; then the other said it was the Left, when in fact it was the Right.

In the end there was nothing of the 'hidden progressive' in Verne, even if his eclectic relationships with Leftists (such as the Reclus brothers) served to temper his basically moderate anti-Dreyfus and anti-*communard* views. Rather, he is a lone, non-conformist Conservative like Kamylk Pasha, whose description in *Master Antifer* (*cf.* Chapter V above) a self-portrait of Verne, not only on the psychological and emotional levels, but on the political level as well. Kamylk Pasha. By remaining faithful to Constantinople, cuts himself off from the Arab nationalist movements in Syria and Egypt, draws down upon himself the wrath of Mehmet Ali, and thus risks his property and life. The progressive study of Verne's personal papers may one day perhaps allow us to relate him to the other solitary figures of the nineteenth century, the other 'intractable reactionaries' such as Gobineau[139] or Villiers de L'Isle-Adam.[140]

Finally, a novel such as *Family without a Name*, which has often been neglected and considered to be marginal, 'not particularly interesting', is of great significance as a pointer to the secret trends in the author's political temperament. The case of the French Canadians allows Verne to give free rein simultaneously to two apparently contradictory propensities in his political and social thinking. As a Breton, a Catholic and a Conservative he feels very close to the peasantry of Quebec. He quotes with obvious satisfaction those nineteenth-century authors who describe French Canada as 'a France from the olden days when the *fleur de lys* flew over it,' or as

> A refuge for the *ancien régime*, like Brittany or La Vendée sixty years ago, stretching away on the other side of the ocean. On that American continent, the inhabitants have preserved with jealous

care the habits of mind, the naïve beliefs and the superstitions of their fathers.

The word 'Vendée' does not figure here accidentally: in his youth, Verne had written a romantic tale about the Royalist insurrection of 1793, *The Marquis of Chantelaine*; he still had friends among the small country squires of Western France. But the French Canadians whom Verne regards as the heirs of ancient France and of the Celtic soul, are also rebels, people who defy law and order, the police and the army. They are, moreover, friendly towards the young American Republic, i.e. towards the most modern and most futurist society of the nineteenth century. *Family without a Name* stands precisely at the crossroads of the basic lines of thought in the *Voyages extraordinaires*, and helps us to come closer to the apparent paradox of a Jules Verne who is both a traditionalist and a friend of rebels and insurgents, both Conservative and non-conformist.

Thus it is not possible in any schematic way to describe Verne's private political thinking (if indeed this existed at all at the level of full consciousness). The *Voyages extraordinaires* cannot be defined either as the direct reflection of a Vernean political system, or as its transposition into the negative, like the 'Left backlash' of conservative bourgeois thought in the nineteenth century. At the end of our analysis, it is equally impossible to reduce to a single formula both 'the man' and 'his work', or to establish any automatic relationship between them. If we have in many cases been led to attribute to Verne as an individual certain characteristics suggested by the text, this is merely by stylistic convention.

Indeed we are much too ignorant of the motives which might have led Verne to slant one of his novels in this or that political direction, or of the political opinion he might have held about any of his works. It does seem clear that he was fascinated and worried at the same time about the possible political implications of his works. When Hetzel entrusted him with Pascal Grousset's manuscript, to rewrite it under his own name, he hesitated before finally accepting the task which was to result in *The Begum's Fortune*. He was perfectly conscious of the *political* interest of the subject:

> I could see that the author had attempted to deal with certain political and philosophical questions. In my opinion, however, that was what he had tried to do, but had not done.[141]

On the other hand, he firmly refused to give any shade of political colour to the character of Captain Nemo, the very one of his heroes whose political significance seems most obvious to us today:

> I do not want this book to have any political colour ... the reader may think what he likes according to his temperament.... I definitely do not want to indulge in politics, a thing for which I have little aptitude, and politics has no place in the book anyway.... Our hero becomes a dispenser of justice only through the force of circumstances.[142]

The fact that we can find no definite, automatic link between Verne's novels and the author's conception of the world, is also the result of the method he used in writing them. We have little information on his working habits, but enough to say that his work was fairly far from being dictated by a sudden, strong inspiration, fairly far from taking on its final shape straight away. Specialists – provided sufficient documentary material becomes available – will one day slog away in an attempt to establish minutely which ideas are Verne's own, and which were borrowed elsewhere (or borrowed by others on his behalf). He himself made no secret of the fact that he took his material where he found it, and that he had no objection to writing imitations or 'sequels'. He writes 'like' Dickens in *The Green Ray*; like Erckmann-Chatrian in *Flight to France*; like Hoffmann* in *Carpathian Castle* or *Master Zacharius*; like Jack London in *The Volcano of Gold*. In *Mathias Sandorf* his inspiration comes from Dumas' *Monte-Cristo*; he even confirms the fact by a dedication to the younger Dumas. *Second Fatherland* and *An Antarctic Mystery* were explicitly written as sequels respectively to Wyss' *Swiss Family Robinson* and Edgar Allan Poe's *Arthur Gordon Pym*. So much for direct borrowing from books already published. His working methods, however, led him also to incorporate into his novels elements suggested to him by his friends and relations. Three names stand out in this context, and perhaps it will become possible to add others in future: Hetzel, Grousset and Michel Verne.

Verne's relationship with his publisher was a very close one, and he was happy to accept the latter's advice and criticism; he had no hesitation in making extensive alterations in certain manuscripts. The correspondence between Hetzel and Verne shows, for example, that a real 'negotiation' took place between them in the matter of Captain Nemo's political identity. Hetzel thought that Nemo's actions could best be justified by attributing them to his fight against slavery, but Verne refused: he insisted that Nemo should sink the English ship simply because he has been provoked. Verne wrote:

> You have told me that the abolition of slavery is the most important economic fact of our time. I agree. But in my opinion, that has

---

*E. T. A. Hoffmann, 1776–1822, German imaginative writer.

nothing to do with the present case. I was pleased with the forceful conciseness of the John Brown incident, but I think it rather diminishes the captain.

A little later, when the novel was nearly finished, he declared:

> If I am not to explain his hatred, then I must either be silent about its cause as about all the rest of my hero's past, his nationality, etc., or if necessary I must alter the dénouement.

Verne then made a counter-proposal: turn Nemo into a Polish nobleman

> whose daughters have been raped, his wife hacked to pieces with an axe, his father beaten to death, a Pole whose friends have all perished in Siberia, and whose nationality is about to disappear under Russian tyranny.[143]

Then it was Hetzel's turn to refuse, for fear of reducing the sale of his books in Russia, and Nemo does not finally receive a national identity until several years later, in the last chapters of *The Mysterious Island*.

The possible influence exerted by Grousset on Verne has also been the subject of much discussion. The two men certainly were not close friends, but both of them collaborated in the production of Hetzel's *Education Magazine*. Grousset knew that it was Verne who had re-written and published under his own name the two manuscripts which were to be known as *The Begum's Fortune* and *The Southern Star Mystery*. In 1885 both authors put their names to *The Wreck of the 'Cynthia'*, a novel which would doubtless have been considered as purely Vernean, had it been officially included in the *Voyages extraordinaires*. The theory that Grousset, who had been one of the leaders of the *Commune* and a Deputy of the extreme Left during the Third Republic, had acted as a sort of 'Left-wing' double for Verne, his Dr Jekyll (or his Mr Hyde, according to the point of view), is enjoying a certain vogue at present; but such documents as are available do not allow us to go as far as that. Nevertheless, Grousset's influence in the production of a certain number of Verne's works was far from negligible.

It seems that this was also the case with the author's own son, Michel Verne. Though no serious study has been devoted to him, he is known to have participated in the composition of some of the texts while his father was still alive. Did he re-write, if indeed he had not written them in the first place, important sections of Verne's later novels, and precisely those which are often of the greatest political interest: *The Survivors of the 'Jonathan'*, *The Barsac Mission* and *The Hunt for the Meteor*, etc.? This is not the place to discuss the thorny question of the authenticity of Verne's posthumous novels. *Grammatici certant*. Marcel Moré and Mme S. Vierne are on the side of authenticity, which E. M. Marucci, for instance, tends to question; these problems have been discussed at length in both the old and the new series of the *Bulletin de la Société Jules Verne*. Rather than accusing Michel Verne of being less than conscientious in his duties as his father's heir and of making easy money by hastily writing books and pretending that the texts were those of his illustrious deceased father, would it not be preferable to consider the possibility that the son, then in the strength of his maturity, had exerted an intellectual and political influence over a writer who was already growing old and who was attached to him by the bonds of a lively affection? It seems likely that it was a real influence, particularly in the case of the late novels of the *Voyages extraordinaires*, although this does not mean in any way that Verne would not have looked upon them as entirely his own once they were finished.

Such borrowings, influences and experiments are the concern of specialists in literary history in the technical sense of the term, but they do not basically alter our opinion regarding Verne's writings as they have come down to us in their final form. In the end, our Nemo turns out to be neither an anti-slavery champion, nor a Polish prince, but an implacably defiant character, the embodiment at one and the same time of the '48 dream of liberty for all peoples, the anti-colonialist struggle, and the libertarian rejection of all authority.

'The reader may think what he likes according to his temperament.' When Verne explained in these terms his hesitation to make a political figure out of Nemo, was he not inviting us to a very different reading, an *autonomous* reading? We read Verne at a distance of a hundred years; our point of view is very different from that of his contemporaries, our perceptions are far removed from those with which the author himself looked upon his work and his times. Our tastes and our judgments are formed by all that is best and worst in the twentieth century: the rising tide of popular struggles in the third world and the revolution in science and technology, the cancerous growth of the American megamachine and the increasing defiance of authority, the responsibilities of the scientist and his dependent status, the setbacks to the creation of an international inter-state society and the prospect of an irreversible deterioration in our natural ecological surroundings, the artificial exploits of the cosmonaut *supermen* and their ridiculous inadequacy in face of the true aspirations of simple people, the vicissitudes of model political societies and the stubborn search for new solutions.

If Jules Verne and his *Voyages extraordinaires* are still alive for us, it is because they – and with them the whole of that fascinating nineteenth century – were already posing the problems which the twentieth century has not been, and will not be, able to avoid.

NOTES TO THE TEXT

Chapter I

1. V. Marguerite, *Aristide Briand*, p. 20.
2. It is unnecessary to recall Jules Verne's biography here. *Cf.* the study by his niece, Mme Allotte de La Fuÿe, of which the 'orthodox' tone is very revealing about Verne's social and family circles, but which was based on many family records: *Jules Verne, sa vie, son œuvre*, Paris 1928. *Cf.* also the study by B. Franck, *Jules Verne et ses voyages*, Paris 1941.
3. Mme Allotte de La Fuÿe, *op. cit.*, p. 94.
4. Mme Allotte de La Fuÿe, *op. cit.*, p. 139.
5. Letter to Hetzel, 1871.
6. Undated letter to Hetzel (filed under 1874, probably in error).
7. Letter dated 11 February 1899.
8. Letter dated 30 November 1898 (*Bulletin de la Société Jules Verne*, August 1936, no. 4).
9. Letter dated 29 December 1898.
10. Letter to Turiello, 17 May 1904.
11. Letter dated 10 July 1899.
12. *Le très curieux Jules Verne*, pp. 101–103: 'Towards 1888, he became more and more interested in politics, and even in revolutionary politics.' According to Moré, his candidacy revealed 'political opinions which the creator of Captain Nemo held, but which had been kept secret until the moment for their expression'.
13. Mme Allotte de La Fuÿe, *op. cit.*, pp. 181–182.
14. Letter dated 20 February 1896.
15. Letter to Hetzel's son, 1897.
16. Reply by M. Jules Verne to M. Gustave Dubois, *Mémoires de l'Académie d'Amiens*, 1875, pp. 103–112.
17. Prize-day speech at Amiens, 29 July 1893.
18. This point was carefully noted by G. de Diesbach, *Le Tour de Jules Verne en 80 livres*, chapter IV, 'Les loyaux serviteurs'. Almost two centuries after the night of 4 August, the nobility retains an unusual sensitivity regarding all that separates it from the bourgeoisie.
19. Letter dated 25 May 1902 (*Bulletin de la Société Jules Verne*, August 1936, no. 4).
20. Letter dated 5 November 1897.
21. Letter dated 18 January 1897.
22. Letter dated 10 April 1895.
23. Mme Allotte de La Fuÿe, *op. cit.*, p. 188.
24. Reproduced in a special number of *Arts et Lettres* devoted to Jules Verne, 1948, no. 15.
25. Still current practice, for example, in the Soviet Union; there it is the state publisher of children's literature which has published the interesting work of literary criticism by Eugene Brandis, one of the better Soviet writers on Jules Verne.
26. Letter from R. Roussel in 1921, quoted in *Arts et Lettres*, no. 15.

27 'Le Point suprême et l'âge d'or à travers quelques œuvres de Jules Verne', *Répertoire I*.
28 'Le mythe de Vulcain chez Jules Verne', *Arts et Lettres*, 1948, no. 15.
29 M. Cellier, 'Les Thèmes initiatiques chez les romantiques', *Cahiers internationaux du symbolisme*, 1964, no. 3; M. Brion, 'Le Voyage initiatique', *L'Arc*, second quarter 1966, special number devoted to Jules Verne; S. Vierne, 'Deux voyages initiatiques en 1864, *Laura* de George Sand et *Le Voyage au centre de la terre* de Jules Verne', *Mélanges George Sand*, Paris 1969, pp. 101–114.
30 *Le très curieux Jules Verne*, Paris 1960; *Nouvelles explorations de Jules Verne*, Paris 1963.
31 *Pour une théorie de la production littéraire*, Paris 1966. I refer at length to the analyses of P. Macherey in chapter II.

Chapter II

32 P. Sorlin, *La Société française (1870–1914)*, Paris-Grenoble 1969.
33 *Cf.* the article by P. Versins, 'La Sentiment de l'artifice', published in the special number of *L'Arc* (no. 29); pp. 59–65 of this article contain an interesting synoptic table of the novels of the future by Jules Verne in which certain themes had already been published in France or abroad.
34 'Once a man has enough money to feed and clothe his family, he interests himself less in the sciences which can increase his comfort and the pleasures of life in general, and more in those which relate to nature as a whole, and to his situation in the universe', says Kenneth Allott (*Jules Verne, his life and works*, p. 150) to explain Verne's predilection for astronomy.
35 'L'Age d'or et le point central à travers quelques œuvres de Jules Verne', *Répertoire I*, p. 134.
36 *The Adventures of Captain Hatteras*. One cannot refrain from associating this with famous passages in Marx, explaining that the reversion to desert of the great Central Asian empires has socio-historical causes, not climatic ones.
37 A. Jacobsen, *Des anticipations de Jules Verne aux réalisations d'aujourd'hui*, Paris 1935 (Preface by Georges Claude).
38 On the connections between mechanization and surplus value, compare the study by J. Fallot, *Marx et le machinisme*, Paris 1966.
39 Jules Verne was seduced by the personality of Leonardo, and in his youth dedicated a comedy in verse to him, which Verne read to a meeting of the Académie d'Amiens in May 1874 (*Bulletin de la Société Jules Verne*, February 1936, no. 2, p. 92); the text remains unpublished. Jules Verne and Leonardo both had an encyclopaedic cultural range; they were both excited by flying machines and obsessed by the fluid element (Leonardo wrote a treatise on water). Both had initially been convinced of the power of human knowledge, and moved later towards pessimism. *Cf.* the parallel between the two men suggested by G. de Diesbach at the end of his study (*op. cit.*).

Chapter III

40 This Vernean political pantheon does not strike the attention of Professor Arronax, involuntary guest of Captain Nemo, until later ('several etchings which I had not noticed on my first visit hung on the partition wall'). This discreet reference, very much in Jules Verne's manner, does not in the least signify that it is a question of a secondary trait in Captain Nemo's character, but on the contrary, a fundamental element of his personality.

41 The 1848 character of Captain Nemo was noted by Mme Allotte de la Fuÿe, niece and biographer of Jules Verne: 'Nemo, the man of '48 transfigured. He pursued the despots and upheld nationalist principles. Inflexible, he sinks the frigate of the oppressors and magnificently carries the treasures to those who fight for their independence. This genius of the seas is of the same generation as his author and publisher.' (*Jules Verne, sa vie, son œuvre*, p. 122).
42 Mme Allotte de la Fuÿe, *op. cit.*, p. 116.
43 *Ibid.*, pp. 31–32.
44 Letter from Jules Verne to Hetzel, 6 December 1851.
45 A. Parménie and C. Bonnier de La Chapelle, *Histoire d'un éditeur et de ses auteurs, P. J. Hetzel*, p. 91 et seq.
46 *Ibid.*, p. 431.
47 Mme Allotte de la Fuÿe, *op. cit.*, p. 116.
48 I am indebted to E. Brandis, Soviet specialist on Jules Verne, for these pointers to relations between Verne and Marko Vovtchok.
49 Mme Allotte de la Fuÿe, *op. cit.*, p. 116 (information from Verne's nephew, Maurice, who took several sea cruises with him).
50 For Verne's taste in music, *cf.* M. Moré, *Nouvelles explorations de Jules Verne*, chapter II.
51 The interest in this idea of the study of connections between national liberation movements and social conflicts was heightened at the time of the discussions of the International History Commission on Social Movements, presided over by Professor Labrousse (Tunis, April 1964).
52 *Le Tour de Jules Verne en 80 livres*, p. 107 et seq.
53 Kenneth Allott (*Jules Verne*, London 1940) is alone among commentators on Verne's work to emphasize at length his romantic side, to the extent of seeing in it the essential character of the *Voyages extraordinaires*.
54 Jean Cassou, *Anatomie des révolutions. Quarante-Huit*, Paris 1939.
55 *Cf.* chapter VII ('Le Paysage') in R. Escaich's study *Voyage au monde de Jules Verne*, Paris 1955; the author does not perceive the romantic character of Verne's landscapes, but his chapter IX ('Les Eléments déchaînés') presents a rich inventory of the earthquakes, tempests, thunderstorms, floods, typhoons and cyclones and other expressions of the savagery of nature, such as those which Verne has described in his works.

CHAPTER IV

56 The formulas, in fact, are due to the lyricism of Enfantin.
57 S. Charléty, *Histoire du saint-simonisme*, Paris 1965, p. 38.
58 *Ibid.*, p. 49.
59 S. Charléty, *op. cit.*, p. 34.
60 *Mémoires de l'Académie des Sciences, des lettres et des arts d'Amiens*, 3rd series, vol. II, Amiens 1875, pp. 347–378.
61 P. Machérey, *Pour une théorie de la production littéraire*, Paris 1966, p. 197.
62 S. Charléty, *op. cit.*, pp. 94–95.
63 A singular anticipation since, at the time the novel appeared in 1892, the Trans-Siberian Railway had not been completed. One knows that a track – resembling somewhat the plan made by Verne – from Lanchou to Alma-Ata, was projected in 1950; it was three-quarters complete before the 1960 Sino-Soviet rupture.
64 'This substratum', said Jules Verne concluding his description of an abandoned mine, 'could provide accommodation for an entire population. And who knows if the poorer classes of the United Kingdom will not find refuge in these surroundings, with a constant temperature, at the bottom of the mines of Aberfoyle,

as well as those of Newcastle, Alloa or Cardiff, when the seams are exhausted?' (*Black Diamonds*). These perspectives of class segregation may possibly have influenced H. G. Wells (who, one knows, read Verne with pleasure). In *The Time Machine* he postulates a category of workers adapted to underground life, and clearly separated from the leisured people on the surface.

65 *Le très curieux Jules Verne*, Paris 1960.
66 Title of part four of the book by S. Charléty quoted above.
67 For example, in *Upside Down*; similarly, Nemo said of Lesseps (*20,000 Leagues under the Sea*): 'He is a man of more honour to a nation than the greatest captains! He began like so many others with anxieties and rebuffs, but he triumphed, as he had the volunteer spirit.' In *The Invasion of the Sea*, Verne attributes to Lesseps the idea of a canal project linking the Gulf of Gabès and the Shotts of southern Tunisia; I have been unable to verify this.
68 Mme Allotte de la Fuÿe, *Jules Verne, sa vie, son œuvre*, p. 129.
69 G. Weill, *L'Ecole saint-simonienne*, p. 287.
70 In 1848 he was Secrétaire-générale du Ministère de l'Instruction Publique, alongside Hippolyte Carnot, also a member of the Ecole; he was the author of *Souvenirs d'un prédicateur saint-simonien*.
71 Son of Charles Duveyrier, who was the close friend and disciple of Enfantin. Henri Duveyrier travelled widely in North Africa.
72 'The most redoubtable aspect of this brotherhood is that it leads to absorption and unification, bending the strong and numerous religious associations of Islam to its retrograde, dominating and aggressive views', declares Henri Duveyrier in a booklet of the Société de géographie. *La Confrérie musulmane de Sidi Mohammed ben Ali es-Senoussi*, Paris 1884.
73 Duveyrier insists, in his 'Premier rapport sur la mission des chotts du Sahara de Constantine' (*Bulletin of the Société de géographie*, May 1873), insists on the fact that the sea was recently present in that region.
74 F. David, early converted to Saint-Simonian ideas, accompanied Enfantin in Egypt, and brought back from there his opera *The Desert*.
75 On Dr Guépin, *cf.* the thesis of Guy Frambourg, *Un philanthrope et démocrate nantais, le Dr Guépin, 1805–1873*, Nantes 1965.
76 Quoted by G. Weill, *op. cit.*, p. 170.
77 To my knowledge, in his preface to the Soviet edition of Jules Verne in 12 volumes, the Soviet writer Cyril Andreiev was the first to point out the possibility that the utopian ideals advocated by some socialists are directly descended from Verne. This preface was translated into French in the review *Europe* in April 1955, a special number devoted to Jules Verne.

CHAPTER V

78 Mme Allotte de la Fuÿe, *op. cit.*, pp. 115 *et seq.*
79 Verne was obsessed with the theme of the outlaw, whether unscrupulous bandits or occasionally chivalrous terrorists. They were not ordinary criminals sought by the police, but intractable men who declined social power (M. Carrouges, *op. cit.*), but the analytical method chosen by the author leads him to define this fact in terms of 'myths' instead of examining its concrete social content.
80 The accuracy of the Verne story is doubtful; the term Wang designates the leaders of the rebels, not the dynasty which they wished to set up; Shanghai was taken in 1853 by the rebels of the Small Sword, one of the branches of the Triad, who did not co-operate with the Taiping, though they profited from their success. The four banners of different colours belonged to the White Lotus, another secret society.

81 *Mémoires de l'Académie d'Amiens*, public meeting on 18 December 1881. (*Cf.* P. Terrasse's study in the *Bulletin de la Société Jules Verne*, new series, 3rd-4th quarter 1968).
82 On the 'free environments' *cf.* J. Maitron, *Histoire du mouvement anarchiste en France, 1880–1914*, p. 355.
83 'The island is [for Jules Verne] the symbol of independence, the sole possibility of its complete realization, far from corrupt governments and badly made laws; the man worthy of the name can find there conditions necessary for the creation of the ideal society.' (G. de Diesbach, *Le Tour de Jules Verne en 80 livres*, p. 47.)
84 *Cf.* particularly E. Girault, *La Bonne Louise* (p. 96) revived by F. Planche, *La Vie ardente et intrépide de Louise Michel*, p. 208.
85 Mme Allotte de la Fuÿe, *op. cit.*, p. 128.
86 Hem Day, 'Louise Michel, Jules Verne, de qui est *20,000 lieues sous les mers?*', *Les Cahiers Pensée et Action*, no. 9, January 1959.
87 *Le très curieux Jules Verne*, p. 153.
88 A. Parménie and C. Bonnier de La Chapelle, *Histoire d'un éditeur et de ses auteurs, P.-J. Hetzel*, p. 94.
89 He presided over the Amiens regional Esperanto group and planned an Esperanto novel (Ch. Lemire, *Jules Verne*, Paris 1908, p. 118); no Verne specialist has yet investigated the bulletins and Esperanto material of this time.
90 The Nadar archives have recently been given to the Bibliothèque Nationale, Paris.
91 M. Marcucci, *Bulletin de la Société Jules Verne*, no. 6.
92 R. Escaich, *op. cit.*, p. 159.
93 Jean Orth, born 1852 (Archduke Jean Nepomucène Salvador de Habsburg), spent some years period in the Austrian Army; in 1889 he abandoned his rank and dignities and disappeared on board his ship.
94 Mme Allotte de la Fuÿe, *op. cit.*, p. 170.
95 Hem Day, *op. cit.*
96 On the anarchist criticism of universal suffrage, *cf.* J. Maitron, *op. cit.*, p. 457.

CHAPTER VI

97 *Cf.* the interesting study of the representation of Dahomey in French opinion at the time of its conquest (Véronique Campion-Vincent, 'La Belle Epoque', *Les Temps modernes*, August 1968, pp. 317–45); this purports to quote as evidence the racism which marks the moral and physical portraits of the Negroes, and abounds in formulas literally identical to those used by Verne.
98 This short story was republished with the novel *The Chancellor*.

CHAPTER VII

99 Quoted by A. Parménie and C. Bonnier de La Chapelle, *op. cit.*, p. 489.
100 Correspondence between Hetzel and Jules Verne.
101 Verbal information from Ch. Dollfus.
102 *Cf.* Mme Allotte de la Fuÿe, *op. cit.*, pp. 56, 80, etc. The author points out, however, very discreetly, that Jules Verne ceased to practise in his mature years (*ibid.*, p. 211).
103 *Le très curieux Jules Verne*, p. 84.
104 Allusion to a novel published in 1950 by Vercors. The 'tropis' are an intermediate race between men and apes. 'Tala' is student slang for someone who goes *tà la messe*, i.e. a devout Catholic.

105 'Le Point suprême et l'âge d'or à travers quelques œuvres de Jules Verne', *Répertoire I*, paragraph V: 'La Providence'.
106 *Ibid.*, p. 150.
107 *Nouvelles explorations de Jules Verne*, p. 89.
108 Mme Allotte de la Fuÿe, *op. cit.*, p. 81.
109 *Le très curieux Jules Verne*, pp. 222–23.
110 *Cf.* the detailed comparison of the two versions, *Bulletin de la Société Jules Verne*, no. 5, November 1936.
111 'The spirituality of Jules Verne, far from being Catholic, approaches that of Victor Hugo, for whom he had a great admiration.' (*Nouvelles explorations de Jules Verne*, p. 232.)

CHAPTER VIII

112 *Cf.* especially G. de Diesbach, *op. cit.*, p. 63, and M. H. Huet, *La Machine à modifier le temps*, p. 75.
113 A. Gramsci, *Œuvres choisies*, Paris 1959, p. 480. The anglophobia expressed by Verne is typical of a deeply ingrained characteristic of the French people; it progresses in the making of modern France from Joan of Arc to the French Revolution and to Napoleon.
114 Correspondence between Hetzel and Jules Verne.
115 This point has been underlined by G. de Diesbach, *op. cit.*, p. 99 ('His Frenchmen occupy only an intermediate place, usually modest and almost always subordinate.').
116 M. H. Huet, *op. cit.*, p. 100.
117 When Antiochus of Syria sought to avoid giving an undertaking to cease hostilities against Rome's ally, Ptolemy of Egypt, the Roman envoy M. Popilius Laenas drew a circle around Antiochus and warned him not to step out before making his decision.
118 In fact, since the novel was written, the Danish Antilles have been purchased by the United States of America.

CHAPTER IX

119 This little story (*An Express of the Future*) is known only in its English version, published in *Strand* magazine, London, July-December 1895 (pp. 638–40).
120 René Rémond, *Les Etats-Unis devant l'opinion française (1815–1852)*, Paris 1962, 2 volumes, p. 769.
121 Marcel Moré, *op. cit.*, p. 196.
122 One should note that the Indian wars and the Indian resistance to American expansion, which played so great a role in the development of American militarism, are completely omitted from the *Voyages extraordinaires*. The Indians appear solely as pillaging Sioux who attack Phileas Fogg's train (*Around the World in Eighty Days*). As a good Saint-Simonian, Verne no doubt thought of the elimination of the Indians as a harsh necessity.

CHAPTER X

123 Yet Hetzel was tempted to soften the charge of anti-semitism: 'I warned Verne, I toned down more than one passage, but he was so insistent that such alterations were difficult.' (Letter from Hetzel to his son, 6 June 1877.)

124 M. Carrouges, *op. cit.*, has noted in Jules Verne 'the disquieting fascination which arises from gold prospecting'; he has noticed that 'the power of gold is one of the constant themes in the work of Jules Verne'. But he does not attempt to seek a wider meaning, and neglects the social content in these constant references to gold.

125 It is about the young Robert Grant who crosses Australia with a group of friends, in search of his father.

126 This 'rich Syrian' could easily prefigure Kamylk Pasha, whom one encounters again at the beginning of the plot of *Master Antifer*. It is generally considered that Verne has only made occasional use of 'the reappearance of characters' (Nemo, Robur, Barbicane). In fact, the connections between the novels are much more numerous, but often concealed in a devious paragraph: for example, when Mrs Barnett (*The Fur Country*) evokes the possibility of building a floating island, later to form the theme of *Propeller Island*. No attempt has been made to deal with the problems of literary treatment in this book.

CHAPTER XI

127 S. Vierne, 'L'authenticité de quelques œuvres de Jules Verne', *Annales de Bretagne*, 1966. Mme Vierne, basing her work on a study of the Hetzel dossier deposited in the Bibliothèque Nationale, has similarly established that Jules Verne had 'adapted' *The Southern Star Mystery* (which Grousset had also made over to Hetzel) on the same terms.

128 This includes the German occupation forces in France. In 1940, *The Begum's Fortune* was on the 'Otto list' (proscribed works), and a copy of the book in the Bibliothèque Nationale still carries the official mark.

129 *La machine à modifier le temps*, pp. 181–85.

130 'A great fabulous island and volcano, home of magic and initiation, engulfed in the turbulence of a great eruption; this is the epitome of the most obvious legendary prototype of the Vernean island.' (M. Carrouges, 'Le Mythe de Vulcain chez Jules Verne', *Arts et Lettres*, Paris 1948, no. 13).

131 In particular, M. Moré, *Nouvelles explorations de Jules Verne*.

CHAPTER XII

132 Letter dated September 1894 quoted by Mme Allotte de la Fuÿe, *op. cit.*, p. 191.

133 *La machine à modifier le temps*, p. 72.

134 This fact is recognized with some embarrassment by his biographer, Mme Allotte de la Fuÿe.

135 M. Carrouges, *op. cit.*, pp. 52–54.

136 'Par où commencer', *Poétique*, 1970, no. 1, pp. 3–9.

137 *Critique*, April 1969 and January 1970.

138 For example, in the original version of chapter 5 published as 'Critique sociale et thèmes anarchistes chez Jules Verne', *Le Mouvement social*, July 1966.

139 In her thesis, Mlle Huet compares Jules Verne's image of the Celtic race with the ideas of Gobineau, but without slanting the analysis in that direction. *Cf.* Jeannine Buenzod, *La Formation de la pensée de Gobineau*, Paris 1967.

140 In his works, M. Moré repeatedly compares Jules Verne and Villiers de l'Isle-Adam.

141 Letter supplied by Mme S. Vierne.

142 *Ibid.*

143 Text and information kindly supplied by Mme S. Vierne.

Bibliography

LES VOYAGES EXTRAORDINAIRES

1863	Five Weeks in a Balloon (Cinq semaines en ballon)
1864	Journey to the Centre of the Earth (Voyage au centre de la Terre)
1865	From the Earth to the Moon (De la Terre à la Lune)
1866	Adventures of Captain Hatteras (Voyages et aventures du capitaine Hatteras)
1867–68	The Children of Captain Grant (Les Enfants du capitaine Grant)
1870	Twenty Thousand Leagues under the Sea (Vingt mille lieues sous les mers)
	Round the Moon (Autour de la Lune)
1871	A Floating City (Une ville flottante)
1872	Measuring a Meridian (Aventures de trois Russes et de trois Anglais dans l'Afrique australe)
1873	The Fur Country (Le Pays des fourrures)
	Around the World in Eighty Days (Le Tour du monde en quatre-vingts jours)
1874	Doctor Ox (Le Docteur Ox)
1874–75	The Mysterious Island (L'Ile mystérieuse)
1875	The Chancellor (Le Chancellor)
1876	Michael Strogoff (Michel Strogoff)
1877	Hector Servadac (Hector Servadac)
	Black Diamonds (Les Indes Noires)
1878	The Boy Captain (Un Capitaine de quinze ans)
1879	The Tribulations of a Chinese Gentleman (Les Tribulations d'un Chinois en Chine)
	The Begum's Fortune (Les Cinq cents millions de la Bégum)
1880	The Steam House (La Maison à vapeur)
1881	The Giant Raft (La Jangada — Huit cents lieues sur l'Amazone)
1882	Robinsons' Island (L'Ile des Robinsons)
	The Green Ray (Le Rayon vert)
1883	Keraban the Inflexible (Kéraban le Têtu)
1884	The Southern Star Mystery (L'Etoile du Sud)
	Islands on Fire (L'Archipel en feu)
1885	Mathias Sandorf (Mathias Sandorf)
1886	The Clipper of the Clouds (Robur le Conquérant)
	A Lottery Ticket (Un Billet de loterie)
1887	Flight to France (Le Chemin de France)
	North against South (Nord contre Sud)
1888	Two Years' Holiday (Deux ans de vacances)
1889	Upside Down (Sens dessus dessous)
	Family without a Name (Famille sans nom)
1890	Caesar Cascabel (César Cascabel)
1891	Mistress Branican (Mistress Branican)

1892	*Carpathian Castle* (*Le Château des Carpathes*)
	Claudius Bombarnac (*Claudius Bombarnac*)
1893	*Foundling Mick* (*P'tit Bonhomme*)
1894	*Master Antifer* (*Les Mirifiques Aventures de Maître Antifer*)
1895	*Propeller Island* (*L'Ile à Hélice*)
1896	*Clovis Dardentor* (*Clovis Dardentor*)
	For the Flag (*Face au Drapeau*)
1897	*An Antarctic Adventure* (*Le Sphinx des glaces*)
1898	*The Superb Orinoco* (*Le Superbe Orénoque*)
1899	*An Eccentric's Will* (*Le Testament d'un excentrique*)
1900	*Second Fatherland* (*Seconde patrie*)
1901	*Village in the Tree Tops* (*Le Village aérien*)
	The Tales of Jean-Marie Cabidoulin (*Les Histoires de Jean-Marie Cabidoulin*)
1902	*The Brothers Kip* (*Les Frères Kip*)
1903	*Travelling Scholarships* (*Bourses de voyages*)
1904	*Master of the World* (*Maître du monde*)
	A Drama in Livonia (*Un Drame en Livonie*)
1905	*The Invasion of the Sea* (*L'Invasion de la Mer*)
	The Lighthouse at the End of the World (*Le Phare du bout du monde*)
1906	*The Volcano of Gold* (*Le Volcan d'or*)
1907	*Thomson and Co.* (*L'Agence Thomson et Co.*)
1908	*Hunt for the Meteor* (*La Chasse au météore*)
	A Danube Pilot (*Le Pilote du Danube*)
1909	*The Survivors of the 'Jonathan'* (*Les Naufragés du 'Jonathan'*)
1910	*Wilhelm Storitz' Secret* (*Le Secret de Wilhelm Storitz*)
	Yesterday and Tomorrow (*Hier et demain*)
1920	*The Astonishing Adventures of the Barsac Mission* (*L'Etonnante Aventure de la Mission Barsac*)

WORKS ON JULES VERNE

Mme ALLOTTE DE LA FUŸE, *Jules Verne, sa vie, son œuvre*, Paris 1928 (new ed. 1953)

ANDREIEV, C., 'Préface à l'édition soviétique de Jules Verne', *Europe* (special number on Jules Verne) 1955

BRANDIS, E., *Ioul Vern, evo jizni i torchtchestvo* (Jules Verne, his life and work), Moscow 1962

BUTOR, M., 'Le Point suprême et l'âge d'or à travers quelques œuvres de Jules Verne', *Répertoire* I, Paris 1962, pp. 130–62

CARROUGES, M. 'Le Mythe de Vulcain chez Verne', *Arts et Lettres*, Paris, 1948, No. 15 (devoted to Jules Verne)

CHESNEAUX, J., 'La Pensée politique de Jules Verne', *Les Cahiers rationalistes*, Sept.-Oct. 1967

CORBOR, M., 'Le Voyage au centre de la Terre', *Action et Pensée*, September 1896

DIESBACH, G. DE, *Le Tour de Jules Verne en 80 livres*, Paris 1969

ESCAICH, R., *Voyage à travers le monde vernien*, Paris 1951

FAIVRE, J.-P., 'Les Voyages extraordinaires de Jules Verne en Australie', *Australian Journal of French Studies*, 1968 No. 2, and 1969 No. 1

FRANCK, B., *Jules Verne et ses voyages*, Paris 1941

HEM DAY, 'Louise Michel, Jules Verne: de qui est *Vingt mille lieues sous les mers*?', *Les Cahiers Pensée et Action*, No. 9, January 1959

HUET, M. H., 'La Machine à modifier le temps, les Voyages extraordinaires de Jules Verne' (unpublished thesis, Faculté des lettres, Bordeaux), 1968
JACOBSON, A., and A. ANTONI, *Des anticipations de Jules Verne aux réalisations d'aujourd'hui*, Paris n.d. (*c.* 1935)
MACHEREY, P., 'Jules Verne, ou le récit en défaut', *Pour une théorie de la production littéraire*, Paris 1966, pp. 183-266
MORÉ, M., *Le très curieux Jules Verne*, Paris 1960; *Nouvelles explorations de Jules Verne*, Paris 1963
PARMENIE, A., and C. BONNIER DE LA CHAPELLE, *Histoire d'un éditeur et de ses auteurs, P.-J. Hetzel*, Paris 1953
SERRES, MICHEL, 'Un voyage au bout de la nuit (*Les Indes Noires*)', *Critique*, April 1970; 'Œdipe-Messager (*Michel Strogoff*)', *Critique*, January 1970
VERSINS, P., 'Le sentiment de l'artifice', *L'Arc*, No. 29 (devoted to Jules Verne)
VIERNE, S., 'L'authenticité de quelques œuvres de Jules Verne', *Annales de Bretagne*, 1966, pp. 445-58; 'Deux voyages initiatiques en 1864: *Laura* de George Sand et le *Voyage au centre de la Terre* de Jules Verne', *Mélanges George Sand*, Paris 1969, pp. 101-14

List of illustrations

The engravings reproduced are taken from the original editions of the following novels:
Around the World in Eighty Days
  Phileas Fogg at the Reform Club (p. 62)
The Begum's Fortune
  The city of Franceville (p. 71)
  The city of Stahlstadt (p. 177)
  The formidable guards of Stahlstadt (p. 183)
Black Diamonds
  Miners' dwellings in the subterranean Coal City (p. 73)
Caesar Cascabel
  The touring company being turned back by Russian officials at the Alaska border (p. 159)
The Carpathian Castle
  Frantz de Telek looking towards the mysterious castle of Rodolphe de Gortz (p. 65)
The Clipper of the Clouds
  Robur's *Albatross* (p. 153)
An Eccentric's Will
  Crowds watching the game of 'Goose' invented by William J. Hipperbone (p. 163)
Family without a Name
  The hero, Jean-without-a-name (p. 50)
  Jean and Clary plunging to their deaths over the Niagara Falls (p. 66)
  A meeting of the British Governor, Commander-in-Chief and Chief of Police (p. 101)
Five Weeks in a Balloon
  Dr Fergusson and his companions crossing the Niger (p. 27)
A Floating City
  The giant liner *Great Eastern* (p. 41)
For the Flag
  The pirate Ker Karraje (p. 92)
Foundling Mick
  Lord and Lady Piborne and their son (p. 55)
From the Earth to the Moon
  The firing of the projectile (p. 32)
  View of the cannon proposed by J. T. Maston (p. 81)
The Fur Country
  Lt Jasper Hobson looking out for a relief ship in the Polar regions (p. 79)
The Green Ray
  The scientist Aristobulus Ursiclos taking measurements by pacing (p. 187)

Hector Servadac
    Weighing the comet Gallia (p. 25)
    Title-page from the first edition (p. 63)
    The Prussian moneylender, Isaac Hakhabut (p. 166)
Islands on Fire
    A battle scene, showing the phil-hellenic French officer, Lt Henry d'Albaret (p. 59)
Journey to the Centre of the Earth
    Professor Liddenbrock and Axel discover the runic inscription 'Arne Saknussem' (p. 134)
Keraban the Inflexible
    The hero, Keraban (p. 97)
A Lottery Ticket
    Professor Hog examining the winning ticket (p. 168)
Mathias Sandorf
    'Dr Antekirtt' overlooking the fortifications of Antekirtt (p. 75)
    The acrobats Pointe Pescade and Cap Matifou (p. 89)
    Mathias Sandorf is found guilty of treason (p. 123)
Measuring a Meridian
    Explanatory diagram to show the method of triangulation (p. 29)
    The meeting of members of the international expedition (p. 31)
Michael Strogoff
    Ivan Ogarev blinding Michael Strogoff (p. 115)
The Mysterious Island
    Cyrus Smith gives a lecture on how a grain of corn will proliferate (p. 35)
    The death of Captain Nemo (p. 133)
The Steam House
    The train in the form of Hindu temples drawn by an elephant (p. 40)
    Brahmins inciting the Sepoys in the Indian Mutiny (p. 118)
The Tribulations of a Chinese Gentleman
    Wang and Kin Fo strolling along a quay at Shanghai (p. 124)
Twenty Thousand Leagues under the Sea
    Captain Nemo and his black flag bearing the letter 'N' (p. 99)
    The ruins of Atlantis (p. 190)

Index

Numbers in italics refer to the illustrations

advertising 164
Africa 36
agriculture 80, 85
Alaska 157, *159*
Allotte de la Fuÿe (family) 11, 18
American Civil War 57ff., 103, 146, 150, 156f.; *see also* United States of America
Amiens 14, 15, 182; Academy 13, 74, 88
Ammianus Marcellinus 192
anarchism 100, 104ff.
anglophobia 61, 140ff.; *see also* Great Britain
Antilles 149f.
anti-semitism 167f.; *see also* prejudice, racial
Anville, Jean-Baptiste d' 192
archetypes, theory of 200
aristocracy, attitude to 54, 55
Asia 37
astronomy 30; comets 24, *25*, 29, 61
Atlantis 190ff., *191*
Australia 76f., 120f., 171
Avezac de Castera Macaya, Marie Armand Pascal d' 192

Bailly, Jean Sylvain 190
Bakunin, Mikhail Alexandrovich 103
Ballanche, Pierre Simon 202
balloons 27, 40; *see also* flight, powered
Baltic provinces 52
Balzac, Honoré de 24, 203
banks 179
Barthes, Roland 201
Bougainville, Louis Antonine de 112
bourgeoisie 11ff.; attitudes to money 164ff.
Briand, Aristide 11, 18
Brion, M. 20

Brown, John 45, 57f., 157
Buffon, Georges Louis Leclerc, Comte de 192
Bulgarian independence 49
Butor, Michel 20, 30, 85, 130

Cabet, Etienne 71, 154
Canada 173; nationalism 49, 50f., 90, 100, 156, 204f.
canals 36, 80f., 179
Capek, Karel 197
Carrouges, M. 20
cartography 28
Cassou, Jean 64, 202
Cellier, M. 20
Celtic peoples 144f.; *see also* Ireland; Scotland
Chance 132ff., *168*, 169, 176
Charton, Edouard 83
chauvinism 21, 121, 140, 145, 199
Chevalier, Michel 82, 152
China 36f., *124*, 125, 165
Church, Roman Catholic 127ff.
colonialism 21, 76ff., 112ff., 181f.; British 49, 53
colonies, scientific 70; *see also* societies, artificial
comets 24, *25*, 29, 61
commerce 165ff.
Commune (1871) 13, 15, 104, 207
Cooper, James Fenimore 113, 151
copyright, author's 16
crime and criminals 90ff.; *see also* outlaws
Crimean War 145

David, Félicien 83
Day, Hem 99
Delibes, Léo 12
Denmark 148

221

Destiny 132 ff.
diamonds 173 f.; synthetic 24, 31
Dickens, Charles 203, 206
Diesbach, Ghislain de 54, 143
disasters, natural 24 f., 190 ff.
Dreyfus, Alfred 13 f., 104
Dubois, Gustave 15
Dumas, Alexandre 206
Duveyrier, Henri 83

Eiffel, Gustave 44, 178
elections 109
electricity, applications of 43, 74, 164
Enfantin, Prosper 76, 77, 82, 83, 84, 86, 178
entertainers 88 f., *89*
equality 60
Erckmann-Chatrian 143, 206
Eskimos 113, 119
Esperanto 103 f., 149
exploration 30, 69, 134

Fashoda incident 141
Fate 132 ff.
Ferry, Jules François Camille 13
flags, symbolism of 99, 100, 156
flight, powered 24, 40 f., 100, 151, *153*
Follie, Louis Guillaume de la 23
Fourier, Charles 82, 83, 85, 86
France 13 ff., 45 ff., 60, 143 f.; as colonial power 116, 119 f., 122, 148
Franco-Prussian War 143
fraternity 60 f.
freedom 47, 48, 60, 96 ff.; sea as symbol of 47, 87; U.S.A. as land of 157
Freemasonry 138

geography 28
geology 29, 33, 131
Germany 142 f.; as colonial power 147; and Slav peoples 52 f.
Girardin, Emile de 12
Gobineau, Joseph Arthur, Comte de 204
gold (as monetary standard) 96, 105 f., 165 ff.
Gramsci, A. 142
Great Britain: as colonial power 100, 140, 147 f.; and Crimean War 145; and Ireland 49, 53, 55
Great Eastern (ship) 39, *41*, 151
Greece 49, 51
Greenland 48
Grousset, Pascal 182, 205, 206, 207
Guépin, Dr 83 f., 86

Guéroult, Adolphe 12, 83
Guizot, François 165

handwriting, analysis of 19 f.
Hero of Alexandria 44
Hetzel (publisher) 11 f., 20, 23, 29, 46 f., 98, 103, 127, 142, 182, 206 f.
Hignard 12
Hoffmann, E. T. A. 206
Holland 148
hospital, mental 90 f.
Hudson's Bay Company 60, 77, 96, 119, 120, 156
Huet, Marie-Hélène 144, 188
Hugo, Victor 45, 68, 138, 202
Humboldt, Alexander von 192
Hungarian nationalism 48, 49, *123*, 124 f.
hygiene 72

Iamblicus 192
Indian Mutiny 117 ff., *118*
Indians, American 62, 113, 119
industry, heavy 177 f., 182 f.; *see also* science; technology
insanity 90 f., 186
internationalism 140 ff.
Ireland 48 f., 53 ff., 139

Joessel 12

Laffitte, Jacques 170
Lamartine, Alphonse de 46
land, ownership of 95, 105, 106, 111
landlords, absentee 53
landscapes, romantic 64 f.
language: Esperanto 103 f., 149; interpretation of Verne's use of 201; in monkeys 24
law 90, 91; chance and 132
Lebaudy, Paul 185
Lemercier 24
Leo XIII (pope) 13, 104, 127
Leonardo da Vinci 44, 178
Lesseps, Ferdinand Marie de 82 f.
London, Jack 173, 206
Loubet, Emile 14
Louis-Salvador (of Habsburg) 12, 109
Louÿs, Pierre Louis 19

Macé, Jean 47
Macherey, P. 21, 30, 43
machines and machinery 23 ff.; ideal functions of 38 f.; man as 41 f.; and Nature 38 f., 42

222

Magasin d'Education et de Récréation 47
Magellan territories 106f., 147
Mahdist movement 83
Malte-Brun, Konrat 192
man: brotherhood of 60f.; as machine 41f.; and Nature 33ff., 69ff.; *see also* social organization; societies, artificial
Mandrin, Louis 94
Maoris 119, 123, 129f.
marriage and divorce, attitudes to 157f.
Marucci, E. M. 207
Marx, Karl 174
Massé, Victor 12
master and servant relationships 17f.
Merle, Robert 93
Michaux, Henri 20
Michel, Louis 98f.
Michelet, Jules 68
militarism 145f., 161, 182, *183*
money, power of 158ff., 165ff.
moneylenders 167f.
Moré, Marcel 14, 18, 20, 82, 102, 157, 207
Morel, Honorine (*née* du Fraysne de Viane) 11, 19
music 47, 83

Nadar (Félix Tournachon) 47, 83, 100, 104, 127, 146
Nantes 11, 19
Napoleon III 46
nationalist movements 48ff., 68, 116ff., 140ff., 198
Nature: as creative force 135, 189; machines and 38f., 42; man and 33ff., 69ff.
newspapers 160f., 164
New Zealand 119, 171
Niagara Falls 66, 151
Nogaret, François-Felix 23
Nisard, Désiré 14
Northwest Passage 85
Norway 56; independence 48

Oceania 121, 147
Origen 192
Orleans, House of 12
Orth, Jean 109
outlaws 92f., 98, 104ff.
ownership, collective 109

Papin, Denis 84
Papuan Islands 147
Pelouze, Théophile-Jules 12

Péreire, Jacob Emile and Isaac 78, 82
pessimism 181ff.
photography 164
pirates 92f., 100; *see also* outlaws
Plato 190, 202
Pliny the Elder 192
Poe, Edgar Allan 135, 136, 206
Poincaré, Raymond 14
Polar regions 24f., 33f., 60, 79, 162
police 90, 110
political opinions, Verne's 13ff., 45ff., 102f.; political analysis of the *Voyages extraordinaires* 196ff.
Porphyrius 192
Portugal 57f.
Posidonius 192
prejudice, racial 112ff., 167f.
prisons 91
Producer, The 78
prophecy, scientific 21, 23, 188; U.S.A. as setting for 151
Proudhon, Pierre Joseph 96
Providence 127ff.

railways 78f., 151
Raoul-Duval 12
Reclus, Elisée and Onésime 100, 103
religion 82, 127ff.
Rémond, René 152, 154
resources, natural 34, 36, 37, 69
Revolution, French (1848) 45ff.
romantic themes 26, 47, 64
Roudaire, François-Elie 77f., 83
Rousseau, Jean-Jacques 14
Roussel, Raymond 20
Russia: colonialism 114, *115*, 116, 146, 157; and Crimean War 145

Saint-Simonian ideas 69, 70, 76, 82ff., 129, 202f.; and U.S.A. 152ff.
Sand, George 68, 202
Sandor, Rosza 94
satire, use of 129, 130, 162f., 188
Schœlcher, Victor 57
Schweitzer, Albert 128
science: in literature 23ff., 84; and militarism 161; money and 170ff.; perversion of 186; and society 69ff., 138, 158, 181ff.
sciences, natural 29f.
Scotland 48, 198
sea (as symbol of freedom) 47, 87f.
seas, artificial 77, 78, 80
Second Empire 45ff.

223

Senussi movement 83, 125
Serres, Michel 202, 203
servants 17f.
ships 39, *41*, 87; discipline on 93
slavery 57, 58, 157
Slav peoples 52
socialism, utopian 69ff.; *see also* Saint-Simonian ideas
social organization 60f., 70ff., 96ff., 104f., 107, 109, 160f., 181, 182; military training in 78; tribal 112ff., 189
societies, artificial 34, 69ff., *71*, *73*, 184ff., 197
society: evolution of 193; future of 181f.; women's role in 16, 82
Sorlin, P. 21
sovereignty, territorial 96, 105, 107, 147f.
space travel 29, *32*, 61, *63*, 150
Spain 148
steam power *40*, 69
Stendhal 203
submarines 39, 42
suffrage, universal 109
surveying 24, 29, *31*
Swedenborg, Emanuel 202
Syria 101f., 204

tabu 115
Taiping rebellion 95
Talabot, Paulin 78, 82
Tatars 95, 114, 125
technology 34, 70, 183f.; in U.S.A. 150f.; *see also* science
telecommunications 42f., 154, 164

Tertullian 192
Theopompus 190
Thiers, Adolphe 46
Tour du Monde, Le 83
Tournefort, Joseph Pitton de 192
transport and travel 42, 43, 87ff., 164; in space 29, *32*, 61, *63*, 150; *see also* balloons; flight, powered; railways
triangulation 24, 29
Tristan, Flora 68
Tuaregs 113, 119
Turiello, Mario 13, 14, 18
United States of America 21, 71, 76, 150ff.; *see also* American Civil War
Unknown, the 132ff.

Vailland, Roger 102
Verne, Michel 11, 206, 207, 208
Verne, Paul 20
Veuillot, Louis 127, 137
Vidal de la Blache, Paul 28
Vierne, S. 20, 200, 207
Villiers de l'Isle-Adam, Auguste de 202, 204
Vovtchok, Marko 47

weapons 186; scientific uses *32*, 79f., *81*
Wells, H. G. 197
women: female characters in novels 67, 82; role in society 16, 82
work, attitude to 69ff.; *see also* Saint-Simonian ideas
working classes 82; insurrection by 54
Wyss, Rodolphe 206

Zola, Emile 203